Preserving the Past & Engaging the Future

Theology & Religion in American Special Collections

EDITED BY M. PATRICK GRAHAM

ATLA OPEN PRESS

Chicago – 2021

atla Open Press

Published by Atla Open Press, an imprint of the American
Theological Library Association (Atla), 200 South Wacker Drive,
Suite 3100, Chicago, IL 60606-6701 USA

Published in the United States of America in 2021.

ISBN-13 978-1-949800-17-3 (PDF)
ISBN-13 978-1-949800-18-0 (EPUB)
ISBN-13 978-1-949800-16-6 (Paperback)

Cover design: Simply Aesthetic Design

Contents

Foreword

The expression "People of the Book" (هل الكتاب) comes from Qur'an 98:6, where it is used to describe adherents of religions that revere a book or, more specifically, a revealed scripture. It is a unifying expression that forges links among the monotheistic belief systems of Judaism, Christianity, and Islam. I think, however, we may extend the notion to other faiths, most of which have texts and traditions that make their communities, too, "People of the Book."

We may further expand the term in a most apt and appealing way to designate special collections librarians—particularly those in the realms of theological librarianship—who devote their careers to collecting, preserving, making accessible, and celebrating important theological books.

Having spent the better part of my life in this field and often competing with such acquisitive giants as Pat Graham, the editor of this collection, and Steve Crocco, one of its authors, I am immodestly proud of the work of such "turn-of-the-century" librarians in building up stupendous collections of religious rare books and manuscripts. The work must continue, however, and not only by fostering creative and aggressive collection development, but also by finding new ways to promote and encourage study of America's significant theological special collections. It is delightful, therefore, to see in these essays a new generation of people of the book who understand the cultural heritage they protect, who champion teaching and engagement with primary sources, and who are making the collections they care for accessible in new and innovative ways.

VALERIE HOTCHKISS
University Librarian and Professor of English, Vanderbilt University
March 16, 2021

Preserving the Past & Engaging the Future

Introduction

M. PATRICK GRAHAM

*T*wo of the greatest threats to the historic efforts of librarians and others to preserve print special collections and archives have been intentional efforts at their destruction and benign neglect. Richard Ovenden's recent publication, *Burning the Books: A History of the Deliberate Destruction of Knowledge* (Belknap/Harvard, 2020), offers a timely survey of the former, and all librarians have lived the quotidian struggle with the latter. Among the more striking passages in the volume by the Bodleian library director is the description of the savage attack in 1992 on the National and University Library of Bosnia and Herzegovina; much of its special collections and other holdings and much of its building were destroyed. The firefighters and librarians struggling to rescue its collections were even targeted by snipers (Ovenden 2020, 153).

This collection of ten articles is written by those who not only lament the destruction chronicled by Ovenden but have devoted their professional lives to resisting it. The volume began as an initiative by the editorial board of Books@Atla Open Press, which invited me to serve as editor. In response to a call for proposals in late 2019, eighteen submissions were received. In order to meet the contours of the volume projected, the hard work began to select about ten for inclusion. These would represent some of the variety in the association, the sorts of materials found in American special collections, and the sorts of activities that occupy special collections staff. The spread of the COVID-19 virus created difficulties for all the authors, as libraries and other institutions closed temporarily, restricted staff access to collections, or otherwise made research more difficult. I am deeply grateful for the dedication and resourcefulness of the contributors to complete their projects in a timely manner and for the families, librarians, and others who supported their work.

The articles have been divided into three groups: 1) those with a particularly retrospective focus, 2) those devoted to current efforts to use special collections for teaching and institutional outreach, and 3) those devoted to collection development and the future of special collections. This is by no means a tidy arrangement, since each article was written with its own distinctive aim and not as part of a more specific organizational plan for the volume. Consequently, the articles typically range across past, present, and future, just as librarians—regardless of job assignment—move back and forth through these. Nevertheless, there is a dominant element in each, and this has governed the current arrangement.

Special Collections Retrospective

The first two articles in this section deal with the sixteenth century and the German Reformation of Martin Luther. Armin Siedlecki begins his contribution, appropriately enough, with a quotation from the reformer himself that includes a phrase suitable for the present volume—"that the good books may be preserved and not lost." What follows is a description of the history, scope, and mission of the Richard C. Kessler Reformation Collection at the Pitts Theology Library. The collection was built on the holdings of the Hartford Seminary Library, which came to Emory University in 1976, but it is now more than three times the size of Hartford's Reformation collection and includes works by Catholic authors and other Protestant reformers who engaged Luther. This essay also outlines current efforts to make the collection available to researchers and to nourish university education and the life of the church. In addition to alerting librarians to this rich resource, it may also be that efforts at Pitts to promote the use of the collection will be useful for others seeking to leverage their own collections to the benefit of their clienteles.

The second piece is also devoted to one of America's foremost German Reformation collections, assembled by the Folger Shakespeare Library in Washington, DC. This collection is substantially based on the library's purchase of the Phillipps and Stickelberger collections. Caroline Duroselle-Melish writes about those collections in her investigation of the material features of these books and pamphlets. This includes attention to things that bear witness to the earlier lives of the imprints, such as bindings, indications of earlier ownership, manuscript notes and decoration, censorship marks, indexes and concordances created by owners, and corrections to the printed text. Readers should find this analysis richly informative, facilitating a more intelligent "reading" of their own materials.

The third article in this section is a description of the effort at the Andover-Harvard Theological Library to recreate the library of a nineteenth-century faculty member at the parent institution—namely, Convers Francis. Nell Carlson and Russell Pollard embarked on a complex effort to identify the holdings of the Francis library, which was largely present at the Andover-Harvard Library but also included materials that have been scattered among other Harvard libraries and beyond. Making use primarily of manuscript inscriptions, they were able to compile an impressive list of titles in this early and important addition to the divinity library, to update Harvard's online catalog so that users could benefit from their meticulous research, and then to characterize what could be known of Francis's research interests, reading knowledge of languages, and place within the development of Harvard Divinity School. Most librarians have had their curiosity aroused by such indications of former owners of their own materials, and these two Harvard librarians have done us all a service by sharing their strategies for identification of a collection, documentation of findings in an online catalog, and analysis of the owner's theology, interests, and reading habits.

Finally, Bruce Eldevik and Mary Ann Teske turn our attention to the history of special collections at Luther Seminary and how physical space and special collections have impacted the library's outreach. Most of the library's special collections came as donations from faculty, Lutheran pastors, and area residents and deal with the Lutheran tradition. In addition to the substantial donation of F. A. Schmidt, the Carl Døving Hymnal Collection and the Jacob Tanner Catechism Collection are particularly noteworthy. One of the more interesting developments at the Luther Seminary Library was the renovation of a room that had served as a chapel, a classroom, and then a radio broadcasting studio. This occurred in the 1970s, when the space was transformed into the library's Rare Book Room and began to serve a key role in introducing students and visitors to the world of manuscripts and rare books. This is a timely reminder of a library's ability to inspire wonder and a sense of awe among visitors and to foster resonance with the church's rich liturgical and educational traditions.

Special Collections at Work in Teaching and Research

The second section of articles focuses on current attempts to use special collections in teaching and in the outreach mission of the library and its parent institution. The Burke Library at Union Theological Seminary (New York) is one of America's largest and most historically significant theological libraries, and today that institution is now a dynamic partner with Columbia University Libraries. After a brief review of the history of Burke special collections, Matthew Baker describes how these materials have "become a cornerstone of the library's overall mission, touching every facet of collection development, management, and planning." This essay provides an incredibly wide-ranging and instructive tour of the ways that special collections may open the eyes of university students and external audiences to the history of the book, the use of archives and other original resources in research, and engagement with contemporary issues. It cannot help but provoke readers to consider possible analogs in their own institutions.

Christopher Anderson shows how the Yale Divinity Library has made its way in a similar effort to introduce primary sources from its collections into traditional and virtual classrooms. The Day Missions Library and Collection is one of the library's most important resources and plays a major role in these activities. In addition to what is done on the Yale campus, the library staff has reached out to other institutions to promote the use of the divinity library's manuscript, print, and digital resources and to provide colleagues elsewhere with interesting possibilities to explore. In all this, Anderson reminds readers of how important it is for audiences to have the experience of handling original materials. When this is not possible, there remain attractive possibilities for leveraging digital means to acquaint students with special collections and to encourage their collaboration with librarians to digitize and manipulate rare or unique materials.

The final essay in this section provides an example of a seminary library working with its school's IT staff and administration to create a digital repository for its special collections so that these materials can be offered without charge to audiences around the world. Jonathan Lawler and Shea van Schuyver of the Southeastern Baptist Theological Seminary provide a detailed, technical description of their work and emphasize the importance of considering institutional context, cooperation among all involved, and attention to the long-term durability of the repository. This piece is a helpful reminder of the importance of libraries in supporting research and instruction with a robust digital infrastructure for special collections and of the fact that even smaller institutions can accomplish significant things through collaboration and careful use of the latest digital tools.

Collection Development and the Future of Special Collections

The final section of the volume is devoted to building library collections for the future. All three articles describe past experiences as the basis for future initiatives. The first essay is by Stephen Crocco and draws on his time at Princeton Theological Seminary, where he built two comprehensive research collections. The first was devoted to Karl Barth, one of the twentieth century's most influential theologians, and the second to Abraham Kuyper, a Dutch pastor, neo-Calvinist theologian, and journalist, who also served his nation as prime minister in the early twentieth century. Both collections were eminently suitable for a Reformed seminary, and Crocco was able to establish the Center for Barth Studies and the Abraham Kuyper Institute of Public Theology at Princeton as well. The "backstories" that

Crocco provides for these collection development initiatives makes for interesting reading, and the "lessons learned" have something to offer every library director.

The next article is based on the Drew University Library's experience with the R. S. Thomas Collection. Brian Shetler and Jesse Mann describe how Drew Theological Seminary alumnus John G. McEllhenney had built his collection of Thomas's poetry and related materials over many decades and finally donated these to Drew. In addition, the Rev. McEllhenney gave a substantial collection of the works of Robert Frost and materials related to Methodism to the university. This experience provides a useful lesson for libraries in the value of their schools' alums for the development of special collections. The authors advance their thesis well and provide helpful guidance to the relevant literature along the way.

Anthony Elia of the Bridwell Library at the Southern Methodist University provides a suitable concluding article for this collection. Entitled "The Millennium Project," Elia's article is a sweeping and ambitious treatment of the setting of special collections and libraries in the "natural" world and at the midpoint of a millennium that began with Gutenberg. Elia urges his readers to balance their interest in the past with a gaze far into the future and to begin developing "collections in and of the present through endowments, commissions, and newly created works of theological expression—in art, music, and literature—with an eye toward our social responsibilities and the environment." Such a creative exhortation may well serve as the altar call to theological and religious studies librarians, who not only want to preserve humanity's literary legacy but also to use these materials for the instruction of generations to come.

Finally, I must acknowledge the support and helpfulness of three who have been closely involved in this project: Christine Fruin, Atla's scholarly communication and digital projects manager; Race MoChridhe, Atla's scholarly communication coordinator; and James Estes, supervisory librarian at the Library of Congress, adjunct associate professor of church history and medieval studies at Wesley Theological Seminary, and Books@Atla Open Press editor. They have been constant in their engagement and faithfully shepherded the project to its completion. I could not have asked for finer colleagues. Vanderbilt University librarian Valerie Hotchkiss kindly agreed to write the foreword for this volume, and for me this was icing on the cake. She has been an Atla friend of more than thirty years and is truly one of America's great scholar-librarians.

Special Collections Retrospective

CHAPTER 1

That the Good Books May Be Preserved

ARMIN SIEDLECKI

The title of this essay is taken from Martin Luther's tract, *To the Councilmen of All Cities in Germany That They Establish and Maintain Christian Schools* (LW 45:373):

> This is essential, not only that those who are to be our spiritual and temporal leaders may have books to read and study, but also that the good books may be preserved and not lost, together with the arts and languages which we now have by the grace of God.

This statement captures the spirit of the Richard C. Kessler Reformation Collection, which has been collecting sixteenth-century imprints and source documents relating to the Lutheran Reformation since 1987 and which continues to grow every year. The collection includes and acquires not only Protestant documents, but it also seeks to represent the context of the Reformation, as well as different positions within the larger discourse of religious reform in sixteenth-century Germany. This essay will outline the historical development of the Kessler Collection in Atlanta and describe its academic importance for Reformation research in North America. An important element that will be discussed is the idea of community outreach in various forms, such as the annual Reformation Day at Emory, concerts, exhibitions, presentations, and publications, all of which characterize the collection and its commitment to promote theological and historical research and make it accessible to wider audiences.

The History of The Kessler Collection

Richard C. Kessler is an American entrepreneur and philanthropist active in the Lutheran Church and various Lutheran organizations, including the Lutheran Brotherhood[1]—an insurance company whose board he chaired. Kessler helped develop the Days Inn hotel chain and served as the company's CEO, president, and chair. When Days Inn was sold in 1984, he developed a line of luxury hotels that constitute part of the Marriott Autograph Collection. He is a descendant of the Salzburgers—a group of Lutherans from Austria and Southern Germany that settled in Georgia near Savannah beginning in 1734 in order to escape religious persecution in Europe.

In October 1987, Richard Kessler and his wife Martha donated their private collection of sixteenth-century documents relating to the Lutheran Reformation to the Pitts Theology Library and so founded the Richard C. Kessler Reformation Collection at Emory University. Twelve years earlier, the Pitts Library had acquired the holdings of the Hartford Theological Seminary, which had been the leading theological library in North America in the late nineteenth and early twentieth centuries.[2] The addition of some 220,000 volumes—including a large collection of rare books—transformed a modest theological library in Georgia into the second-largest theological library at the time and laid the foundation for several of the library's current collections strengths, including hymnody, English church history, and African Christianities. Establishing a Lutheran collection at an historically Methodist institution therefore made sense for the Kesslers, who were Atlanta residents at the time, as Emory University in general and the Pitts Theology Library in particular were developing into a significant research center in the American South.

A formal agreement between the Kesslers and Emory University, represented by Pitts Library director Channing R. Jeschke and Emory University's President James T. Laney (a former dean of the Candler School of Theology at Emory and later US Ambassador to South Korea), was signed to establish a named collection and an endowment to support future acquisitions. An advisory committee with members from Emory University and the Lutheran Church[3] was formed to oversee the future development of the collection. It was decided that the scope of the collection was the Lutheran Reformation in Germany between 1500 and 1570. The reason for beginning with 1500—seventeen years before Martin Luther published his 95 Theses—was to allow for the inclusion of background documents important for the cultural and historical context of the Reformation. This move is indicative of the goal not to build a "fan club" collection, but to establish an academic research collection that documents various perspectives. Thus, from the beginning, there was also a conscious effort to collect not only Lutheran pieces but also materials by Luther's opponents. Materials written by other Reformers (e.g., in the Zwinglian or Calvinist traditions) are included insofar as they respond to the Lutheran Reformation or serve to shed light on the context of the Wittenberg movement.

The existence of an endowment allowed for a robust growth of the collection, which reached one thousand titles in about a decade. In the late 1990s, a four-volume annotated bibliography was compiled, which provided a detailed description of each title, including signature collation and bibliographic references, such as the Weimar Edition of Luther's Works, Josef Benzing's *Lutherbibliographie*, or Karl Hartfelder's *Philipp Melanchthon als Praeceptor Germaniae*. Also provided were an image of the title page, a Kessler number, and the local call number.[4] The work is organized chronologically with one page for each entry. It is unlikely that a bibliography like this would be published in print today, given the current advantages of online searchability, image representation, linked metadata, etc. Although the internet was already being used for academic research, it was still in its early phases of development and many of the possibilities we now take for granted had not been realized. The bibliography is in many ways an unusual, but also remarkable, testimony to the interplay of changing technologies and academic progress, another iteration of which (the development of printing in the fifteenth century and the reform of the university system) had helped set the stage for the Protestant Reformation itself. It is also noteworthy that, due to the fairly rapid growth of the collection, the bibliography was already out of date by the time it was published, the Kessler Collection having added over one hundred other volumes when the bibliography appeared in print in 1999. This problem, in a sense, confirms the success of the collection and brings to mind the words of the Basel printer Adam Petri on the title page to the first volume of his collection of Luther's writings in 1520 (Benzing 9): *Alio tomo, Domino volente, post hac meliora tradem* (the second volume, God willing, should be issued after these better parts). Although Petri went on to print many other works by the Reformer, he never issued a second volume to his *Lucubrationum*, as Luther's prolific output made it virtually impossible for any printer to keep pace and so maintain a comprehensive collection of all his writings as they appeared.

Processing, Preservation, and Maintenance

Materials in the Kessler Collection are cataloged and processed according to RBMS standards. In addition to the standard elements of bibliographic description, a typical entry for a Kessler Collection imprint includes a signature count, a citation or reference (e.g., Benzing, VD16, Hartfelder, etc.), and notes regarding specific print features, such as the use of red and black ink, graphic elements (woodcuts, title page borders, initials), and printed marginal annotations. Copy-specific features such as inscribed annotations or marks of provenance are included if present. Information about binding is of particular significance here, since book printing and binding were separate industries prior to the nineteenth century, and books were bound at the request of their owners after purchase. Furthermore, separate titles and publications were frequently bound together, sometimes for thematic reasons, sometimes for purely practical reasons. The result is called a *Sammelband* or "collected volume." All this copy-specific information underscores an important point for collecting and preserving rare books: it is essential to consider a book not only for its printed content, but also as a unique object in its own right, since marks of provenance may provide important information about the cultural context in which a book was read and interpreted.

While marks of provenance from previous owners are often a welcome feature of a book, processing and preserving a book, once it is added to the Kessler Collection, is based on the idea of leaving the book as unaltered as possible and to make any alteration reversible. Call numbers are written in the book with a #1 pencil, which is softer and erases more easily than the standard #2. A call number flag on acid-free and lignin-free paper is inserted into the book to facilitate shelving and retrieval. A specially designed Kessler Collection bookplate is affixed to the front inside cover of the book with a pH-neutral adhesive, usually hinged at the top edge. If the front inside cover contains any inscriptions or other older marks of ownership, the bookplate is placed elsewhere. The Pitts Theology Library does not have its own preservation department, but any pre-existing damage or instability to a book is examined by conservation experts at Emory University's main library. If necessary, a book is typically stabilized rather than restored, since the latter would represent an alteration.

For many years, the Pitts Theology Library was located in one of the oldest buildings on the Emory campus. The original building housed theology faculty offices and classrooms, a chapel, the office of Emory's chancellor, and the theology library. As the library grew and other spaces became available to Candler, the library expanded to displace most of the other elements (Hauk 2014, 93–105). Special accommodations were made for climate control and security according to modern standards, with a temperature of 65° F and a relative humidity below 50%. A non-water-based FM-200 fire suppression system was installed to avoid possible water damage in case of response to a fire. Access to the collection was restricted to staff working with special collections materials, and patrons would request materials for use in a designated area outside the rare book stacks. While the special collections facilities in the building were designed according to modern standards, the library quickly outgrew the building in general. The lack of a designated special collections reading room, for example, presented challenges for the use and presentation of Kessler Collection materials. The reference reading room (the nave of the original chapel) had a small alcove (the altar space) that allowed for eight glass cases approximately three feet wide and eighteen inches deep, accommodating a small number of books and descriptive labels. Lighting and climate control in these cases was dependent on the environment of the larger room, so that prolonged exposure was not ideal. The move into a new five-storey building in 2014 offered new possibilities. Archives and special collections now has a dedicated floor that even includes a vault area inside the restricted, climate controlled rare book stacks, which allows for the rarest and most valuable materials to be placed inside a doubly secured area with its own FM-200 system. There is an adjacent, dedicated reading room with controlled access, staffed at all times during special collections office hours, usually weekdays from 10:00 a.m. to 4:00 p.m. Use of Kessler Collection and other special collections materials is not restricted to those affiliated with Emory University but is open to anyone after a brief registration protocol.

Academic Significance of the Kessler Collection

Comparing a collection to those held by other institutions always entails difficulties. Every collection is unique and guided by its own parameters and policies. Some may add only Protestant materials but may include Calvinist or Anglican writings unrelated to the Lutheran Reformation. Other collections may focus on materials in a particular language (Latin, German, etc.) or a specific genre (e.g., pamphlets, biblical interpretation). The focus of a collection may be breadth, assembling as many different titles as possible but not allowing for the acquisition of different printings of the same title (which may be important for some research projects), while others may try to collect as many copies of a particular imprint as possible, as, for example, the Folger Shakespeare Library's collection of 1623 Shakespeare First Folios. As stated above, the Kessler Collection includes materials reflecting a variety of positions insofar as they relate to the Lutheran Reformation. It has also consistently tried to achieve a balance of breadth and depth, collecting a variety of titles but also different imprints of the same work. The latter are considered important, because the regional differences of the German language, in which many texts relevant to the Lutheran Reformation were written, were still very pronounced in the sixteenth century.

Since Martin Luther is the central figure of the Kessler Collection, one measure of the collection's academic importance may be a comparison of holdings with other North American libraries. An OCLC search (November 2020) of institutional holdings for books and pamphlets written, edited, or translated by Martin Luther and published between 1515 and 1600 shows that the ten North American libraries with the most holdings are as follows:

Library[5]	Holdings
Kesler Collection (Pitts Theology Library)	1069
Harvard University Libraries[6]	573
Yale University Libraries	419
Columbia University	373
Folger Shakespeare	372
Princeton University	348
Concordia Seminary, St. Louis	314
Library of Congress	180
United Lutheran Seminary	159
Huntington Library	128

The Kessler Collection is not only the sole institution in the American South on this list, but it tops the list by a fairly wide margin. With the exception of the combined holdings of several libraries at Harvard University, the Kessler Collection has more than twice the number of sixteenth-century Luther imprints than any other leading institution in North America.

A comparison with institutions outside North America is a different matter. One would naturally expect European and especially German libraries to have substantially more holdings, partly due to the geographic proximity of the original place of publication and also because these institutions had several more centuries to develop and maintain their collections. The leading library here is the Herzog August Bibliothek in Wolfenbüttel, Germany, which was founded in 1572 and early on incorporated the collections of such Reformation figures as Johannes Aurifaber or Matthias Flacius (Linder 1997). Another dominant institution is the Bavarian State Library in Munich, which serves as the home to such resources as VD16 (*Verzeichnis der im deutschen Sprachbereich erschienenen Drucke des 16. Jahrhunderts*, initially published in print, now available online, where it is continually updated) and which spearheads several digitization projects (Bayerische Staatsbibliothek n.d.). A search (October 2020) of holdings registered in VD16 for books and pamphlets written, edited, or translated by Martin Luther and published before 1570 has the following institutions as the ten leading libraries with regard to Luther holdings.

Library	Holdings
Herzog August Bibliothek, Wolfenbüttel	2226
Bavarian State Library, Munich	1798
Lutherhalle, Wittenberg	1340
Herzogin Anna Amalia Bibliothek, Weimar	959
Sächsische Landes- und Universitätsbibliothek, Dresden	950
University & State Library Saxony-Anhalt, Halle	929
University Library Heidelberg	919
State Library, Berlin	909
Protestant Seminary Library, Wittenberg	902
Research Library, Gotha	896

These figures place the results of a comparative search of North American libraries in context. They confirm that the holdings of Luther imprints at European institutions eclipse those of their North American counterparts, as one might expect, but they also show that the Kessler Collection does place among the leading libraries for Reformation research, not only in North America, but also world-wide. Only three institutions have more registered Luther holdings: the Herzog August Bibliothek in Wolfenbüttel, the Bavarian State Library in Munich, and the Lutherhalle in Wittenberg.

Select Highlights of the Kessler Collection

As of December 2020, the Kessler Collection holds a total of 3,980 titles. These include two indulgences, a plenary indulgence issued by Pope Leo X, and a special indulgence for clerical benefits issued by Albrecht of Brandenburg. It holds thirteen Lutheran church-orders (*Kirchenordnungen*), more than forty Protestant and nine Catholic catechisms, and several early Lutheran hymnals, including the *Acht-*

liederbuch (a proto-hymnal with eight hymns printed in 1524) and the only known copy of a 1536 printing in Low German of the *Enchiridion geistliker Leder vnde Psalmen* (also known as the *Slüter Hymnal*). The collection includes the first Latin and German editions of the Augsburg Confession, the first edition of the revised Augsburg Confession (Variata), and several later printings of either edition. There is the first edition of Philipp Melanchthon's *Loci communes* and more than thirty other printings of this work of systematic theology, which the reformer kept revising throughout his life. Space does not permit a full description of key holdings but, to demonstrate the importance of the collection in preserving and making available rare source documents of the Reformation and to illustrate why these pieces are important for research, a closer look at some exceptional pieces in two different areas may be helpful: the works of Martin Luther and early printed Bibles.

Martin Luther

With 1,069 imprints, writings by Martin Luther comprise over one quarter of the total holdings. According to an OCLC search (December 2020), over 20% of these are not held by any other North American library. There are two specimens of Martin Luther's handwriting in the collection. The first is a seven-line note in Latin about computing the age of the world (image 1). The note is specifically in reference to one of Luther's books from 1541 (image 2), in which he attempts to determine the second coming of Christ and the end of the world. Luther's calculations were not accepted by everyone in the Wittenberg circle, including his fellow reformer Philipp Melanchthon, and the seven-line note was most likely part of a larger conversation in which Luther was trying to justify his position.

Another item in the collection that contains an inscription in Martin Luther's own hand (image 3) was only recently identified as such, and the discovery helped determine the author of a previously pseudonymous tract.

This pamphlet had been in the Kessler Collection since the early 1990s and, while it was known that the title page contained an inscription in a sixteenth-century hand, the inscriber had not been identified. Furthermore, the author of this tract was unknown, since both names mentioned on the title page (Curtius Malaciola and Johannes Coticula) were clearly pseudonyms. Earlier speculations re-

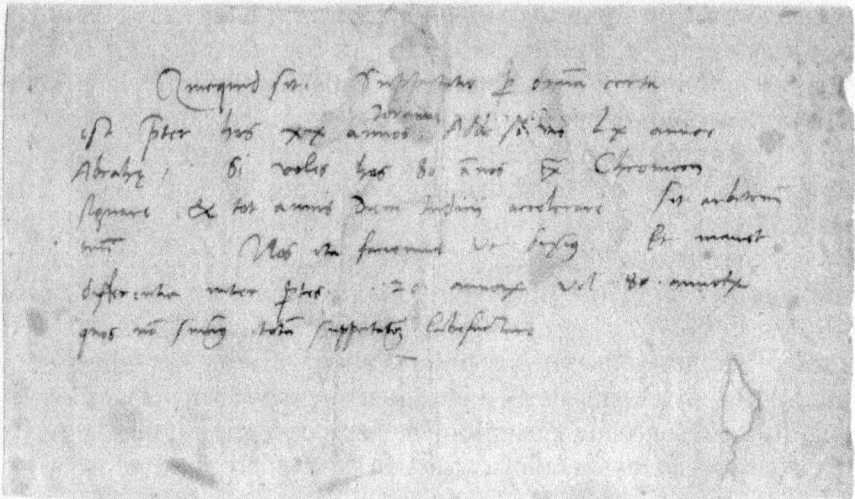

Image 1: Martin Luther manuscript, ca. 1541.
(Note on the computation of the world. 11 x 20 cm; 7 lines in Latin. MSS 090.)

garding the author of this tract had included the satirist Ulrich von Hutten and Johannes Caesarius, but no conclusive evidence could be found. In 2017, Dr. Ulrich Bubenheimer determined that a three-line gift inscription on the title was in Martin Luther's own hand and transcribed the note as follows: *idest p.[atris] lectoris / Betzensteynn / priori Volfgango Volprechto N[urenbergensi]* (= This is Pater Lector Betzensteynn, for Prior Wolfgang Wolprecht of Nuremberg). The figures mentioned in this note are known: Wolfgang Wolprecht was the prior of the Augustinian monastery in Nuremberg, and Johannes Petzenstein was a fellow Augustinian who had come to Wittenberg from Nuremberg to serve as lector and who was later one of Luther's two travel companions (with Nikolaus Amsdorff) on his return to Wittenberg from the Diet of Worms. This allows for the following reconstruction of events: the pamphlet was given by Martin Luther to Wolfgang Wolprecht, and Luther reveals to him the identity of the pseudonymous author as a monastic brother well known to both of them. The identification of Petzenstein also explains the name Johannes Coticula printed on the title page, since the Latin *coticula* means "whetstone" or *Wetzstein* in German, which becomes *Betzstein* or *Petztstein* in some German dialects.

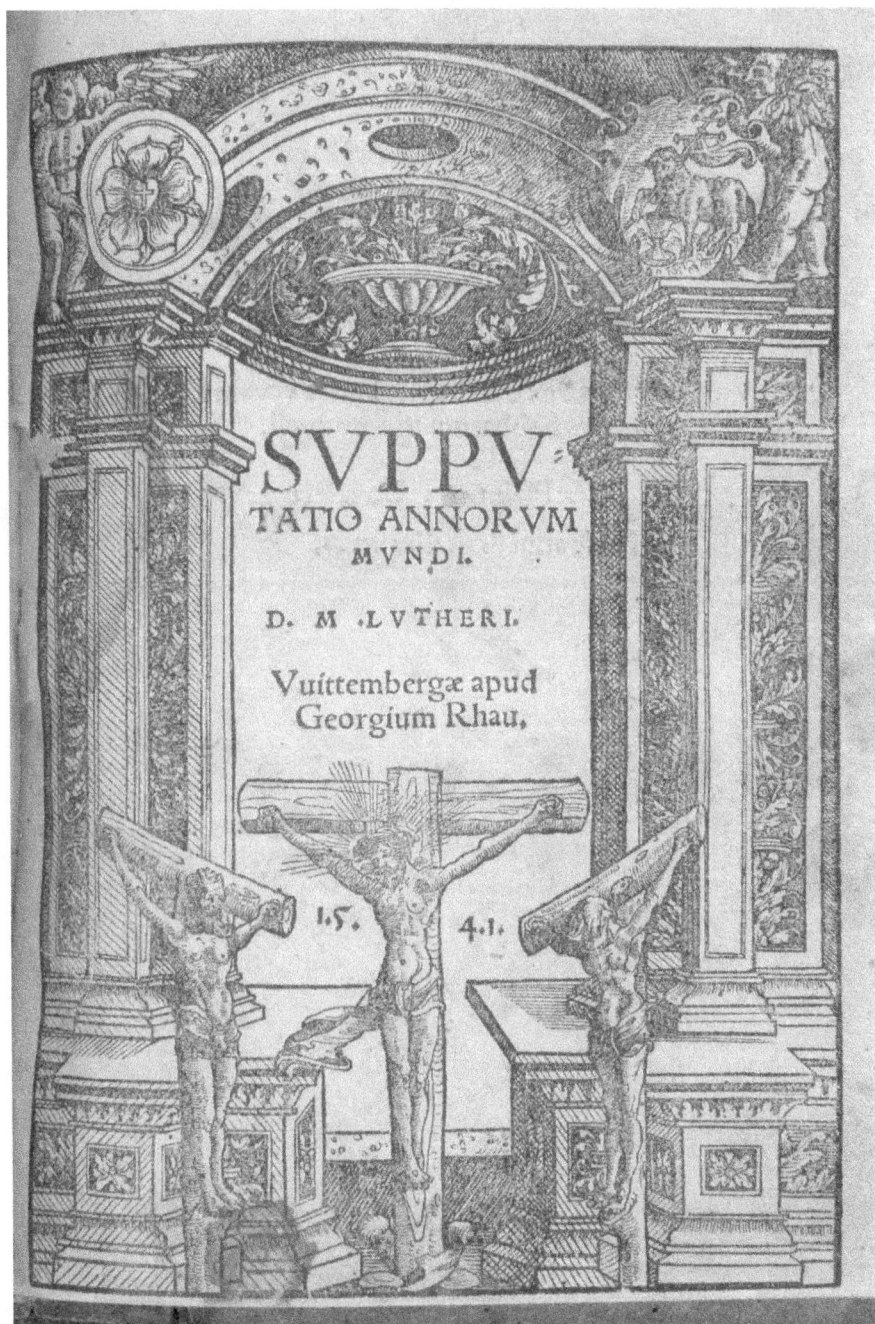

Image 2: Title page of Luther's *Supputatio annorum mundi* (1541). (Martin Luther, *Supputatio annorum mundi* (*Computation of the age of the world*) (Vuittembergae: apud Georgium Rhau, 1.5.4.1.) [204] p.; 21 cm (4to); Benzing 3366, VD16 L 6716; title within architectural woodcut border; initials. 1560 ASPH:2.)

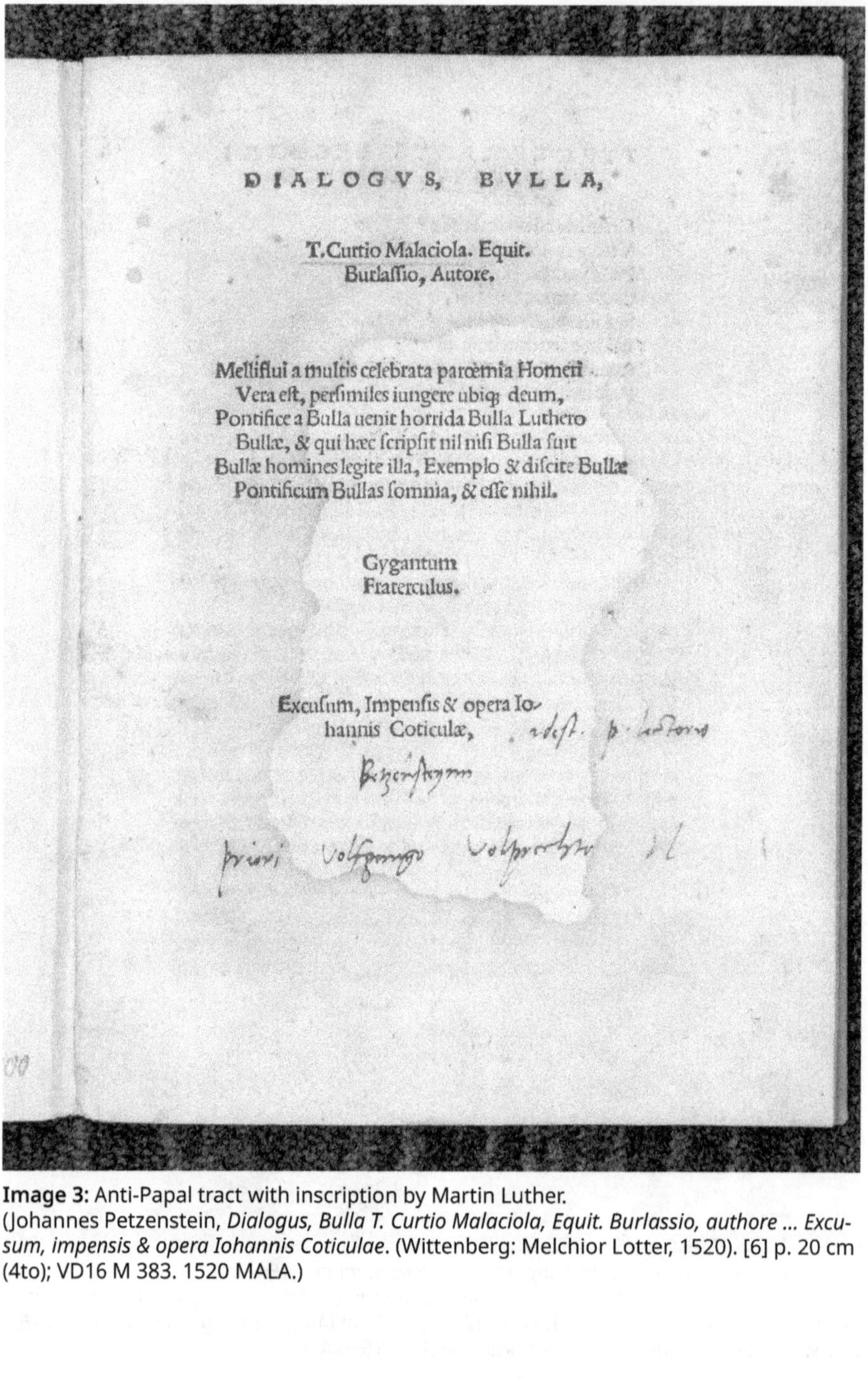

DIALOGVS, BVLLA,

T.Curtio Malaciola. Equit.
Burlaſſio, Autore.

Mellifluì a multis celebrata parœmia Homeri
Vera eſt, perſimiles iungere ubiq; deum,
Pontifice a Bulla uenit horrida Bulla Luthero
Bullæ, & qui hæc ſcripſit nil niſi Bulla fuit
Bullæ homines legite illa, Exemplo & diſcite Bullæ
Pontificum Bullas ſomnia, & eſſe nihil.

Gygantum
Fraterculus.

Excuſum, Impenſis & opera Iohannis Coticulæ,

Image 3: Anti-Papal tract with inscription by Martin Luther.
(Johannes Petzenstein, *Dialogus, Bulla T. Curtio Malaciola, Equit. Burlassio, authore ... Excusum, impensis & opera Iohannis Coticulae*. (Wittenberg: Melchior Lotter, 1520). [6] p. 20 cm (4to); VD16 M 383. 1520 MALA.)

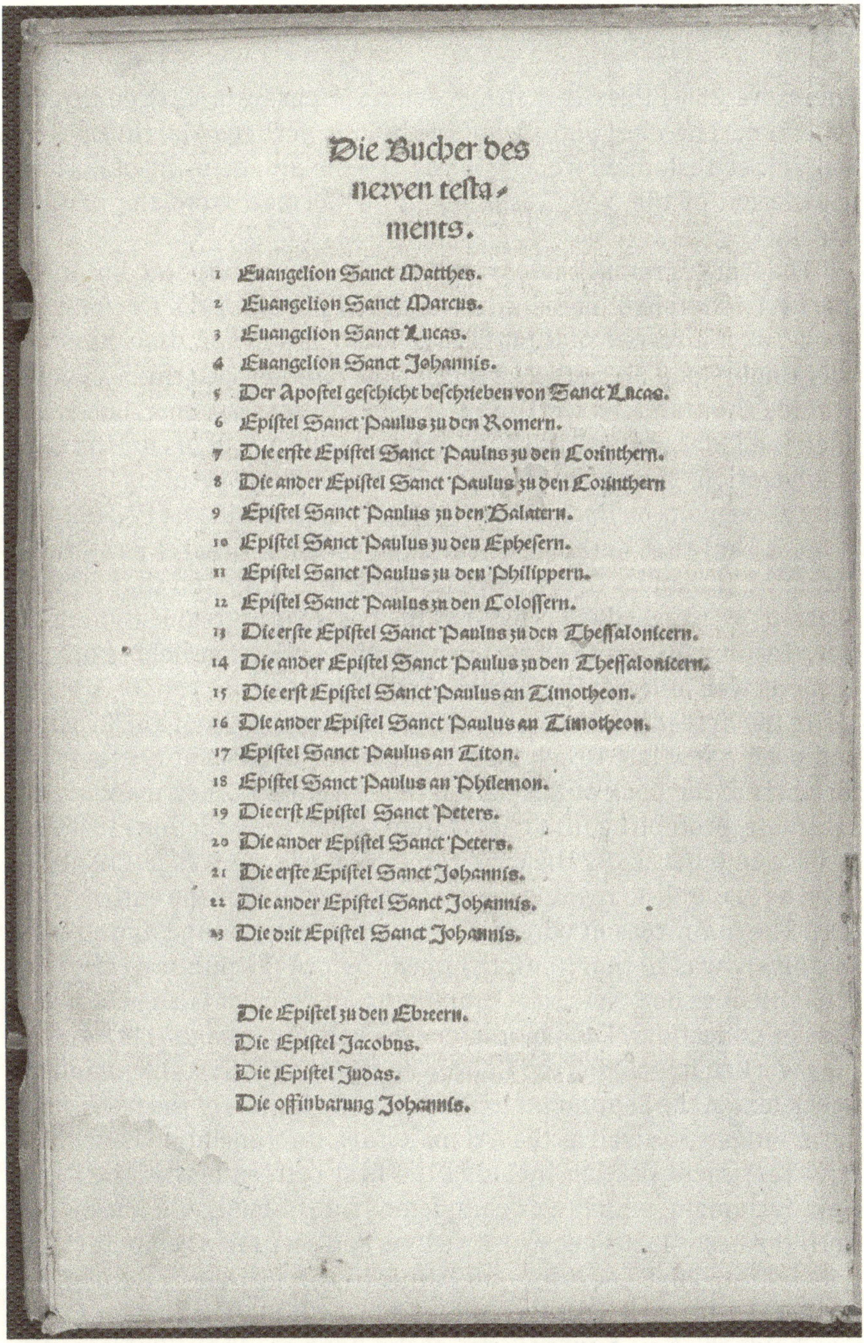

Die Bucher des nexven testaments.

1. Euangelion Sanct Matthes.
2. Euangelion Sanct Marcus.
3. Euangelion Sanct Lucas.
4. Euangelion Sanct Johannis.
5. Der Apostel geschicht beschrieben von Sanct Lucas.
6. Epistel Sanct Paulus zu den Romern.
7. Die erste Epistel Sanct Paulus zu den Corinthern.
8. Die ander Epistel Sanct Paulus zu den Corinthern
9. Epistel Sanct Paulus zu den Galatern.
10. Epistel Sanct Paulus zu den Ephesern.
11. Epistel Sanct Paulus zu den Philippern.
12. Epistel Sanct Paulus zu den Colossern.
13. Die erste Epistel Sanct Paulus zu den Thessalonicern.
14. Die ander Epistel Sanct Paulus zu den Thessalonicern.
15. Die erst Epistel Sanct Paulus an Timotheon.
16. Die ander Epistel Sanct Paulus an Timotheon.
17. Epistel Sanct Paulus an Titon.
18. Epistel Sanct Paulus an Philemon.
19. Die erst Epistel Sanct Peters.
20. Die ander Epistel Sanct Peters.
21. Die erste Epistel Sanct Johannis.
22. Die ander Epistel Sanct Johannis.
23. Die drit Epistel Sanct Johannis.

Die Epistel zu den Ebreern.
Die Epistel Jacobus.
Die Epistel Judas.
Die offinbarung Johannis.

Image 4: Table of contents from Luther's September Testament.
(*Das Newe Testament Deuotzsch*. (Vuittemberg: [Melchior Lotther for Christian Döring and Lukas Cranach, September 1522]). [222] leaves; 31 cm (folio in 6's and 4's); VD16 B 4318, Darlow & Moule 4188; woodcuts, initials, bound in blind-stamped, bleached pigskin of the 17th century over wooden boards. 1522 BIBL:1.)

Bibles

There are 286 Bibles in Latin, German, Hebrew, and Greek in the collection. The most significant of these is perhaps Martin Luther's September Testament (images 4 and 5)—the first printing of Luther's translation of the New Testament into German from the original Greek.

The work is remarkable from a theological standpoint, but it also marks a watershed moment in the development of the German language, as it ensured that Luther's Thuringian-Saxon dialect, which was understood in both Northern and Southern Germany, would provide the standard for High German in years to come. Lucas Cranach the Elder provided twenty-one full page woodcuts for the Book of Revelation. The work is bound with a 1522 Basel printing by Adam Petri of sermons by the medieval mystic Johannes Tauler (VD16 J 785).

It is said that Luther was inspired to learn Greek by the publication of Erasmus's Greek New Testament in 1516 and that he used Erasmus's second edition (1519) as the basis for his translation of the New Testament into German. The Kessler Collection holds both editions, as well as the third, fourth, and fifth editions.

In the first edition of his Greek New Testament (image 6), Erasmus had used a few late Greek manuscripts as the basis of his text, and for parts of the Book of Revelation there were no Greek manuscripts available, prompting him to translate the missing sections from Latin back into Greek. By the time the second edition was published in 1519, he was able to include manuscript evidence for the entire Greek text. The main reason why the 1516 edition was edited and printed so quickly was so that it might appear before the publication of Cardinal Jimenez de Cisneros's Complutensian Polyglot (also held by the Kessler Collection). The Complutensian Polyglot (image 7) is a six-volume work that included the Hebrew text of the Old Testament and the Greek text of the Septuagint to the right and the left of the traditional Latin Vulgate,[7] as well as the Aramaic Targum translation below. The New Testament portion included the first printed text of the Greek New Testament, which was completed in 1514 but could not be sold until the early 1520s because Erasmus had secured a temporary monopoly from Pope Leo X for publishing his Greek New Testament.

Regarding early editions of the Hebrew Bible, the Kessler Collection holds the first four editions of the Rabbinic Bible. Published in

Image 5: Woodcut illustration by Lucas Cranach the Elder in Luther's September Testament (Four Riders of the Apocalypse).

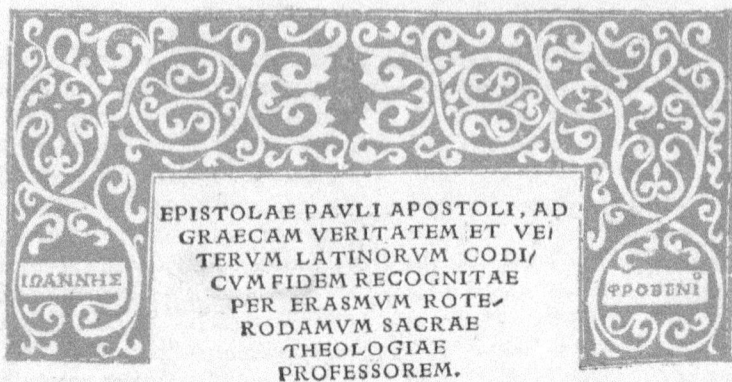

EPISTOLAE PAVLI APOSTOLI, AD
GRAECAM VERITATEM ET VE/
TERVM LATINORVM CODI/
CVM FIDEM RECOGNITAE
PER ERASMVM ROTE-
RODAMVM SACRAE
THEOLOGIAE
PROFESSOREM.

ΠΑΥΛΟΥ ΤΟΥ ΑΠΟΣΤΟΛΟΥ Η
ΠΡΟΣ ΡΩΜΑΙΟΥΣ ΕΠΙΣΤΟΛΗ

EPISTOLA PAVLI APO/
STOLI AD ROMANOS.

Image 6: First page of Paul's letter to the Romans in Erasmus's Greek New Testament (1st ed.)

(*Nouum instrumentu[m] omne diligenter ab Erasmo Roterodamo recognitum & emendatum. (Apud inclytam Germaniae Basilaeam: in aedibus Ioannis Frobenij Hammelbergensis, mense Februario. Anno M.D.XVI).* [28], 324, 672 [i.e. 636], [3] pages; 32 cm (folio in 6's and 8's); Darlow & Moule 4591, VD16 B 4196; bound in blind-stamped, polished calf over wooden boards; old ownership mark: "Ex Bibliotheca Sci[en]tiae SS. Joan. Bapt. & Jan. E. in Haugis. Herbipoluis," manuscript marginalia. 1516 BIBL B.)

Preserving the Past & Engaging the Future

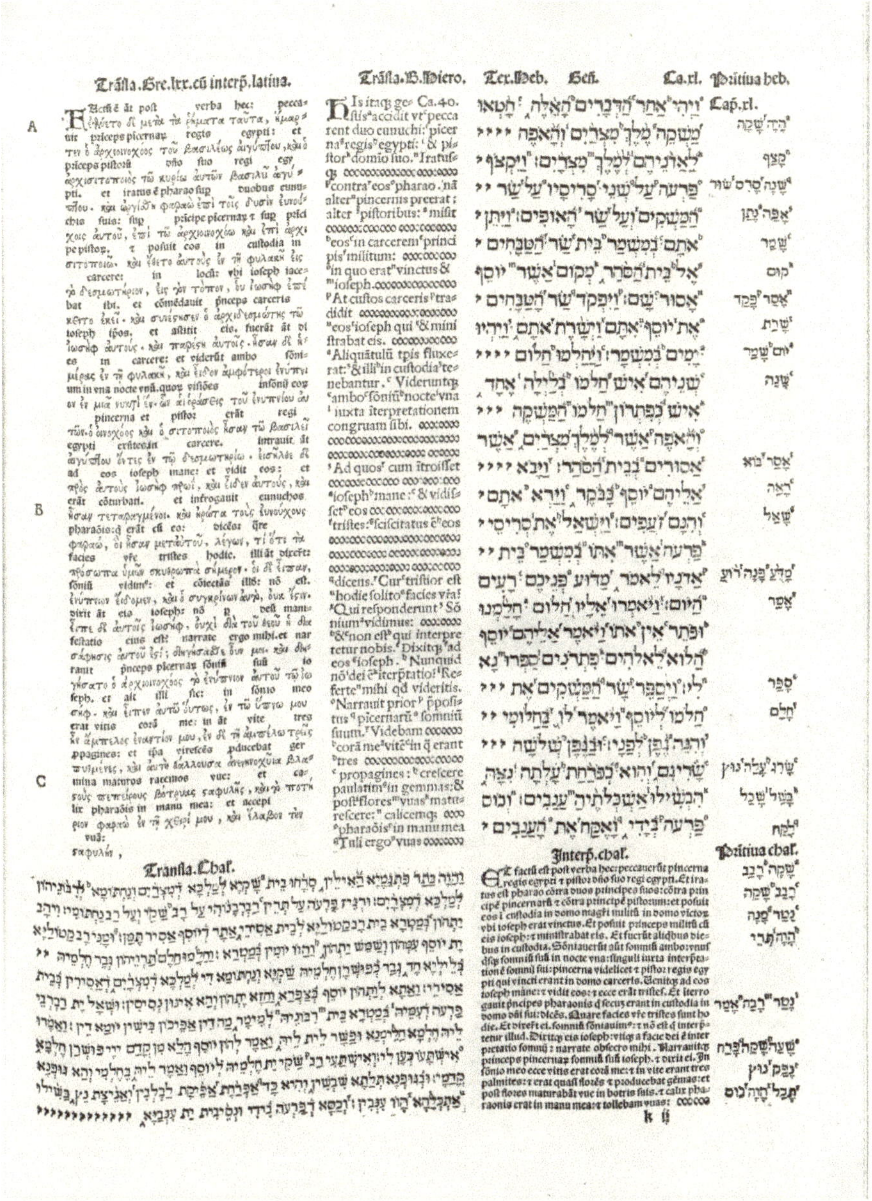

Image 7: A page from the book of Genesis in the Complutensian Polyglot (1514). (*Uetus testamentu[m] multiplici lingua nu[n]c primo impressum* [v.1] ... ; *Nouum testamentum grece et latine in academia complutensi nouiter impressum* [v.5]. Academia Complutensi: Industria Arnaldi Guillelmi de Brocario, in Academia Complutensi, [1514–1517]. 6 vols.; 39 cm (folio in 8's and 6's); Darlow & Moule 1412; title page in red and black with coat of arms of Cardinal Jiménez, surrounded by ornamental engraved, woodcut border. 1514 BIBL V.1–6.)

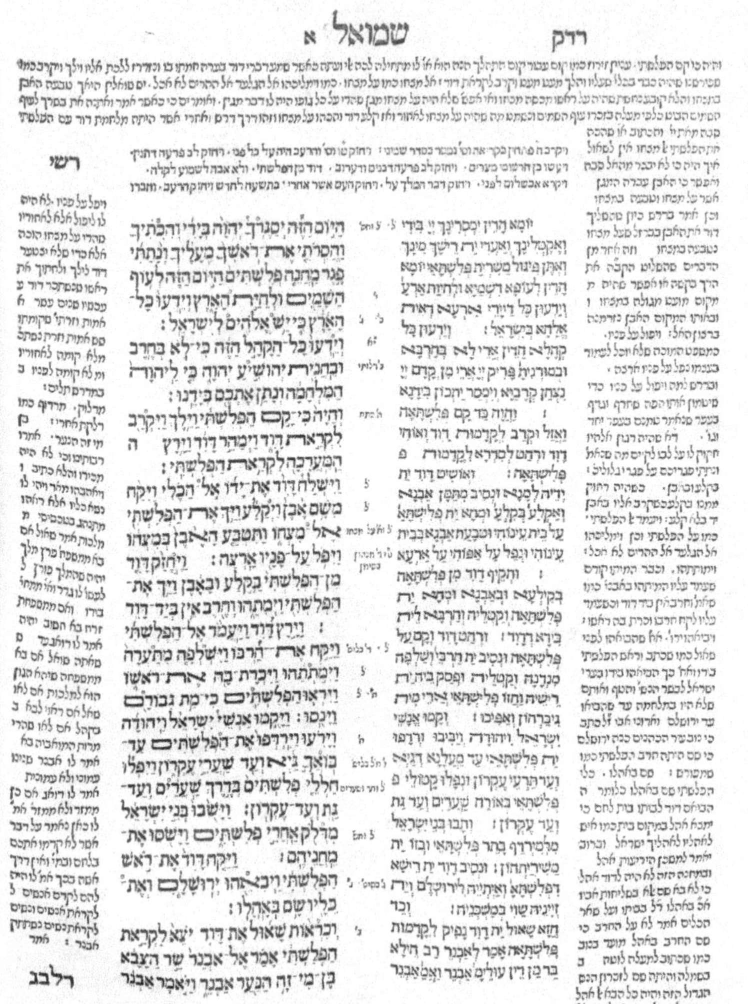
שמואל א
רדק
רשי
רלבג

Image 8: A page from the First Book of Samuel in the first Rabbinic Bible, edited by Jacob ben Hayyim (1524).
(תרה נבים וכתובים. Venice: Daniel Bomberg, 1524. 4 vols.; 39 cm (folio); Haberman 93; 1524 BIBL V.1–4.)

Venice in 1517, 1525, 1547, and 1567, it combined the biblical text along with rabbinic commentary (Rashi, Ibn Ezra, Nachmanides, etc.).

The first edition (1517) was edited by Felix Pratensis, a Sephardic Jew who had converted to Catholicism. That, and the fact that the printer—Daniel Bomberg—included a dedication to Pope Leo X, led to a general rejection of the work in Jewish circles. The second edition of 1524, on the other hand, was edited by the Masoretic scholar Yaaqov Ben Hayyim. It was much better received, and some would discount the 1517 printing altogether and consider the 1524 edition as truly the first Rabbinic Bible. It became the standard text of the Hebrew Bible and was the version that many Christian translators used in the sixteenth century and beyond.

Outreach and Research Initiatives

As mentioned above, the Kessler Collection is primarily an academic research collection, but from the beginning there has been a conscious effort to broaden access to the collection beyond Emory University. Presentations to church groups and schools are quite common and encouraged. In addition, there are several other outreach initiatives, including an annual celebration of Reformation Day at Emory, and exhibitions of materials from the collection, publications, and digitizations.

Beginning in 1988, Pitts Library has hosted an annual celebration of Reformation Day. The program for this day has changed several times over the years but has typically included a church service and sermon, one or more lectures on a specific Reformation topic, a presentation of new acquisitions for the collection, and often a Reformation-themed concert, connecting the music of the Lutheran composer Johann Sebastian Bach to a particular piece in the collection. The goal of this celebration was to raise awareness of the collection as well as to raise funds for future acquisitions. In recent years, friends of the collection have been offered the opportunity to "adopt" a volume in the collection for which they would have their names inscribed on the Kessler Collection bookplate and entered into the catalog record, indicating that the item was acquired with their subvention.

The 2020 COVID-19 pandemic presented a number of challenges. A traditional gathering for Reformation Day was impossible, but considerations to move the celebration to a virtual environment also prompted a new program—the Kessler Conversations (Pitts Theology Library n.d.). In the fall of 2020, a series of three online interviews was conducted by Pitts Library director Bo Adams with a focus on the relationship between Reformation theology and infectious disease. A conversation with Anna Johnson (Garrett-Evangelical Theological Seminary) focused on Martin Luther's sermon, "Whether One Should Flee the Deadly Plague," and other related writings. A second conversation with Erik Heinrichs (Winona State University) dealt with medical and cultural responses to plagues in sixteenth-century Germany, while the final interview, with Ronald Rittgers (Valparaiso University), explored the theology of suffering in relation to the plague as a central theme in sixteenth-century religious thought. Moving to an online format offered greater flexibility in terms of scheduling speakers and made the program accessible to people who might not otherwise have been able to attend. Each of the three interviews was live-streamed as well as recorded for future viewing. The program was well received, and a new series of conversations with a focus on poverty in the Reformation and today was scheduled for the Spring of 2021.

The construction of a new library building in 2014 included a twelve-hundred square foot gallery space with twenty-two custom display cases, facilitating the exhibition of Kessler Collection materials in ways that were not previously possible. The library usually has three exhibitions per year, featuring different collections from its special collections holdings. The fall exhibition has traditionally included materials from the Kessler Collection, as it coincides with the annual celebration of Reformation Day at Emory, and the focus usually aligns with the theme chosen for the year. Since 2017 marked the 500th anniversary of Martin Luther's 95 Theses, all three exhibitions were Kessler-themed. The first of these was "Law and Grace: Martin Luther, Lucas Cranach, and the Promise of Salvation" (October 11, 2016–January 16, 2017) and was done in collaboration with four German museums from the heartland of the Reformation: the State Museum of Prehistory in Halle, the Luther Memorial Foundation of Saxony-Anhalt (which includes the Luther House and the Melanchthon House), the German Historical Museum in Berlin, and the Foundation Schloss Friedenstein in Gotha. This exhibit was part of a larger initiative by the German state department, called "Here I Stand," which also included Luther exhibitions in New York ("Word and Image: Martin Luther's Reformation," Morgan Library & Museum, New York City, October 7, 2016–January 22, 2017) and Minneapolis ("Martin Luther: Art and the Reformation," Minneapolis Institute of Art, October 30, 2016–January 15, 2017). The centerpiece was an oil painting by Lucas Cranach the Younger, entitled *Law and Grace*, which depicted a tree that is dead on one side (law) and flourishing on the other (grace), surrounded by religious symbolism illustrating this theological dichotomy.[8] The last exhibition of 2017 celebrated the 30th anniversary of the establishment of the Kessler Collection.

Occasional publications provide another opportunity for outreach. There are two irregularly published series that have focused on materials from the Kessler Collection. The first is Emory Texts and Studies in Ecclesial Life, which issues larger book projects and includes the four-volume annotated Kessler Bibliography mentioned earlier. Another series—Occasional Publications of the Pitts Theology Library—includes shorter publications, often translations into English or Spanish of pamphlets held by the Kessler Collection. Another recent translation project should be mentioned in this context: *Luther as Heretic: Ten Catholic Responses to Martin Luther, 1518–1541*, a collection of translations from Latin or German into English of texts written by Martin Luther's contemporary opponents (Graham and Bagchi 2019). The goal of this and other translation projects is to make texts previously unavailable in English accessible for research and study.

The discovery, noted earlier, of a previously unknown Luther inscription in 2017 gave rise to a promising research initiative. Ulrich Bubenheimer, who had identified the inscription, was invited to Atlanta to visit the Pitts Library and explore other contemporary inscriptions and marks of provenance in the Kessler Collection. In addition to a detailed report, Dr. Bubenheimer also co-curated an exhibit in the fall of 2019, entitled "A Book More Precious than Gold: Reading the Printed Book Alongside Its Previous Owners and Readers" (Pitts Theology Library n.d.). To encourage further research on Reformation source documents, a research fellowship was established that included an honorarium as well as the cost of expenses for young scholars in the field of Reformation studies.

In 1999, the Kessler Collection had begun digitizing woodcut images and engravings found in its books. The focus was specifically on images rather than text, and the audience for the Digital Image Archive was an informed laity rather than academic specialists. The images, which could be downloaded freely for non-commercial use in JPG or PDF format, were particularly popular with churches, which would use them as illustrations for Sunday bulletins. For use in publications, a high-resolution TIFF image could be provided for a nominal fee. The DIA eventually grew beyond the Kessler Collection to include other books from Pitts special collections and now has over sixty-five thousand images.

More recent digitization projects have focused more heavily on texts or a combination of text and images. Technological developments in recent years have also opened up new possibilities. Thus, unlike the DIA, which scanned and preserved images in black and white, recent digitization efforts by the Pitts Library are in color and may include hyperlinked background information. A good example of future initiatives is a project currently under development but available in its beta version (Adams 2019). The work in question—*Passional Christi vnnd Antichristi* (*Passion of Christ and Antichrist*)—is an anonymous polemical pamphlet, often attributed to Martin Luther, with woodcut engravings attributed to Lucas Cranach the Elder. It is a series of thirteen contrasting image pairs with scenes from the Passion of Christ on the left side and scenes from the life of the pope on the other, culminating in the final juxtaposition with Christ ascending to heaven and the pope moving in the opposite direction.

Since the work may be analyzed from a variety of angles, there are various annotations provided by experts in the field, including an art-historical explanation of graphic features in the engravings, historical and theological background and context, as well as a transcription of the sixteenth-century inscribed annotations found in the copy held by the Pitts Theology Library. The goal is to provide a multi-layered, interactive digital work, which offers the reader a thick description of the content and context of the sixteenth-century work.

Conclusions

When Luther wrote to the "councilmen of all cities in Germany" of the importance that "the good books may be preserved and not lost," he was not referring to his own books but to the books that he deemed essential for a good Christian education, including works on the arts and languages. He was thinking of a solid, humanist education in the biblical languages and classical authors, along with the early Christian writers and, of course, Scripture itself. Regarding his own books, he wrote in 1545, one year before his death: "I wished that all my books were buried in perpetual oblivion, so that there might be room for better ones." This self-deprecating judgment appears in the preface to the first volume to the Latin portion of his collected works published in Wittenberg (LW 43:327–8). The paragraph before the statement explains his reluctant approval to the publication of his writings:

> For a long time I strenuously resisted those who wanted my books, or more correctly my confused lucubrations, published. I did not want the labors of the ancients to be buried by my new works and the reader kept from reading them. Then, too, by God's grace a great many systematic books now exist, among which the *Loci communes* of Philip excel, with which a theologian and a bishop can be beautifully and abundantly prepared to be mighty in preaching the doctrine of piety, especially since the Holy Bible itself can now be had in nearly every language. But my books, as it happened, yes, as the lack of order in which the events transpired made it necessary, are accordingly crude and disordered chaos, which is now not easy to arrange even for me.

As Luther's writings, as well as those of his friends and opponents, have become an important chapter in the history of Christianity and, as such, indispensable reading for any student and scholar of religious history, it is fortunate that his books were not buried in perpetual oblivion. The Richard C. Kessler Reformation Collection plays an important part not only in preserving these documents but also in making them accessible in North America and beyond.

References

Adams, Bo. 2019 *"Passional Christi vnnd Antichristi." https://boadams01.github.io/passional/pages.*

Bayerische Staatsbibliothek. n.d. "Verzeichnis der im deutschen Sprachbereich erschienenen Drucke des 16. Jahrhunderts (VD 16)." Accessed February 1, 2021. *https://www.bsb-muenchen.de/sammlungen/historische-drucke/recherche/vd-16.*

Benzing, Josef & Helmut Claus, 1989. *Lutherbibliographie: Verzeichnis der gedruckten Schriften Martin Luthers bis zu dessen Tod.* 2.

Auflage, Bibliotheca Bibliographica Aureliana; 10, 143. Baden-Baden: V. Koerner.

Briggs, Kenneth A. 1976. "Prized Theological Library Sold To Emory U. for $1.75 Million." *New York Times*, August 21, 1976. *https://www.nytimes.com/1976/08/21/archives/new-jersey-pages-prized-theological-library-sold-to-emory-u-for-175.html*.

Bugenhagen, Johannes. 1996. *A Christian Sermon Over the Body and at the Funeral of the Venerable Dr. Martin Luther.* Translated by Kurt Hendel. Atlanta: Pitts Theology Library.

Crist, Stephen A. 1994. *Enchiridion Geistliker Leder Unde Psalmen.* Emory Texts and Studies in Ecclesial Life, 2. Atlanta: Scholars Press.

———. 2007. "Early Lutheran Hymnals and Other Musical Sources in the Kessler Reformation Collection at Emory University." In *Music and Theology: Essays in Honor of Robin A. Leaver*, edited by Daniel Zager, 9–30. Lanham: Scarecrow Press.

Graham, M. Patrick, ed. 2017. *Renewing Church and University: The Twenty-seventh Annual Reformation Day at Emory.* Emory Texts and Studies in Ecclesial Life, 7. Atlanta: Pitts Theology Library.

——— and David Bagchi, eds. 2019. *Luther as Heretic: Ten Catholic responses to Martin Luther, 1518–1541.* Eugene: Pickwick Publications.

Grater, Fred A., and William Bradford Smith. 1999. *The Richard C. Kessler Reformation Collection: An Annotated Bibliography.* Emory Texts and Studies in Ecclesial Life, 3–6. Atlanta: Scholars Press.

Hartfelder, Karl. 1964. *Philipp Melanchthon als Praeceptor Germaniae.* Nieuwkoop: B. de Graaf.

Hauk, Gary S. 2014. *Religion and Reason Joined: Candler at One Hundred.* Atlanta: Candler School of Theology, Emory University.

Leaver, Robin. 1995. *Elisabeth Creutziger, the Magdeburg Enchiridion, 1536 & Reformation Theology.* Atlanta: Pitts Theology Library.

Linder, Leo G. 1997. *Die Herzog August Bibliothek und Wolfenbüttel*. Braunschweig: Edition Westermann.

Luther, Martin. 1520. *Synceri lucubrationum: Pars una*. Basel: Adam Petri, 1520.

———. 1883–. *Werke: Kritische Gesamtausgabe*. Weimar: Herman Böhlau.

———. 2017. *Un sermón sobre indulgencias y gracia*. Translated by Alberto Garcia. Atlanta: Pitts Theology Library.

Pelikan, Jaroslav et al., eds. 1955–. *Luther's Works*. Saint Louis: Concordia-Publishing House.

Pitts Theology Library. n.d. "A Book More Precious than Gold." Accessed February 1, 2021. *https://exhibitions.pitts.emory.edu/exhibitions/more-precious-than-gold*.

———. n.d. "Kessler Conversations." Accessed February 1, 2021. *https://pitts.emory.edu/about/news-events/kesslerconversations.cfm*.

Rettberg, Daniel J. 1997. "Melanchthoniana in the Richard C Kessler Reformation Collection." In *Philip Melanchthon (1497–1560) and the Commentary*, edited by Timothy J. Wengert and M. Patrick Graham, 238–97. Sheffield: Sheffield Academic Press.

Tetzel, Johann. 2012. *Johann Tetzel's Rebuttal Against Luther's Sermon on Indulgences and Grace*. Translated by Dewey Kramer. Atlanta: Pitts Theology Library.

———. 2017. *Una refutación contra Lutero concerniente un sermón sobre Indulgencias y gracia*. Translated by Alberto Garcia. Atlanta: Pitts Theology Library.

Zwingli, Ulrich. 2016. *The Implementation of the Lord's Supper*. Translated by Jim West. Atlanta: Pitts Theology Library.

Notes

1   In 2001, the Lutheran Brotherhood merged with the Aid Association for Lutherans to form Thrivent, a not-for-profit organization for financial services.

2   A *New York Times* article at the time of sale noted: "Among the factors that led trustees to choose Emory among several contenders, including Fuller Seminary in Pasadena, Calif., the State University at Stony Brook, and the Billy Graham Center in Chicago, were its respected academic reputation, its financial backing and the character of its existing library (Briggs 1976).

3   The Evangelical Lutheran Church in America (ELCA) was formed a few months later—on January 1, 1988—as a merger of the Lutheran Church in America, the American Lutheran Church, and the Association of Evangelical Lutheran Churches.

4   Call numbers for the Kessler Collection follow the local convention for special collections books at the Pitts Theology Library and consist of the date of publication followed by the first four letters of the main entry (e.g., 1529 LUTH). In situations where the main entry is duplicated, an additional suffix is added, beginning with "A" and proceeding alphabetically, adding double digits when necessary (1529 LUTH B, 1522 LUTH EEE). In a *Sammelband*, where distinct publications were bound together, the call number of the first title bound in the volume is followed by ":1". Each subsequent title bound in the same volume receives the same call number with the number following the colon being successively increased by 1 (e.g., 1521 BIEL:1, 1521 BIEL:2, 1521 BIEL 3, etc.).

5   Unless otherwise indicated, a university's holdings includes the holdings of all its libraries.

6   Harvard includes the holdings of the Houghton Library, the Widener Library, and the Andover-Harvard Theological Library. Other Harvard libraries do not hold sixteenth-century imprints by Luther.

7   The placement of the three language versions in columns with the Vulgate in the center prompted some cynics critical of non-Latin versions of the Bible to remark that the Vulgate appeared like Christ on the cross between the two thieves.

8   This graphic was a popular motif in early Lutheran art and is also seen in several woodcuts and even bindings in books held by the Kessler Collection.

CHAPTER 2

Reading the Materiality of a Pamphlet Collection

The German Reformation at the Folger Shakespeare Library[1]

CAROLINE DUROSELLE-MELISH

he Folger Shakespeare Library in Washington, DC, is well known for its eighty-two copies of Shakespeare's First Folio and its early English book collection, but few people are aware of its collection of sixteenth-century German Reformation pamphlets—one of the largest in North America. While undeniably important, the reputation of the Folger English collections has obscured the existence of significant holdings in other subject areas, which also make up the library's identity. Furthermore, the presence of a German Reformation collection at the Folger Library is unexpected, since most other North American collections on this subject are located in theological libraries (Gatch 2007, 3).

This essay seeks to shed light on a too-little-known collection at the Folger Library. In doing so, it aims to capture the historical complexity of the collection through a close examination of its books' material features. Indeed, the meaning of a collection goes beyond the size and the content of its books; it is also determined by their individual and collective histories. As Aaron Pratt has aptly written,

> early printed books carry with them the years between their original creation and their presence in twenty-first-century institutions and private collections. They are home to bookplates, stamps, labels, shelfmarks, and manuscript inscriptions… many books have seen substantial structural changes… each book's accretions and subtractions have meaning. (Harry Ransom Center, January 27, 2021)

These alterations take on new meaning when a book becomes part of a different collection, small or large. As Ben Kinmont writes, "When the book joins a library, it takes on another voice… [and] becomes part of a communal body that creates something larger than the sum of its parts" (Kinmont 2020, vii).

It is the sum of these individual and collective voices that makes up the significance of the German Reformation collection in the Folger Library.

Foundation of the German Reformation Collection

The Folger Shakespeare Library opened its doors in 1932 with, at its core, the collection of its founders—Henry and Emily Folger—whose interests were focused on Shakespeare and Shakespeariana. With the acquisition in 1938 of Robert Leicester Harmsworth's collection of over twelve thousand English books printed between 1475 and 1640, the library became overnight one of the largest repositories of early English books on either side of the Atlantic. While the Folgers had acquired English works mostly to illuminate Shakespeare's literary world, the Harmsworth acquisition expanded the library's scope to include early modern British culture broadly defined. After World War II, Folger directors and curators kept developing the English collections and extended their acquisitions to works as late as the end of the seventeenth century. By the late 1950s and early 1960s, they had started aggressively acquiring continental books—until then, less of a priority at the Folger Library—and focused on texts that would help to inform English culture. Pamphlets on the German Reformation fell into this category.

The building of the German Reformation collection was intended to support and develop a subject area already well documented
in the collections—namely, the English Reformation. Thanks to the
Harmsworth collection and acquisitions in the 1950s, the library
owned copies of numerous works by English reformers as well as
multiple editions of sixteenth-century English translations of works
by their German and Swiss counterparts.

The acquisition of two major collections established the Folger German Reformation collection: first, the purchase of about 250
pamphlets from Sir Thomas Phillipps's collection in 1958, and then
the purchase of Emanuel Stickelberger's collection almost twenty
years later in 1977.

Both collections concentrate on the early years of the German
Reformation. Most of the Phillipps titles were printed between 1502
and 1550, while the 850 books in the Stickelberger collection were
printed between 1502 and 1658, with 516 titles published before Luther's death in 1546. As Drew Thomas (2019, 276–7) has recently re-
marked, Luther was not only a prolific writer, he was also one of the
best published authors of his time. It is therefore not surprising that
the two collections, with their early chronological focus, include 370
different editions of his works that pre-date his death: that is, about
two-thirds of the total number of Luther's publications produced
during his lifetime (Folger Shakespeare Library 1983).

The works of other early reformers and supporters of the Reformation, such as Andreas von Karlstadt (1486–1541), Wenceslaus Linck
(1483–1547), and Ulrich von Hutten (1488–1523), are also represented
in both collections. Emanuel Stickelberger (1884–1962) was interested in documenting the Reformation movement in Switzerland—his
native country—and collected the works of Swiss reformers, such as
Ulrich Zwingli (1484–1531), Jean Calvin (1509–64), Johann Oecolampadius (1482–1531), and Heinrich Bullinger (1504–75). His collection
is also broader in scope than Phillipps's, which mostly consists of
pamphlets by Luther (190 out of 250 titles total). In addition to sermons, it includes reports on important Swiss disputations, a few early satirical dialogues, mandates, and declarations by the princes of
the Schmalkaldic League and others. It also includes Bibles and psalters, among which are copies of the 1522 second edition of Luther's
New Testament and the first French Protestant Bible, printed in Neuchatel in 1535.

The Folger Library kept acquiring books and pamphlets on the
Reformation after the purchase of the Phillipps and Stickelberger

collections and tried to fill in gaps, while limiting its acquisitions to printed items within the chronological range of the two collections. When doing so, it considered other holdings in the library. Hence, acquisitions of the works of humanist thinkers of the pre-Reformation were guided by the impressive Folger Erasmus collection—now consisting of four hundred different pre-1800 editions. Likewise, acquisitions of works by Catholic authors opposed to the Reformation movement were most likely driven by the recusant literature present in the collections.[2]

One should note that the Folger German Reformation collection is strictly made up of printed books. Only one manuscript—an autograph letter by Philip Melanchthon (1497–1560)—came with the Phillipps collection (Melanchthon c. 1545).[3] Furthermore, most of the books are pamphlets, usually under a hundred pages long, in a quarto or octavo format, and typically written in German.

Collective Voices: The Phillipps Collection

Phillipps's and Stickelberger's collections carry distinct collective voices despite having the same focus. Much, indeed, separated the two collectors: the scale of their collections, their attitude towards collecting, and, most importantly, the circumstances under which they acquired their books. These differences greatly affected the shape of their collections.

Sir Thomas Phillipps (1792–1872) is no doubt one of the greatest collectors of all time, at least in terms of the size of his collection. It was so large—it has been estimated at sixty thousand manuscripts and fifty thousand books—that its dispersal lasted well into the twentieth century. In 1946, Phillipps's great-grandson, Alan Fenwick, sold the remnant of the collection (i.e., another twelve thousand manuscripts and an unrecorded number of books) to the bookseller brothers Philip and Lionel Robinson, who were based in London. It was from Philip Robinson that the Folger Shakespeare Library acquired the Phillipps's collection of Reformation pamphlets in 1958 (Robinson, August 1, 1968). The library had already done business with the Robinsons before World War II, when it had acquired from them the love letters of John Donne, among other manuscripts (Munby 1960, 5:96).

Phillipps's remarkable manuscript collection has overshadowed his printed books and, even within the realm of his printed books, most attention has focused on his collection of incunables. Little appears to have been written on his books printed after 1500, which included historical works on the British Isles, books on colonial America, travel narratives, and many bibliographies and catalogues, some of which are now in the Folger Library collections. Phillips was a voracious acquisitor, but this did not prevent him from having a clear objective: to preserve documents witnessing the history of the British Isles and, more broadly, the origins of a European culture at a time of great transformations (Clemens and Ducharme 2019). Phillipps's interest was primary sources, whether in manuscript form or as printed books. His library catalogues indicate that he owned historical studies on the German Reformation, bibliographies, and catalogues of German and Swiss libraries (Phillipps [1819]; [1824–1825], no. 1614, no. 7730; [1841], 40; [1852], 21–3, 30, 46, 49). His strong interest in the Reformation movement in England (starting with Henry VIII's text on sacraments) and his trips on the Continent between 1822 and 1829 also influenced his acquisitions.

Phillipps was not the only one in Britain acquiring Continental material during this period. British collectors and libraries greatly benefitted from the upheavals happening on the Continent in the late 1700s and early 1800s: the French Revolution, the Napoleonic Wars, the dissolution of monastic institutions, and the reshaping of Western European states. No other period in European history had ever known such a large destruction and circulation of books. A. N. L. Munby, in his Phillipps Studies, mentions that, of the thirteen million books in France before the French Revolution started in 1789, ten million were either destroyed or changed hands within five years— i.e., by 1794 (Munby 1954, 3:19). Germany was not immune to these events: in 1803, monastic institutions were dissolved, books moved from private hands to institutional ones, governing units were reshaped, and political systems changed.

German Reformation pamphlets seem to have circulated mainly within Germanophone countries in the early modern period (Guilleminot 2017, 2). It is thus in the early 1800s that they started being collected in earnest in other parts of the Western world, mainly in Britain and, a couple of decades later, in the United States (Gatch 2007, 38–9).[4]

The provenances of Phillipps's Reformation pamphlets are illustrative of these changes. In 1824, while in Darmstadt during one of his trips to Germany, Phillipps acquired part of the collection assembled by Leander van Ess (1772–1837). Van Ess had been deeply affected by German political and societal transformations. After having been a Benedictine monk until the dissolution of monasteries, a pastor, and then a professor of Catholic theology at the University of Marburg and a Catholic pastor in the same city, he had retired to Darmstadt, where he was working on a German translation of the Old Testament (Gatch 2007, 10–12, and Gatch 2021). The German scholar seems to have benefitted from the turmoil around him to amass an extensive book collection, part of which he was trying to sell when he met Phillipps.

Van Ess sold to the British collector numerous manuscripts, incunabula, early printed Bibles, and Luther pamphlets—the last now in the Folger collections (Gatch 2007, 33). A decade later, in 1838, he sold to the Union Theological Seminary in New York the rest of his books, including the largest part of his Reformation pamphlets collection, made up of approximately 1,250 items (Gatch 2007, 49).

The Phillipps pamphlets from the Van Ess collection can be identified by the numbers inscribed or pasted on a small square or round label on their title pages (these correspond to the numbers in Van Ess's catalogue of pamphlets) (Gatch 2007, 50). Some of these items also carry numbers inscribed by their previous owners, which Van Ess sometimes crossed out in red pencil. Others have an inscription "Dupl" indicating that the German collector mostly sold duplicate copies to Phillipps. Gatch's extensive research on this collection has determined that the Van Ess Reformation pamphlets came from the Marienmünster monastery library near Paderborn, where the collector had been a monk.

Some Phillipps pamphlets have provenance marks reflecting their recent dispersal from different collections. Phillipps likely acquired them through various agents, such as the importers Williams and Norgate, whose ticket is pasted in one of the Luther pamphlets (Luther [1521a]), and at various auctions in Britain and on the Continent. He thus must have purchased at auctions several books from the Van de Velde collection, from which he also acquired fifty manuscripts in 1833 (Munby 1956, 4:206). Jan Frans van de Velde was a Belgian Catholic cleric and librarian at the Catholic University of Louvain who had lost his position when the Habsburg emperor Joseph II closed the university in 1788. Earlier, the librarian-bibliophile had helped his institution obtain manuscripts from Belgian monasteries dissolved by the same Joseph II. In 1797, though, when the Belgian

Preserving the Past & Engaging the Future

states were annexed by the French revolutionary government, Van de Velde, fervently anti-revolutionary, fled to Germany. This was where he became interested in Luther's works and assembled a significant collection on Luther and the Reformation movement throughout Europe (De Schepper, Kelders, Pauwels 2008, 54–6). Some of Van de Velde's books carry the marks of other collections recently dispersed, such as the bookplate of chaplain Henricus Vanden Block—a Belgian bibliophile who had lost his fortune during the French Revolution and whose collection was partly sold in 1808 (Cochlaeus 1529 and Linnig 1906, 112–13).

Other marks of provenance on Phillipps pamphlets include the stamp of the Munich University Library: "ad. Bibl. Acad. Land." or "biblioth. Acad. Ingolst." Founded in Ingolstadt in 1472, the Bavarian university had been moved to the town of Landshut in 1800 due to the threat of the Napoleonic army, before being transferred in 1826 to Munich. Its library was among those state institutions that received large quantities of books from nearby dissolved monasteries (Munby 1954, 3:19–20). In order to make space for the newly arrived books (and also, no doubt, for financial gain), the university library undertook a campaign to deaccession duplicates, stamping them as such.

Some pamphlets, in addition to various marks documenting their recent provenance, bear Thomas Phillipps's shelfmark with a roman numeral, a letter, and a number inscribed either on the title page or on the front board (image 1). This shelfmark is distinct from the one the collector assigned to his manuscripts.[5]

Many of the pamphlets in the Phillipps collection can be identified by their uniform, gray-printed three-quarter boards with a manuscript paper label on their spine (image 2). The fact that they have the same decorated boards as the Van Ess pamphlets at the Union Theological Seminary underlines their shared provenance. It also indicates that their bindings date prior to their acquisi-

Image 1: Example of Phillipps shelfmark inscribed on the title page of a pamphlet.

Image 2: Example of a gray printed three-quarter board with a paper label pasted on the spine, covering a Phillipps pamphlet.

tion by the British collector and the New York library (Gatch 2007, 50–4).

Phillipps had a utilitarian approach to the binding of pamphlets. He preserved the ones that were sound and replaced with his Middle Hill boards those that no longer efficiently protected the textblocks. Indeed, the books in his collection that he had bound or rebound were uniformly covered with a distinct, plain-colored paper, either salmon pink or yellow over millboard without pastedowns or other endpapers (image 3). Such bindings were similar to those found on books of popular literature at the end of the eighteenth century in England, although they generally included endpapers. Publishers commissioned these covers for their trade editions but rarely did collectors have their books bound in such a way (Stuart 2004, 80–96). Phillipps's preference for unadorned paper covers (instead of leather) was therefore unusual for a collector of his wealth. No doubt, these preferences were driven by his desire for economy, like publishers. Several pamphlets in Middle Hill boards have blue endpapers, which must have been elements carried over from their previous bindings. Clearly, Phillipps instructed his binder to use the cheapest cover method possible and to reuse whatever material could be preserved.

The most likely explanation for the presence of pamphlets in the collection left disbound or unbound with a simple paper spine is that Phillipps's binder ran out of time or money to work on these items. It should not be perceived as a desire to

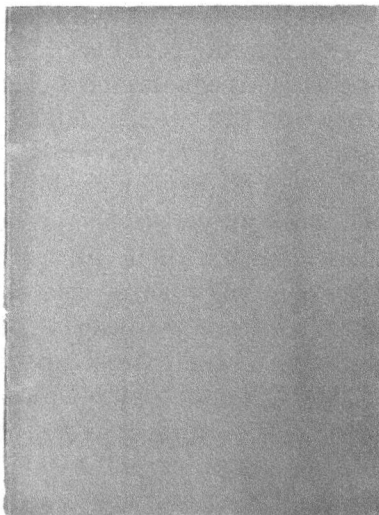

Image 3: Example of a pink salmon Middle Hill board covering a Phillipps pamphlet.

preserve historical evidence; Phillipps's concern was in preserving texts, not their materiality.[6]

Collective Voices: The Stickelberger Collection

Emanuel Stickelberger collected German Reformation literature in a very different context from Phillipps. At the end of the First World War, he left his career as a chemical engineer to write historical fiction, short stories, a book on Hans Holbein the Younger (Stickelberger 1942), and historical plays on early German and Swiss reformers. Although his family ties to Holbein may have played a role in his interest in this historical period, his main motivation seems to have been a wish to inform his Protestant fellows about early figures of the Reformation movement. Clearly, his own works and his collection informed each other.

Unlike Phillipps, who collected voraciously and acquired collections *en bloc*, Stickelberger collected selectively, acquiring only authors and editions that specifically appealed to him. His main collecting interest was the Swiss Reformation movement and the works of German reformers who held views similar to those of their Swiss counterparts (Seebass and Tammann-Bertholet 1977, 5).

Stickelberger also collected Swiss imprints and seventeenth- and eighteenth-century German literature.[7] In 1944, he founded the Swiss bibliophile society named after Sebastian Brant's *Stultifera Navis* (the Ship of Fools). The Folger Library purchased the portion of his collection on the Reformation after his death in 1977 through the Basel firm Erasmushaus, Haus der Bücher, with whom the collector had done business throughout his life.

Stickelberger's books have more varied modern provenances than Phillipps's because he acquired them individually or in small groups. Yet some books bear the same marks as those in the Phillipps collection, such as the Van de Velde inscription or the stamp of the Munich University Library (*Das Alt Testament zü teütsch...* 1527). The fact that the same marks of ownership are found in both collections is evidence of the steady circulation through the 1900s of books from collections dismantled in the early 1800s.

Many Stickelberger pamphlets have an institutional provenance showing that the sale of duplicates was a common practice of German university and public libraries throughout the nineteenth and early twentieth centuries. Their marks also reflect the turmoil of the Swiss collector's lifetime: many of these volumes came from German institutions affected by the political changes occurring between the First and Second World Wars. Their stamps can sometimes help determine the period of their deaccession from institutions and the approximate period of their acquisition by Stickelberger. The books with a stamp from the "Martin Luther University of Halle-Wittenberg," for example, must have been sold after 1933—the year in which the Nazi regime renamed the university. Likewise, books from the State Library of Breslau were likely deaccessioned before 1945, when Breslau became part of the Republic of Poland and the library took its Polish name: "City Library in Wroclaw" (later renamed the Wroclaw University Library). Closer to home, Stickelberger also acquired many duplicates from the Basel Public Library in his hometown.

Stickelberger's collection also includes books from private theological collections built in the nineteenth century, such as that of the Swiss historian of Protestantism Gaspard Ernest Stroehlin (1844–1907). Although the bulk of Stroehlin's collection was sold to the municipal library of Geneva after his death in 1907, Stickelberger was later able to buy a group of books remnant from it. Other North American libraries with German Reformation material also include books from this private library. The Pitts Theology Library at Emory University, for example, owns five books from the Stroehlin collection.

Like the books from Phillipps's collection, those from Stickelberger's are distinguished by their bindings. Most of the pamphlets are in decorated paper boards or wrappers, following bibliophilic tastes from the first part of the twentieth century. Stickelberger's binder used leaves from incunables and books from the early 1500s to cover many of these items and, in doing so, renewed the tradition of early binders, who used leaves from manuscripts and printed books no longer thought to be of value themselves; the leaves might be used as covers, pastedowns, or guards on the newer books. But while the early binders did this for economic reasons, Stickelberger's binder used printed leaves for aesthetic purposes: the beauty of their typography, the whiteness of their paper, their decorations, or their woodcuts. This practice also reveals the collector's complex attitude towards early books. He did not hesitate to have his pamphlets bound with leaves separated from books printed less than fifty years earlier. Only in a few cases was attention paid to the printed text of the leaves or to the subject of their woodcuts. Hence a leaf with a large wood-

Image 4: Large leaf with woodcut depicting St. Augustine preaching, used to cover a pamphlet written by Luther's opponent, Johann Eck (Eck [1519?]).

cut depicting Saint Augustine as a preaching bishop appropriately covers a text written by Johann Eck (1486–1543), a theologian and opponent to Luther (Eck [1519?]) (image 4).

Manuscript leaves were also used as covers, here again with little to no consideration of their content. In one instance, several manu-

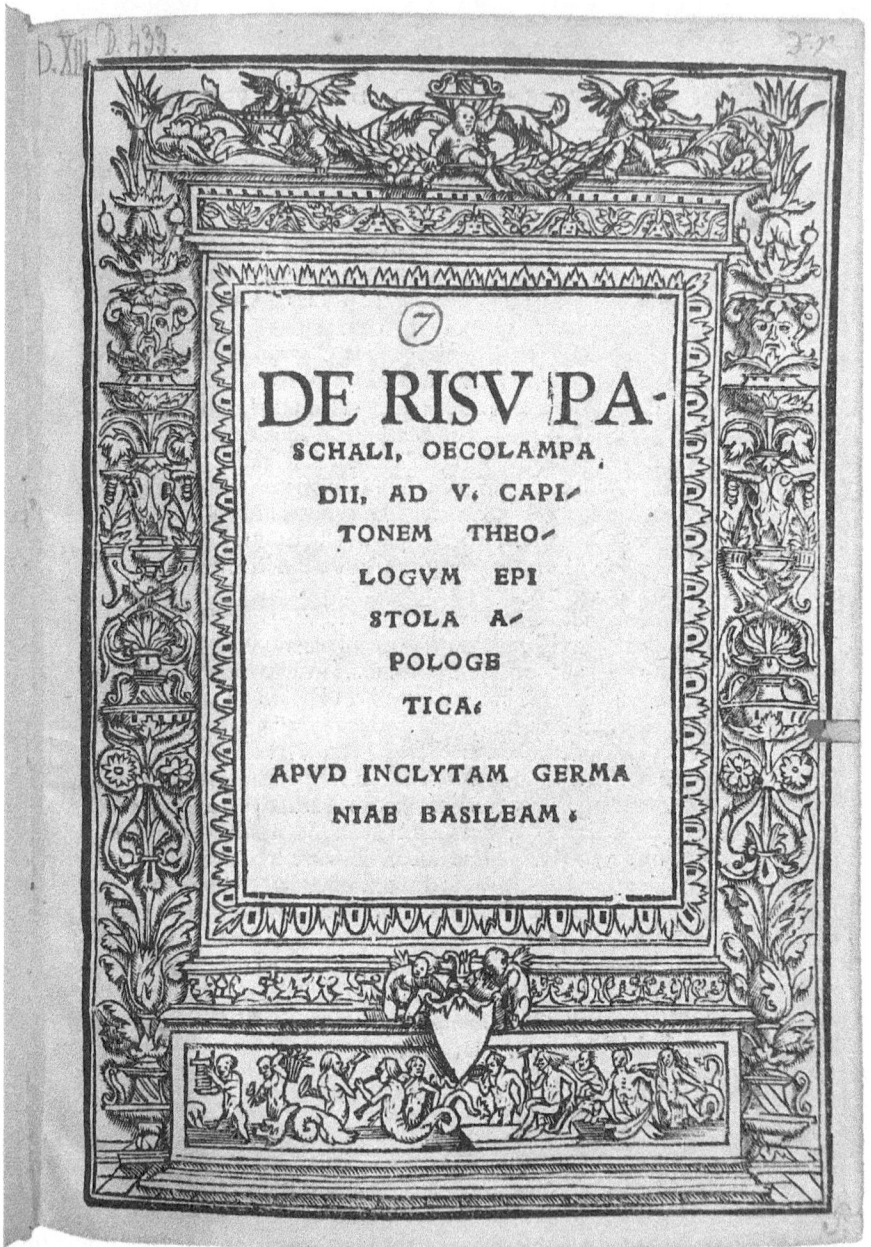

Images 5: Title page of a pamphlet by Johann Oecolampadius (Oecolampadius 1518).

Preserving the Past & Engaging the Future

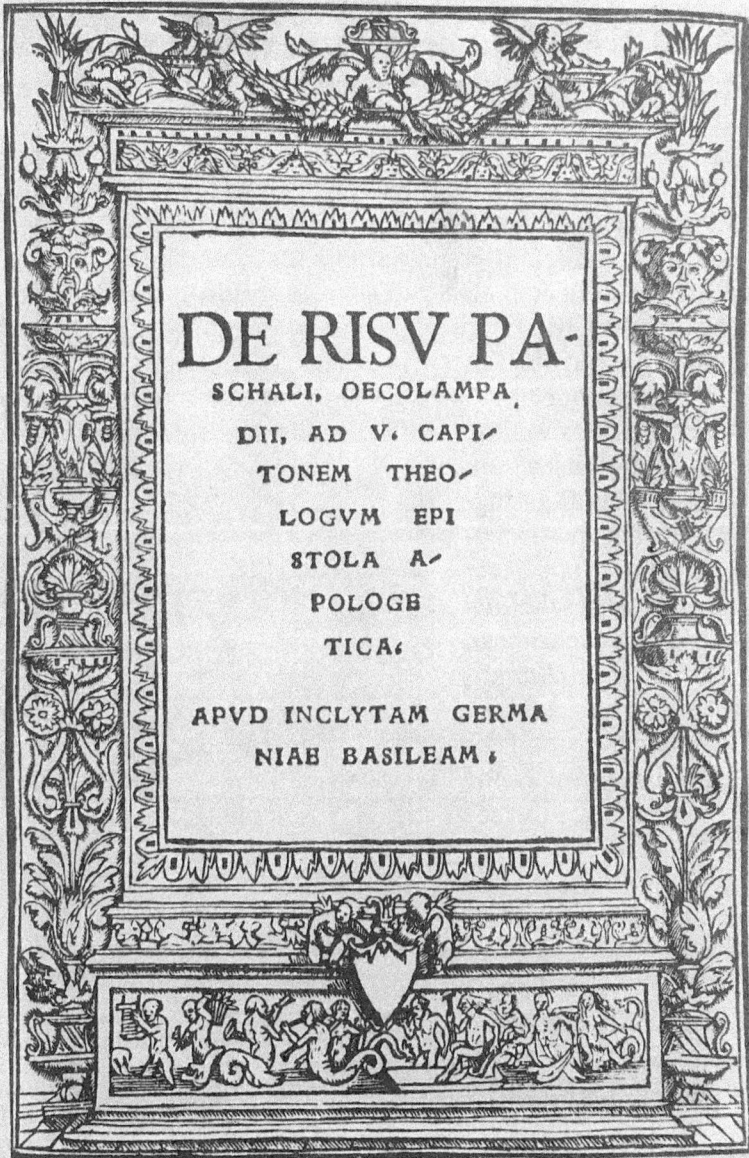

Images 6: The cover of the pamphlet in Image 5 by Johann Oecolampadius with drawing that copies the printed title page (Oecolampadius 1518).

script fragments written in different hands and from different time periods were used to cover a pamphlet, as pastedowns, and as spine reinforcement (Eck 1526).

The collector's sister is thought to have been responsible for the calligraphic inscriptions and drawings on the spines of many books and pamphlets.[8] She may have been the calligrapher who copied onto several modern vellum bindings the printed text of their title pages. Covers were then turned into pages of text, celebrating the typographical quality of Reformation pamphlets (Oecolampadius 1518) (images 5 and 6). The collector also had several binding stamps created, including one with his armorial design, which were placed on modern parchment and on original early bindings. These gilt stamps imitated those of early modern collectors while adding a decorative element, though sometimes with doubtful results: the stamping of the collec-tor's armorial on a cover made of a manuscript leaf rendered its design indecipherable (*Ein Christenlich gespräch gehallten zü Bern[n] Zwüschen den Predicanten vn[d] Hansen Pfyster Meyer von Arouw ...* [1531]) (image 7).

Stickelberger was far from being the only collector to have his books bound following his own tastes and perception of his books. Those he acquired from the Ernest Stroehlin collection were bound in goatskin (often referred to as morocco) by Hans Asper, a prominent

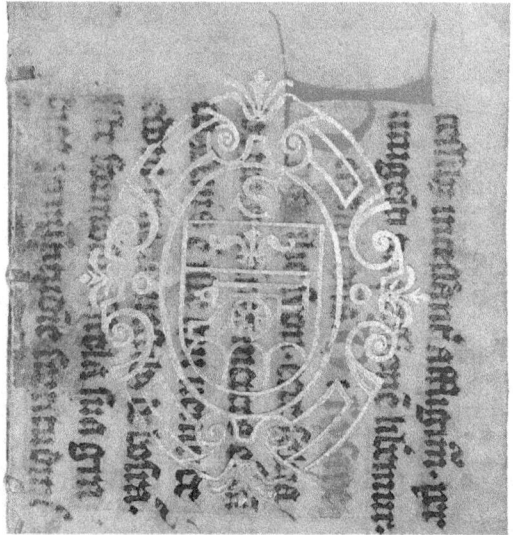

Image 7: Stickelberger's armorial stamp on a manuscript leaf, used to cover a pamphlet and rendering the stamp's design indecipherable (*Ein Christenlich gespräch gehallten zü Bern[n] Zwüschen den Predicanten vn[d] Hansen Pfyster Meyer von Arouw... [1531]*).

Swiss binder active in the late 1800s and early 1900s. Asper's most sophisticated binding represented in the Folger Library collections was for a copy of the first edition of Henry VIII's *Assertion of the Seven Sacraments*, which used a modernist design to highlight the historical importance of this text (Henry VIII 1543) (image 8). Collectors then regularly mixed artistic styles from different time periods on their books. Stickelberger thus did not hesitate to place his modernist

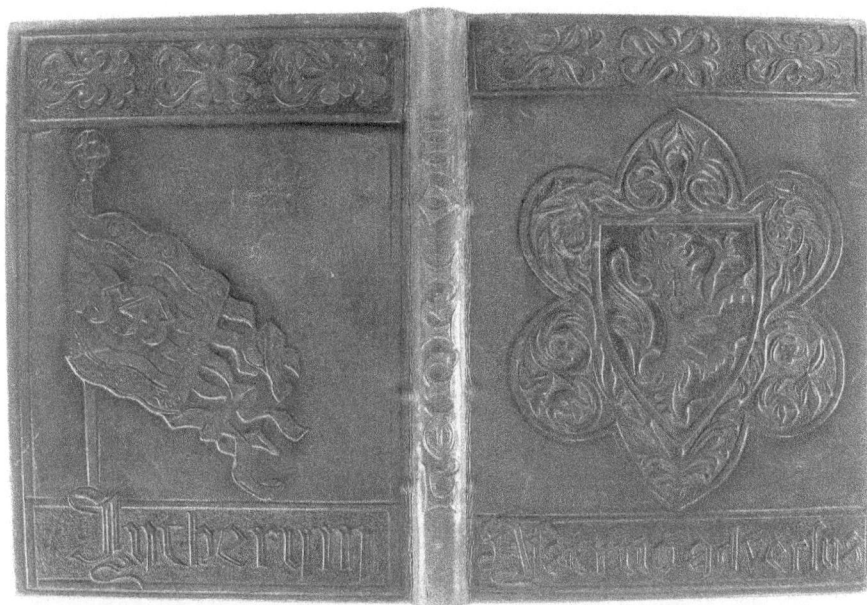

Image 8: Binding by Hans Asper covering Henry VIII's *Assertion of the Seven Sacraments* (Henry VIII. 1543).

bookplate in sixteenth-century books. Besides changing their covers, he extra-illustrated some of his pamphlets, pasting onto their end-leaves either early modern single-sheet prints or cutouts from books depicting their authors.

Early Accretions and Subtractions

In addition to the qualities specific to the most recent collections they came from, the Folger Reformation pamphlets also display charac-teristics of their earlier lives. Hence, while the majority of the pam-phlets in the Phillipps and the Stickelberger collections are bound individually, many show evidence of having been bound with other texts in composite volumes (or *Sammelbände*) at an earlier time.

The remnants of finding tabs are the most common traces of these earlier groupings. Finding tabs were used to easily retrieve the section of a text in a book or the beginning or the end of a pamphlet in a volume (image 9). Made of parchment or paper in various colors (white, brown, or green), they were pasted on title pages or the last leaves of text.[9]

Image 9: Finding tab on the title page of a pamphlet by the poet and opponent to the Reformation Thomas Murner (1475–1537) (Murner 1522).

The manuscript pagination superimposed over the printed one in numerous pamphlets and the traces of offset ink on pages—i.e., text or image transferred from one page to the opposite page—also indicates their binding with other texts in the same volumes.[10]

Phillipps and Stickelberger acquired their pamphlets after they had been broken up from volumes. Most Phillipps pamphlets were disbound before they became part of the Van Ess collection (Gatch 2007, 50–4). The practice of breaking up volumes had started in the eighteenth century and reached its height a century later, when numerous institutional libraries wished to introduce a new order and accessibility to their collections. These were the reasons why, for example, Armand d'Artois (1845–1912), the curator of the Mazarine Library in Paris, broke up thousands of volumes of Mazarinade political pamphlets and arranged them on shelves in alphabetical order by title (Duroselle-Melish 2017a, 191). One may suspect that the same fate befell many Stickelberger pamphlets in German institutional libraries in the nineteenth century.

A few Reformation pamphlets in the Folger library collection also show evidence of having been simply stitched before having been bound more formally. Indeed, not all pamphlets were bound either individually or in composite volumes when acquired by their early owners. Many must have been first used without a cover, although few are extant in such condition (most likely because, without covers, they were more at risk of being lost or destroyed), and their number should not be underestimated. The mark of a fold, for example, in the center of the twenty-page-long biblical commentary by Ludwig Hätzer (c. 1500–29)—now bound in a modern binding—reveals how this pamphlet spent a significant part of its earlier life folded and unbound (Hätzer 1523). Other pamphlets in the collection have soiled first and last leaves, showing that these leaves served as de facto covers.

While Phillipps and Stickelberger did not hesitate to have their pamphlets bound, they were more circumspect with books of a larger size.[11] Stickelberger, hence, kept some of his books in their original state without any alteration. In doing so, he preserved evidence of pre-1800 binding production and of owners' attitudes towards their books, including their practice of having separate texts bound together.

For example, a *Sammelband* with four texts printed in 1561 and 1562 is in its sixteenth-century binding with decorated blind tooling. The texts are all in German and share an intellectual unity, demonstrating the intentionality of their grouping in one volume. Far from writing in isolation, Reformation authors were in dialogue with one another and responded to one another's arguments, whether in agreement or not, through the print medium. This interrelationship sometimes led to the binding of these texts together. The volume starts with a 1561 translation of a biblical commentary on the Lord's Supper, first written in Latin by the Swiss reformer Heinrich Bullinger (1561). The second text—a defense of the Holy Eucharist doctrine from 1562 by the German reformer Johannes Brenz (1499–1570)—is directed against Bullinger's text (Brenz 1562). The third one is Bullinger's response to Brenz, also from 1562 (Bullinger 1562). The volume ends with a sermon on the Apostles' Creed by the Swiss humanist and reformer Johannes Montanus Fabricius (1527–66) (Fabricius 1562). Although Fabricius's text is not directly related to the previous ones, its printing date (1562) and an inscription on its title page (indicating that it was a gift from the author) signal the owner's likely intention to store it securely with pamphlets recently acquired.

Another composite volume with two texts is in an elaborate binding with gold-stamped decorations and gauffered gilt edges from the late seventeenth or early eighteenth century. The first bound text is a revised edition of the French version of the Geneva Bible prepared by Theodore de Bèze (1519–1605) and other theologians (*La Bible, qui est toute la Saincte Escriture du Vieil & du Nouueau Testament...* 1588); the second is a translation of the Psalms by the same author and Clément Marot (1496–1544) (Marot and de Bèze 1587).[12] The most intriguing feature of the volume is its yellow paper (image 10). Other examples of Bibles on yellow paper exist, although none in either edition of these texts. This suggests that the coloring in this Stickelberger volume was applied when the texts were to be bound together. Such embellishment might have been intended to imitate the brightness of gold. The yellow paper, which at first must have looked much brighter, paired well with the gilt binding of the book to create a striking effect (Duroselle-Melish 2017b).

Original bindings from the Stickelberger collection sometimes provide direct information about their early owners. Hence the name of a woman, Helena Fürstenhauserin, has been stamped on the front cover of a binding with the date (most likely of its making) 1588 (image 11). The text it covers was printed in 1584 and written by the reformer Urbanus Rhegius (1489–1541) (Rhegius 1584). Although nothing is known about this female owner, her elaborate binding shows her social standing and points to the type of Reformation texts

Preserving the Past & Engaging the Future

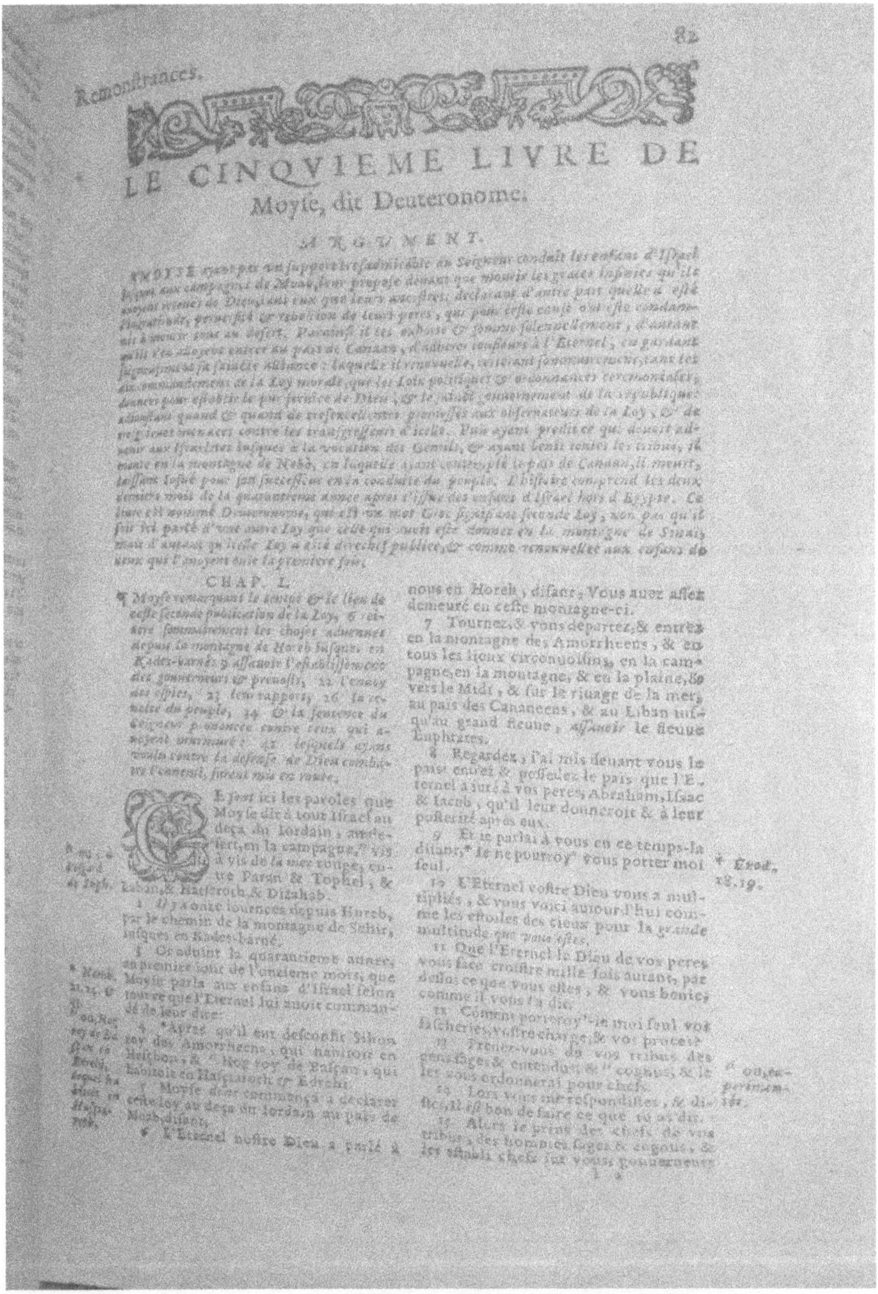
Remonstrances. 82

LE CINQVIEME LIVRE DE
Moyse, dit Deuteronome.

ARGVMENT.

CHAP. I.

Image 10: Page from a copy of the French version of the Geneva Bible on yellow paper (*La Bible, qui est toute la Saincte Escriture du Vieil & du Nouueau Testament...* 1588).

Image 11: Binding with name of its owner, Helena Fürstenhauserin, stamped on it (Rhegius 1584).

women read. Rhegius's book was extremely popular in the late six-teenth and seventeenth centuries. Written in the form of a dialogue between the author and his wife, it explained numerous prophecies found in the Old Testament. Rhegius's inclusion of a female character and his didactic style may indicate that he also aimed for his book to reach a female readership.

Some books have less elaborate early bindings than those discussed above, but they nonetheless provide information about their early owners. A copy of Calvin's commentary on the epistles of Paul, for example, is in a plain German binding, providing a durable method to protect a text frequently used (Calvin 1548; image 12). One of its sixteenth- or early seventeenth-century owners assertively signed his name on the title page.

Image 12: German binding with thin wooden boards and quarter vellum over parchment covering a copy of Calvin's commentary on the epistles of Paul (Calvin 1548).

Phillipps's and Stickelberger's books include traces of their early lives, not only on their covers but also on their pages with manuscript notes. These inscriptions help clarify the reception of Reformation texts over three centuries and suggest that early editions of the Reformers' works were read and used until the late eighteenth and early nineteenth centuries.

The most common type of manuscript notes found throughout the collection are ownership inscriptions. They record, often on the title page, the various transactions involving the books (e.g., a purchase, or a gift from the author or a friend). They also document the transmission of volumes over centuries from one owner to another, either within the same family or not.

Members of several generations of the same family inscribed their names in Stickelberger's copy of the first French Protestant Bible printed in Neuchatel (*La Bible qui est toute la Saincte Escripture, en laquelle sont contenus...* 1535). The earliest inscription seems to be contemporary with the printing of the book and records a mother and her son (image 13). By contrast, the Bible on yellow paper discussed earlier displays an ecclesiastical connection between two of its successive owners: an archdeacon gave this copy to a pastor.

Reformation books and pamphlets in the Folger collections also exhibit the coats of arms of their early owners, either drawn or stamped on their leaves. These might be drawn in a blank space intentionally left by printers for this purpose on title page borders,

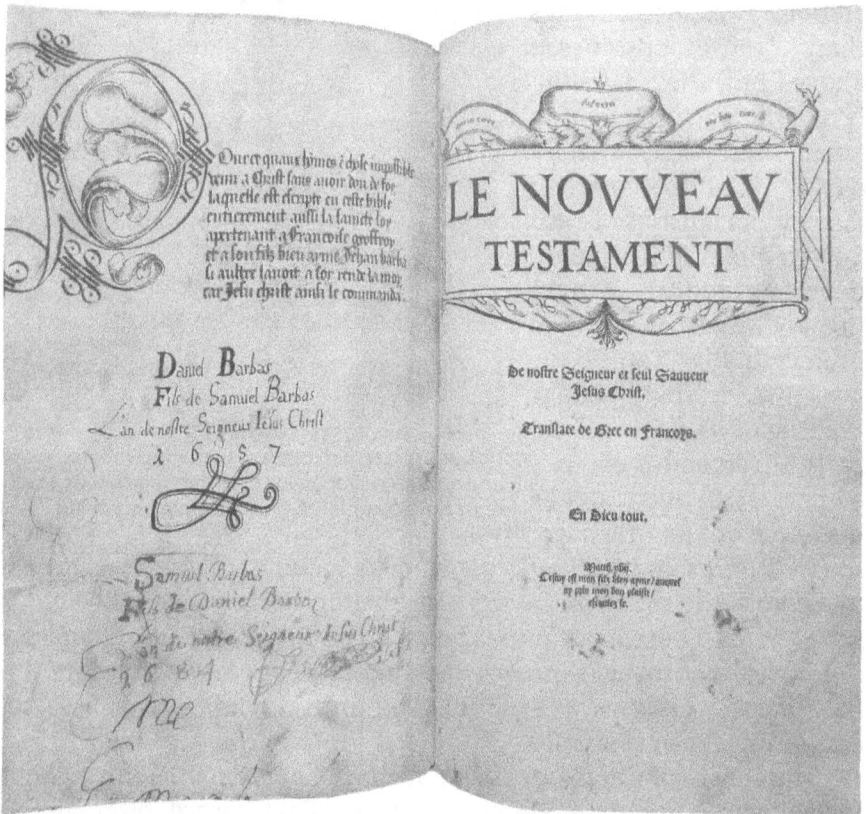

Image 13: Françoise Geoffroy and her son Jehan Barbas appear to have been the first owners of this copy of the first French Protestant Bible, printed in Neuchatel in 1535 (*La Bible qui est toute la Saincte Escripture, en laquelle sont contenus...* 1535). The exquisite calligraphic style of their inscription sharply contrasts with the more standard one of their heirs.

or they might be stamped (image 14). Coats of arms are also depicted on bookplates, such as in the Stickelberger copy of a text by the Augsburg evangelical weaver Ulrich Utz Richsner (n.d.), with the bookplate of Martin II Gerbert—abbot of the Saint Blaise Abbey in the Black Forest from 1764 to 1793—thus recording the eighteenth-century ecclesiastical provenance of this Reformation pamphlet (Richsner 1524).

Owners also recorded the date of purchase and the price paid for their books, whether new or used. Hence a certain Jean Boisnard, perhaps from the Huguenot community in England, recorded how much he paid in 1696 in London for a copy of Calvin's *Sermons in French* (Calvin 1563).

Those who belonged to a learned circle sometimes wrote the Latin inscription *Et amicorum* in their books, wishing to record their adherence to the Renaissance literary ideal of book sharing between literati friends (for example Brenz 1523).

Image 14: Large armorial design of the Gufer von Reinhardsberg family from Bamberg, active at least until the early eighteenth century, stamped on the verso of a pamphlet by Andreas von Karlstadt (Karlstadt 1520). Above, the stamp of the Basel Public Library crossed out with the inscription "Dupl."

Beyond ownership inscriptions, the Folger Reformation pamphlets include many notes recording the interactions of readers with their texts. These paratexts could range from non-verbal marks to elaborate commentaries. Readers corrected typographical errors, underlined words or sentences, traced vertical marks, or drew manicules by the text they wished to highlight. Sometimes they recorded when they had completed the reading of a text with the Latin word *perlegi* ("I have read this") and a date (for example, Luther 1520).

Readers also added by hand the author's name and the imprint information often missing from pamphlets' title pages, most likely for easy retrieval.[13] Their notes were either in Latin or in the vernacular (mostly German), independent of the language of the text. They created their own indexes and concordance tables to search texts more efficiently, such as in the Stickelberger copy of Luther's translation of the New Testament issued in December 1522 (Luther 1522).

Overall, few books in the Phillipps and Stickelberger collections include marks of censorship. The majority were written in the vernacular and seem to have circulated in an environment free of censors. Ecclesiastical libraries sometimes owned a few, or collections of, Reformation pamphlets (at least in the late seventeenth and eighteenth centuries), but they must have kept these texts behind locked doors, restricted to a few.[14] Hence the inscription *Prohibitus* on the title page of a copy of Calvin's commentaries is not necessarily a sign of censorship and may simply indicate that this book was on the Index (Calvin 1561). Likewise, the few readers who crossed out sections of text in their pamphlets did not make those sections impossible to read. They may simply have wished to mark their disagreement with the text. Book owners, certainly, did not hesitate to express their opinions in their books. The owner of a copy of a diatribe against monastic orders by Ulrich von Hutten, for example, added his or her own criticism against monks and nuns (Hutten 1520)

While early owners did not hesitate to cover their texts with manuscript notes, they rarely decorated the pages of their books. Few pamphlets in the Folger Reformation collection have their title page woodcuts hand-colored. Likewise, only a few texts include rubrications. The woodcuts that decorated numerous Reformation pamphlets must have amply satisfied book owners' tastes for ornamentation. Moreover, although printed in black, the high-quality impression of woodcuts sometimes produced striking results and created the impression of color.

Drawn images, though, could be more than simple decorations and could represent a reader's visual response to a text. Hence, if the hand-painted borders on the title page of a Luther pamphlet (image 15) served as a decoration, the allegorical image of the Christian faith drawn on its verso (image 16) can be read as the assertion by its maker of his or her commitment to the Lutheran faith in light of the content of the pamphlet: a response from Luther against two of his opponents fervently opposed to the Reformation, Hieronymus Emser (1478–1527) and Thomas Murner (1475–1537) (Luther [1521b]).

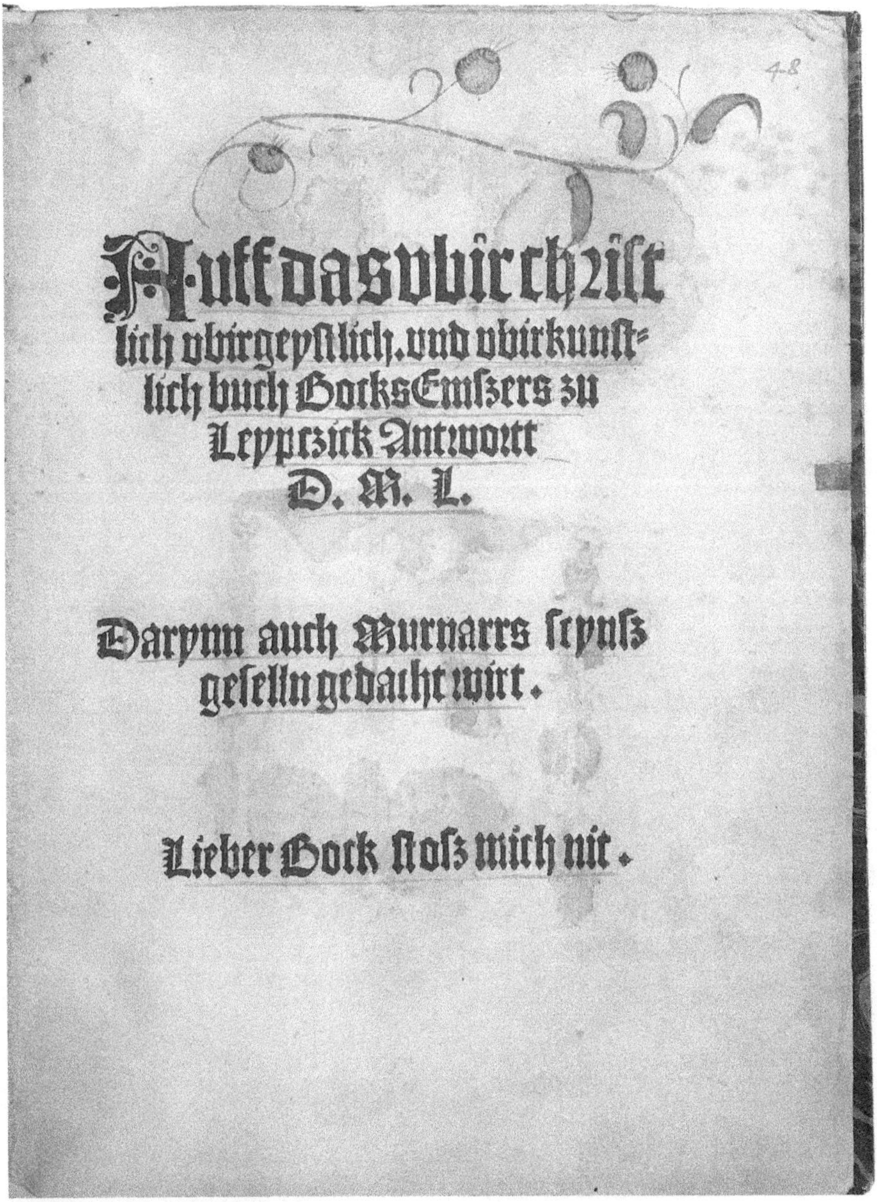

Auff das vbir christ
lich vbirgeyſtlich, vnd vbirkunſt-
lich buch BocksEmſzers zu
Leyptzick Antwort
D. M. L.

Darynn auch Murnarrs ſeynß
geſelln gedacht wirt.

Lieber Bock ſtoſz mich nit.

Image 15: Title page of a Luther pamphlet with hand-painted decorations (Luther [1521b]).

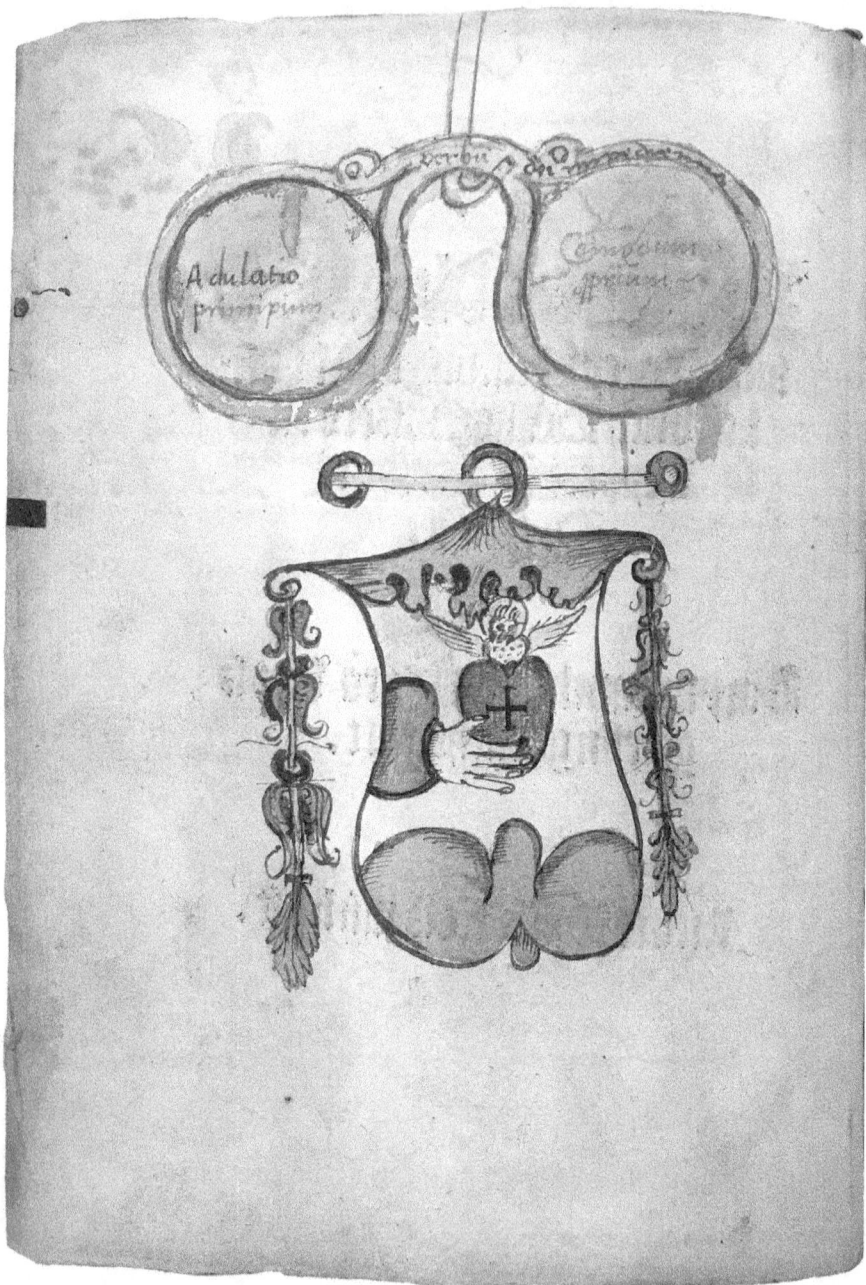

Image 16: A drawn allegory of Christian faith on the verso of the same pamphlet.

Preserving the Past & Engaging the Future

Conclusion

Until recently, readers of Reformation pamphlets at the Folger Library were mostly historians of English religious thought, who studied these items only for their content (Folger Shakespeare Library 1977, 7). By contrast, today's readers are increasingly paying attention to the material features of these printed items in addition to their textual content.[15] These pamphlets are not fixed objects; they were physically changed as they passed through multiple hands, places, and historical periods. Their bindings and the marks on their leaves reflect these various transitions and impact our reception of their texts. From manuscript notes to ownership and non-textual markings, from stitched pamphlets to *Sammelbände* (and their disassembling), from plain to decorated bindings, over the centuries private and institutional owners changed the physical aspect of their pamphlets and, each time, created a different reading experience.

Highlighting the materiality of this Folger collection is especially critical, since copies of Reformation pamphlets are now accessible in multiple ways: in libraries where they have survived in large numbers (Gatch 2007, 5) and in online tools, mostly in the database VD16, which includes digital surrogates of Reformation pamphlets from German libraries (VD16 n.d.). While digitization has greatly supported textual studies, it has also expanded the ways one can examine books by highlighting their unique material features. VD16, for example, includes multiple copies of the same text, underscoring each item's unique story. Yet it includes few digital surrogates of copies from non-Germanophone libraries. It also lacks many texts that are extant only in a few copies and so are not readily available in most collections. If only for these reasons, the in-person consultation of individual copies in libraries remains necessary.

It is also important to acknowledge that the Folger Reformation items share common features with books in other collections—the Union Theological Seminary and the Pitts Theology Library, to name just two. Uncovering the shared material characteristics among collections, as well as the significance of the unique characteristics of each item, would add meaning to Reformation pamphlets well beyond their textual content and help us to better understand their former lives. Ultimately, it would make our collections more meaningful and give them greater visibility.

References

Primary Sources

Das Alt Testament zü teütsch... 1527. Zürich: Christoph Froschauer. Call number 218- 035, Folger Shakespeare Library, Washington, DC.

La Bible qui est toute la Saincte Escripture, en laquelle sont contenus... 1535. Neuchatel: Pierre de Vingle. Call number 218- 037, Folger Shakespeare Library, Washington, DC.

La Bible, qui est toute la Saincte Escriture du Vieil & du Nouueau Testament... 1588. Geneva: [Jérémie des Planches]. Call number 218- 038 item 1, Folger Shakespeare Library, Washington, DC.

Brenz, Johannes. 1523. *Ain Sermon zü allen Christen, von der Kirche...* Augsburg: Melchior Ramminger. Call number 218- 060, Folger Shakespeare Library, Washington, DC.

———. 1562. *Bericht Iohannis Brentzij von dem Büchlein D. Heinrici Bullingeri, des Tittels, Von dem Himmel vnd Gerechten Gottes...* Frankfurt am Main: Nicolas Bassée. Call number 218- 097.2, Folger Shakespeare Library, Washington, DC.

Bullinger, Heinrich. 1562. *Gägenbericht Heinrychen Bullingers, vff den Bericht herren Iohansen Brentzen von dem Him[m]el vnnd der Gerächten Gottes...* Zürich: Christoph Froschauer. Call number 218- 097.3, Folger Shakespeare Library, Washington, DC.

———. 1561. *Von dem Himmel vn[d] der Grächten Gottes...* Zürich: Christoph Froschauer. Call number 218- 097.1, Folger Shakespeare Library, Washington, DC.

Calvin, Jean. 1561. *Commentaires de M. Iehan Caluin sur toutes les epistres de l'Apostre S. Paul, et aussi sur l'Epistre aux Hebrieux...* Geneva: Conrad Badius. Call number 218- 123, Folger Shakespeare Library, Washington, DC.

———. 1548. *Commentarii in quatuor Pauli Epistolas...* Geneva: Jean Gérard. Call number 218- 114, Folger Shakespeare Library, Washington, DC.

———. 1563. *Sermons de M. Iean Caluin sur l'epistre S. Paul apostre aux Galates...* Geneva: François Perrin. Call number 218- 128, Folger Shakespeare Library, Washington, DC.

Ein Christenlich gespräch gehallten zü Bern[n] Zwüschen den Predicanten vn[d] Hansen Pfyster Meyer von Arouw... [1531]. Zürich: Christoph Froschauer. Call number 218- 233, Folger Shakespeare Library, Washington, DC.

Cochlaeus, Johannes. 1529. *Fasciculus calumniarum, sannarum et illusionum Martini Lutheri, in episcopos & clericos...* Leipzig: Valentin Schumann. Call number: 171- 218, Folger Shakespeare Library, Washington, DC.

Eck, Johannes. [1519?]. *Disputatio et excusatio Domini Ioha[n]...* Leipzig: Martin Landsberg. Call number 218- 178, Folger Shakespeare Library, Washington, DC.

———. 1526. *Die falsch onwarhaftig, Verfurisch Leer Vlrich zwingli von Zurch.* Ingolstat: Peter and Georg Apian. Call number 218- 180, Folger Shakespeare Library, Washington, DC.

Fabricius, Johannes Montanus. 1562. *Der Christen Gloub...* Zürich: Christoph Froschauer. Call number 218- 097.4, Folger Shakespeare Library, Washington, DC.

Folger Shakespeare Library. 1977. *Annual Report of the Director for the Fiscal Year Ending June 30, 1977.* O. B. Hardison, Jr., Director. Washington: The Folger Shakespeare Library.

Hätzer, Ludwig. 1523. *Ein vrteil gottes vnsers ee gemahels, wie man sich mit allen götzen vnd bildnussen halte[n] sol...* Zürich: Christoph Froschauer. Call number 218- 241, Folger Shakespeare Library, Washington, DC.

Henry VIII. 1543. *Assertio Septem Sacrame[n]torum aduersus Martin. Lutherum...* Rome: Francesco Priscianese. Call number 218- 251, Folger Shakespeare Library, Washington, DC.

Hutten, Ulrich Von. 1520. *Clag vnd Vormanung gege[n] dem übermässigen vnchristelichem Gewalt des Bapstes zü Rom...* Strasbourg: Johann Knobloch. Call number 218- 279, Folger Shakespeare Library, Washington, DC.

Karldstadt, Andreas Rudoff-Bodenstein von. 1520. *Von geweychtem Wasser und Saltz*. Strasbourg: Martin Flach. Call number 218-045, Folger Shakespeare Library, Washington, DC.

Luther, Martin. [1521a]. *Von der Beycht ob die der Bapst Macht habe zu gepieten*. Wittenberg: [Melchior Lotter]. Call number 171- 046, Folger Shakespeare Library, Washington, DC.

———. [1521b]. *Auf das überchristlich Buch Bocks Emsers Antwort...* Wittenberg: Johann Grunenberg-Rhau. Call number 218- 429, Folger Shakespeare Library, Washington, DC.

———, trans. December 1522. *Das new Testament, yetzund recht grüntlich teutscht...* Basel: Adam Petri. Call number 218- 036.1, Folger Shakespeare Library, Washington DC.

———. 1520. *Warumb des Bapsts vnd seyner Iungerñ Bucher von Doct. Martino Luther vorbrāt seynñ...* Wittenberg: Johann Rhau-Grunenberg. Call number 171- 022, Folger Shakespeare Library, Washington, DC.

Marot, Clément and Théodore de Bèze. 1587. *Les CL Pseaumes de Dauid mis en rime francoise...* Geneva: Jérémie des Planches. Call number 218- 038 item 2, Folger Shakespeare Library, Washington, DC.

Melanchthon, Philipp. Circa 1545. *Letter to Conrad Embecanus at Cologne*. Call number F.c.2, Folger Shakespeare Library, Washington, DC.

Murner, Thomas. 1522. *Ob der Künig vsz engelland ein lügner sey oder der Luther*. Strasbourg: Johann Grüninger. Call number 218-570, Folger Shakespeare Library, Washington, DC.

Oecolampadius, Johann. 1518. *De risu Paschali...* Basel: Johann Froben. Call number 218- 579, Folger Shakespeare Library, Washington, DC.

Phillipps, Thomas, Sir. [1819]. *A Catalogue of Books at Middle-Hill, Worcestershire, 1819*. Salisbury: Printed by J.A. Gilmour. Call number \Phill.\Coll.\08.26\P54\CatB\1819 04/04/96 N 03/26/96 N 03/25/96 X 03/20/96 C, Phillipps Collection, The Grolier Club of New York.

———. [1841]. *Catalogue of Books at Middle Hill: 2nd[-4th] Supplement, 1841.* [Middle Hill: Charles Gilmour?]. Call number \Phill.\ Coll.\08.26\P54\Cat\no. 1 04/04/96 N 04/01/96 X 03/26/96 N, Phillipps Collection, The Grolier Club of New York.

———. [1824–25]. *Catalogue of Printed Books.* Middle Hill: Adolphus Brightley]. Call number \Phill.\Coll.\34.52\MH462, Phillipps Collection, The Grolier Club of New York.

———. [1852]. *Catalogus of Printed Books, at Middle Hill.* [Middle Hill: Typis Medio-Montanis. Call number: \Phill.\Coll.\08.26\P54\ CatB\1852, Phillipps Collection, The Grolier Club of New York.

Rhegius, Urbanus. 1584. *Dialogus von der herrlichen, trostreichen Predigt, die Christus Luce XXIIII...* Wittenberg: Clemens Schleich. Call number 218- 673, Folger Shakespeare Library, Washington, DC.

Richsner, Ulrich. 1524. *Ain hüpsch Gesprech biechlin, von ainem Pfaffen vn[d] ainem Weber, die zůsamen kom[m]en seind auff der strass...* Augsburg: Heinrich Steiner. Call number 218- 676, Folger Shakespeare Library, Washington, DC.

Robinson, Philip. August 1, 1968. *Description of materials sold to the Folger Shakespeare Library.* Call number Acquisitions Files, Folger Shakespeare Library, Washington, DC.

Secondary Sources

Bibliographical Society of America. n.d. "Lenore Coral, 'British Book Auction Catalogues 1801–1900: A Preliminary Version of Munby-Coral 2,' 2014; update: 2016". Accessed January 27, 2021. *https:// bibsocamer.org/bibsite-home/list-of-resources.*

Clemens, Raymond and Diane Ducharme. 2019. *All the Books in the World! An Exhibition at the Beinecke Rare Book and Manuscripts Library, Yale University.* January 18–April 21, 2019. New Haven: Office of the Yale University Printer; West Haven, Connecticut: GHP.

De Schepper, Marcus, Ann Kelders, and Jan Pauwels. 2008. *Les Seigneurs du livre: Les grands collectionneurs du XIXième siècle à la Bibliothèque royale de Belgique du Ier février au 23 août 2008.* Brussels: Bibliothèque royale de Belgique.

Duroselle-Melish, Caroline. 2017a. "Anatomy of A Pamphlet Collection: From Disbinding to Reuniting." *Papers of the Bibliographical Society,* 111:2, 185–202.

———. 2017b. "A Yellow Book," *The Collation* (blog), March 7, 2017. *https://collation.folger.edu/2017/03/a-yellow-book.*

Fabian Handbuch: Handbuch der Historischen Buchbestände in Deutschland, Österreich und Europa. n.d. "The Bodleian Library. 2. Outline of the Collections. Tractatus Lutherani." Accessed January 27, 2021. *https://fabian.sub.uni-goettingen.de/fabian?BodLib2.*

Folger Shakespeare Library. 1983. *Martin Luther (1483–1546): A Jubilee Exhibition at the Folger Shakespeare Library.* Washington DC.: Folger Shakespeare Library.

Gatch, Milton McC. 2007. *The Library of Leander van Ess and the Earliest American Collections of Reformation Pamphlets.* New York: Bibliographical Society of America.

———. n.d. "The Book Collections of Leander van Ess." Accessed January 27, 2021. *https://www.miltongatch.us/the_book_collections_of_leande.html.*

Guilleminot, Geneviève. 2017. "Les éditions de Luther à la Bibliothèque nationale de France." *Revue d'histoire du protestantisme* 2, no. 1/2: 237–47.

Harry Ransom Center, The University of Texas at Austin. n.d. "The Long Lives of Early Printed Books." Accessed January 27, 2021. *https://www.hrc.utexas.edu/long-lives-of-early-printed-books.*

Kinmont, Ben. 2020. *Gastronomy, Catalogue 17.* Austin, Texas: The Antinomian Press.

Linnig, Benjamin. 1906. *Bibliothèques et ex-libris d'amateurs belges aux XVIIe, XVIIIe, et XIXe siècles.* Paris: H. Daragon.

Munby, Alan Noel Latimer. 1951. Phillips Studies. Vol. 1, bk. 1, *The Catalogues of Manuscripts and Printed Books of Sir Thomas*

Phillipps; Their Composition and Distribution. Cambridge: University Press.

———. 1952. Phillips Studies. Vol. 2, bk. 2, *The Family Affairs of Sir Thomas Phillips.* Cambridge: University Press.

———. 1954. Phillips Studies. Vol. 3, bk. 3, *The Formation of the Phillips Library up to the year 1840.* Cambridge: University Press.

———. 1956. Phillips Studies. Vol. 4, bk. 4, *The Formation of the Phillips Library from 1841 to 1872.* Cambridge: University Press.

———. 1960. Phillips Studies. Vol. 5, bk. 5, *The Dispersal of the Phillips Library.* Cambridge: University Press.

Seebass, Adolf, Tilman Seebass, and Verena Tammann-Bertholet. 1977. *Reformation: Katalog der Sammlung Emanuel Stickelberger für die Folger Shakespeare Library, Washington, D.C. = Reformation: Catalogue of the Emanuel Stickelberger Collection Purchased by the Folger Shakespeare Library, Washington, D.C.* Basel: Haus der Bücher.

Stickelberger, Emanuel. 1942. *Der Mann mit den zwei Seelen: ein Holbein-Roman.* Stuttgart: J. F. Steinkopft.

Stuart, Bennett. 2004. *Trade Bookbinding in the British Isles, 1660–1800.* New Castle, DE: Oak Knoll Press; London: British Library.

"Verzeichnis der im deutschen Sprachbereich erschienenen Drucke des 16. Jahrhunderts (VD 16)." n.d. *https://gateway-bayern.de/TouchPoint_touchpoint/start.do?SearchProfile=Altbestand&SearchType=2.*

Thomas, Drew. 2019. "Cashing in on Counterfeits: Fraud in the Reformation Print Industry." In *Buying and Selling: The Business of Books in Early Modern Europe,* edited by Shanti Graheli, 276–300. Leiden, Boston: Brill.

Notes

1   This paper is based on a talk given at the Pitts Theology Library at Emory University on October 29, 2019. The author would like to thank William Davis from Image Services at the Folger Shakespeare Library for his precious help in bringing the author's pictures up to publication quality. She would also like to thank Roger Gaskell for his helpful comments on a draft of this essay and Chandra Wohleber for her in-depth reading. Due to the current pandemic and the closure of most libraries in Washington, DC, the author was prevented from reviewing some primary and secondary sources first consulted in 2019.

2   For this essay, however, I have limited my research to the Phillipps and Stickelberger books, which represent the main part of the Reformation collection at Folger.

3   The British collector must have owned other manuscripts written by German Reformers, which were dispersed prior to the 1950s (see next section on Phillipps's collection).

4   The Bodleian Library, for example, purchased in 1818 through Sotheby's a collection of over 2,500 Lutheran pamphlets from the German collector, professor, and librarian Johannes Gottlob May (1754–1821) (Fabian Handbuch n.d.). The British auction book catalogues also record the sale of several private German collections of theological works during the same period (Bibliographical Society of America n.d.)

5   Phillipps may not have had the time to assign a shelfmark to all his pamphlets.

6   Little work has been done on Phillipps's pamphlets. Further research is needed to confirm these observations.

7   An overview of this portion of Stickelberger's collection can be consulted on the auction website Yumpu (last accessed on January 27, 2021), *https://www.yumpu.com/de/document/read/7537864/bibliothek-emanuel-stickelberger-deutsche-koller-auktionen.*

8   Stickelberger's sister is also thought to have bound most of his Reformation pamphlets. Further research in Swiss archives is needed to confirm this.

9   Peter Stallybrass shared with the author his Powerpoint presentation, "The Materiality of Reading," Goethe-Universität,

Frankfurt, 15 June 2016.

10 Offset printing could happen at the printing or binding stage. It seems related to a combination of factors, including: the manufacture of the ink, how soon it was bound in a composite volume and when the paper was pressed, and the atmospheric conditions in which the book is kept.

11 A practical explanation for this is that it was less time-consuming to bind a pamphlet than a large and thick book.

12 The printer Jérémie des Planches is thought to have printed both works in Geneva, although his name does not appear in the first bound text. Marot's and de Bèze's translation was first printed in 1544.

13 For a discussion on the absence of imprint information on Reformation pamphlets, see Thomas's (2019) "Cashing in on Counterfeits."

14 Gatch (2007, 54–6) has written that few German monastic libraries owned collections of Reformation pamphlets. Yet, it is clear that some did.

15 I thank my colleagues Michele Silverman and Rachel Dankert for their Aeon users' report for the Reformation pamphlets collection from 2017 to 2019.

CHAPTER 3

An Enlightened Ministry

Reconstructing and Exploring the Library of Convers Francis

NELL K. CARLSON AND RUSSELL POLLARD

F rom time to time, staff of the Andover-Harvard Theological Library (AHTL) would notice books inscribed "C. Francis," with special bookplates reading, "Theological School in Cambridge. Bequest of Convers Francis, D.D." Sometimes inscriptions of varying lengths would accompany the signatures. Books with these markings would surface routinely during projects to move older collections offsite. So many were sent to the conservation department over the years that a stock of replacement bookplates was maintained for books that needed to be rebound with new pastedown pages. The frequent appearance of these books hinted at a large collection donated by someone worthy of attention.

Beyond the lovely autographs, these books might appear unremarkable. In fact, they might be lumped into a category of books so many librarians find troubling: too recent to be automatically transferred to special collections, yet too outdated to be of much interest to the current student body. Occasionally identified as duplicates, some were selected for withdrawal. A curious librarian or patron could quickly learn from Wikipedia that Convers Francis was a Unitarian minister and Harvard Divinity School professor closely associated with the founding of American Transcendentalist thought in the mid-nineteenth century, yet, despite these important affiliations, no systematic effort had been made to record the provenance of these books in the online catalog.

Librarians familiar with the contents of the Archives Workroom at AHTL might be able to connect the inscribed books to a bound, manuscript *Catalogue of the Francis Library* from 1864, but twentieth-century library work prioritized textual content over copy-specific features like inscriptions or provenance, and the list probably seemed of little practical use since the books had already been cataloged and integrated into the AHTL collections. Actually, the manuscript catalog might have seemed more notable for the fact that it was written in part by Charles Ammi Cutter, well known to librarians as a pioneer of book classification.

Despite the lack of attention given to it, today even a quick scan of the manuscript catalog suggests that the donation of Francis's books must have expanded the existing divinity school's library significantly. A large proportion of titles are in German or French and, in addition to the expected sermons and works of theology, there are titles on non-Christian religions and titles that suggest a propensity for the contemporary study of philosophy. If his library gift could be reconstructed and studied as a collection, what could be learned about Convers Francis as a minister, scholar, and educator?

Before deciding to embark on a project to reconstruct his library, a review of existing biographical material for Francis was undertaken, carefully noting references to his relationship with books, reading, and scholarship.

Convers Francis (1795–1863)

There is no critical biography of Convers Francis, and an autobiographical manuscript covering his early years has been lost. The main sources are biographical "sketches" and Guy Woodall's publication of Francis's journals (Woodall 1993, 51).

The geography of Convers Francis's career was two towns in Massachusetts: Watertown, where he was minister of First Parish Congregational (Unitarian), 1819–42, and Cambridge, where he was Parkman Professor of Pulpit Eloquence and Pastoral Care at Harvard Divinity School, from 1841 until his death in 1863. His father, a baker in Medford, Massachusetts, recognized his son's interest in learning and surprised him one day by asking if he would like to go to college. As it turned out, his father had been planning for this for some time, had consulted with others, and had arranged for him to start at a nearby preparatory school (Weiss 1863, 16; Vaughan 1944, 5). After graduating from Harvard College in 1815, he remained in Cambridge to study for the ministry. He was awarded an AM degree in 1818, and soon thereafter was examined and approbated to preach. In 1819, he began his twenty-three years of ministry in Watertown, followed by a return to Cambridge in 1842 to begin his twenty-one-year career as a professor at Harvard Divinity School.

Francis was a bibliophile's bibliophile. He loved books: he read them, collected them, loaned them, borrowed them, discussed them, and wrote them. In his autobiography, he confesses that his love of books began at an early age: "I had a sort of passion for reading whatever came in my way; and often, when I was wanted for work, in and about the house, I was found somewhere by myself over a book" (Newell 1866, 7). He not only read for himself but also read to others, including an elderly school mistress and his uncle James, who was blinded by smallpox. At first, his uncle requested Baptist classics, but later Winchester's *Dialogues on Universal Salvation* (Weiss 1863, 8–9; 11–12). Thus, at an early age, he was learning to read a wide range of other points of view beyond what he would have selected for himself. The size and scope of his personal library was perhaps the greatest evidence of his bibliophilia:

> Books were his only luxury. He laid in wait for them in catalogues and auction-rooms and carried off many a rarity whose titles betrayed no values to less instructed purchasers. There are more curious books in his library of seven or eight thousand volumes, than in most other collections of twice or twenty times the size. (Weiss 1863, 51)

In addition to reading books in his own library, the charging lists preserved in the Harvard University Archives show that he charged an average of sixty books per year between 1842 and 1852, his first ten years at Harvard as a professor, and an average of forty books per year after that (Woodall 1981, 282). Many, if not most, of the conversations within his circle of friends were about books. Indeed, "If you met him in the cars, you met also a queer book in his pocket. He would take it out and tell you all about it with a sparkle of fondness, as if it was a favorite child he had in charge" (Weiss 1863, 52).

Francis was also a scholar's scholar. He was well versed in the classics and was especially fond of Cicero, Plato, Sophocles, and Tacitus. He could read Latin, Greek, and Hebrew, as well as French, Italian, and Spanish (Woodall 2000). He could also read German, a relatively uncommon skill among New Englanders in his day. His facility with the language allowed him to access German literature, philosophy, theology, and biblical studies without translations. "By 1835 he had read Herder's *Spirit of Hebrew Poetry*, Berger's *Einleitung in das neue Testament*, De Wette, Ilgen, Eckermann, Bauer, Corrodi, and other Germans" (Pochmann 1957, 581 n. 685). He authored numerous articles, sermons, addresses, and tracts for the American Unitarian Association. All his books were histories, the best known being *Life of John Eliot*. With an established reputation as an historian, he became an active member of the Massachusetts Historical Society, "which he greatly aided in the preparation of its collections" (Vaughan 1944, 16). When Francis returned to Harvard to teach, he was already widely known and respected as a scholar, having received the honor of Doctor of Divinity in 1837 in recognition of his achievements.

He was a founding member of the Transcendental Club, a place for free and unfettered discussions of what were often controversial topics, at the time including Transcendentalism itself—a relatively new and, some believed, radical spiritual philosophy. As a senior member, Francis often moderated these discussions, since he was known for having a generous spirit that was "free of intellectual prejudices and dogmatism" and a manner with an "amiable, neutral, and mollifying quality" (Woodall 1993, 46). His reputation for being able to moderate discussions of controversial subjects was a significant reason for his professorial appointment at the Harvard Divinity School. At the time, Unitarians were divided into liberal and conservative camps:

> In many ways Francis seems to have been the perfect appointment for a denomination split between reason and intuition, Christian revelation and freedom. He was a tolerant moderate Transcendentalist, grounded in institutional loyalty, which meant that he could be trusted by radicals and conservatives alike." (Harris 2017, 128–9)

His moderation was also manifest in his broad-minded style of teaching. Drawing on encyclopedic and wide-ranging knowledge, he would present students diverse points of view and expected them to draw their own conclusions based on their reading and thinking. This approach was both lauded and derided. Some students wanted answers and found him to be "too all sided" (Harris 2017, 124). Others saw his method as a major contribution to a tradition of critical thinking at Harvard Divinity School. After his death, his sister (author and poet Lydia Child) described his manner of teaching and its impact:

> I think few appreciate duly the liberal influence of my brother in his teachings at the University. He never sought to impress his own opinions, or the doctrines of any sect, upon the minds of his pupils; but presented questions from various points of view, and left their minds free to decide which aspect was the true one. Sectarians complained of this, and he had many difficulties to encounter in consequence of their opposition; but he had his reward in the liberalizing effect of his system. (Child 1982; 426)

A notable exception, however, was the subject of slavery. He would not tolerate any argument defending what, to him, was an abominable institution: "I said all I could to encourage them in their resistance to this sin of our land, and told them I hoped every member of the School would go forth into the ministry prepared to set his face as a flint against this terrible iniquity" (Woodall 1982, 258).

Francis's wide circle of intellectual and book-loving friends relied both on his knowledge of books and on the volumes in his library, especially for titles that were hard to find:

> In his acquaintance with books, of which he had a large, and, in many respects, rare collection, accumulated through many years, he had few equals; and admirable was the heartiness with which he communicated his knowledge, and the generous alacrity with which he lent his treasures to all who sought his counsel, suggestion and help. (Newell 1866, 21)

Many of his closest friendships began or were cemented at the Transcendental Club, including Amos Bronson Alcott, Theodore Parker, Frederic Henry Hedge, and Ralph Waldo Emerson.

Francis and Alcott often disagreed. Francis continued to hold more orthodox Christian beliefs and felt Alcott's opinions too often lacked tangible evidence. Still, there was mutual personal appreciation. In fact, Alcott considered Francis one "by whom great principles are honored among us" (Woodall 1993, 47). Francis often loaned Alcott books from his library, including his rare copy of Dr. Henry More's poems, when Alcott wanted to translate "Cupid's Conflict" (1647) for submission to *The Dial*—the journal of the Transcendental Club (Woodall 1993, 48).

His friendship with Theodore Parker began in 1832, when, twenty-one years old and "in homely and awkward dress," Parker appeared on Francis's doorstep and introduced himself: "I am told that you welcome young people, and I am come to ask if you will be kind to me and help me, for I have come to Watertown to try and keep a school. I long for books and I long to know how to study" (Weiss 1863, 67). Francis not only helped Parker establish his school, but later he helped him enter Harvard Divinity School and preached at his ordination. Francis served Parker as a guide to German scholarship. Parker became so proficient that he was able to tutor German and translate German works while a divinity school student. To prepare for his monumental 1843 translation and commentary on De Wette's work (published as *A Critical and Historical Introduction to the Canonical Scriptures of the Old Testament*), Parker read hundreds of German books and consulted Francis's library (Pochmann 1957, 215–16). After Parker became a minister in West Roxbury, Massachusetts, there were years of lively correspondence about subjects such as the basis of religious authority, the composition of the Pentateuch, the nature of Christ, and spiritual philosophy. Despite disagreements (Parker was far more radical) they remained friends. In 1859, Parker wrote Francis:

> I thank you also for the interest you then took in my studies, —for the loan of books, your own, and those from the college library, which I had then no access to. I remember also, with great delight, that, in the conversations of the little club, your learning and your voice were always on the side of progress and freedom of thought. (Newell 1866, 19)

Francis and Frederic Henry Hedge shared a special interest in German language and philosophy. Hedge had studied in Germany as a youth and was so proficient in the language he became known as "Germanicus." Both Francis and Parker looked to Hedge for expertise on the philosophy of Immanuel Kant, which became the fountainhead of American Transcendentalism (Pochmann 1957, 144; Grady 2000; Harris 2017, 125).

Francis knew Emerson from early in his ministry, when Emerson preached for him in Watertown (Myerson 1978, 20). He much admired Emerson's views, knowledge, and exquisite style of writing and speaking. Despite their differences, when he overheard someone question Emerson's sanity, he replied, "I wish I were half as sane" (Myerson 1978, 20). He read everything Emerson wrote and attended many of his lectures, including his famous "Divinity Address" (1838)—Emerson's foundational presentation of Transcendentalist theology. "It was books and the ideas they inspired that joined Francis and Emerson most closely and was at the foundation of their mutual admiration" (Woodall 1993, 31). They discussed philosophy, theology, ethics, literature, and other subjects and authors of substance. Francis helped with Emerson's publication of Thomas Carlyle's *History of the French Revolution*, prompting Emerson to write to Carlyle, "To one other gentleman I have brought you in debt, —Rev. Convers Francis ... who supplied from his library all the numbers of the *Foreign Review* from which we printed the work. We could not have done without his books, and he is a noble hearted man who rejoices in you" (Woodall 1993, 32).

He had a close relationship with his sister, Lydia Maria Child—one based largely on books and scholarship. Throughout their lives, they mutually supported, encouraged, and inspired each other (Weiss 1863, 17). She wrote her first book, *Hobomok* (1824) at the Francis home in Watertown. Child was an outspoken abolitionist. She advocated for women's rights, Native American rights, and opposed American expansion. Francis shared her views and supported her work but was never the activist she was (Goodwin 2001; Teets-Parzynski 2000). One of her books, *The Progress of Religious Ideas, Through Successive Ages* (1855), showed unusual (for that time period) respect for non-Christian religions, describing each religion "in its own light." In writing of "the beauties and the blemishes" of each faith—including Christianity—she promoted tolerance for all religions (Harris 2017, 131). Her more conservative brother was "not altogether pleased" with her criticism of doctrinal theology, yet still "seems to rejoice in my book" (Child 1982, 278).

Having confirmed that books were central to the intellectual life and influence of Convers Francis, could an analysis of his library further enhance the understanding of Francis as a well-read and broad-minded scholar, teacher, minister, or bibliophile? Would an analysis enhance the understanding of the impact of his bequest upon the Harvard Divinity School?

The Case for Reconstructing the Convers Francis Library

Book historian David Pearson explains that the analysis of the books in a person's library "shows up the interests and tastes of the owner, and the texts which may have influenced his thinking" (Pearson 1998, 2). Therefore, if his books are understood to be possible influences upon Francis himself, the books deposited in the library of the divinity school (now AHTL) had the potential to influence contemporary and future students.

Researchers of early Transcendentalist thought and Unitarian history might be interested in knowing what books Francis read. The written correspondence between those in Francis's intellectual circle includes countless references (often incomplete or ambiguous) to books and authors; a list of the contents of his library could enhance understanding of their discussions. For those researching the history of the study of religion, an analysis of Francis's books deposited with the divinity school would provide insight into theological education of the time. If the contents of his library were compiled, Francis's collection could be compared with other private or institutional collections to uncover differences or similarities.

Because Francis wrote in his books, a study of the tangible evidence of his interactions would also be of interest to book historians. Often one cannot tell whether a former owner actually read a book as opposed to just collecting it, but if Francis left such evidence regularly, these books would represent a rich source for the study of nineteenth-century American book history.

The possibilities for research are tantalizing, but how could one study the Francis Library when the collection had been dispersed and untraced for more than a hundred years? Only a handful of the Francis books had been noted in online catalog records over the years, usually updated when more substantial cataloging work was needed. Almost all remaining books remained hidden in plain sight on library shelves.

A recent project to identify the scattered books at Harvard from the library of philosopher William James faced similar challenges yet forged ahead. The project's architect articulates some of the reasons for libraries to identify books of significant provenance that have been dispersed within larger institutional libraries: books can be guarded against theft or loss, the chance of modern readers adding their own marks or annotations to the original owner's is reduced, inadvertent withdrawal is avoided, removal to improved physical preservation conditions can be prioritized, and losses to the material book object through rebinding or excessive handling can be prevented (Algaier 2020, [53]–63). Of these, the threat of inadvertent withdrawal looms large for Francis's books as libraries face pressure to remove print holdings, particularly if the title is available in digital form.

Knowing that the Francis books should have all been given a bequest bookplate and that Francis routinely wrote his name in his books, one way to identify the books from his library would be to review each book physically, one by one. This method was deemed impractical, since the majority of books printed before 1863 (the year of Francis's death) and still circulating are permanently housed in offsite storage. (Almost all AHTL special collections materials were temporarily stored offsite during 2018–21 due to building renovations.) Instead, the manuscript catalog of the original Francis Library was determined to be the best starting point from which to produce a working bibliography with the most likely shelf locations for each. But does this list represent the bulk of Francis's library at the time of his death or only a subset of his collection?

Researching the Gift to the Divinity Library

The *Annual Reports of the President and Treasurer of Harvard College: 1863–64* records the facts of the gift:

> Rev. Dr. Convers Francis having intimated to his children his desire that a part of his library should be given to the University, they have with much care selected about two thousand six hundred valuable works, not in our libraries, and placed two thousand of them in Divinity Hall, and six hundred in Gore Hall. (Harvard College 1865, 6)

It is not obvious why some books were routed to Divinity Hall (which housed the divinity library) and others to Gore Hall (the library of Harvard College), since both gifts include religious works such as sermons (*List of Books Bequeathed* 1886). Later in the report of the Treasurer, they are described as "valuable French and German books" (Harvard College 1865, "Treasurer's Report," 2). The report confirms that, as is commonly the case, it was the family that selected books for donation. It also suggests two important points: first, it may be reasonably assumed that titles already held at Harvard, even if of great importance or value to Francis, would not likely be included in the books donated; and second, that the gift represented a trove of resources previously unavailable to students.

Knowing that his library was estimated to contain about seven to eight thousand volumes, it is clear that only some of the books that belonged to Convers Francis would be identified by the manuscript catalog. Harvard would have received less than half of them. While the project at hand focuses on identifying the books that were given to Harvard Divinity School, researchers interested in the larger, more complete library of Convers Francis will be glad to learn of several other sources.

Seven years after the death of his sister, at least a portion of the books not given to Harvard were sold, along with Child's, at auction. The collection was large enough (1,901 lots) and important enough to warrant a printed catalog but, unfortunately, the auction company did not distinguish between the books of Francis, Child, and "selections from another private library" integrated for the purposes of the sale (*Catalogue* [1887] 1970, 2). The collector George S. Davis appears to have purchased more than a dozen of these books, noting the inscriptions of Convers Francis and later ownership by Child and, for some, noting that the books were part of Child's working library for her book, *The Progress of Religious Ideas* (Davis 1890). Again, it is uncertain whether this lot represented the totality of Francis's books still with the family in 1887 or if, once more, portions were retained or otherwise dispersed. Despite the fact that the auction list includes materials from a third, unnamed collector, it nonetheless suggests the possibility of integration of books between Convers Francis and Lydia Child. The auction catalog does not routinely note inscriptions by Francis or Child, but one wonders if some of those books might bear markings of both, a topic that might also interest scholars of Child.

At least one scholar has reviewed the auction catalog for a study of German influences within American scholarship, noting the broad range of German titles present but observing that "The more recent German theologiual [sic] writers of the Tübingen School are conspicuously absent" (Pochmann 1957, 581 n. 685).

Finally, Francis also donated books to the divinity library during his life. A preliminary scan of early accession records reveals more than two hundred gifts—the earliest in 1827 and the bulk during 1840–50, while he was teaching at the school. Were these books so important Francis thought the school should have them? Or were these books of lesser value and with which he could easily part? One must also wonder whether Francis routinely gave away books to friends, colleagues, or students. Books in these categories might reasonably be excluded if his library is defined as the collection at the time of his death, but they, too, provide insight into his reading habits and relationships with books, as would records of books he borrowed.

The Project Plan

While it is somewhat disappointing to realize that the gift to the divinity library represents a mere portion of the whole collection of books having belonged to Francis, it is, at the same time, encouraging that a contemporary catalog recording bibliographic citations for the books survives with information on at least two thousand pieces from his collection. Convinced that such a project would be worthwhile, a plan was formulated to track down and reunite the books of the Francis Library in a virtual way, to offer initial observations and analysis of the collection, and to suggest possibilities for future research.

The project had the following goals: transcribe the manuscript catalog to produce a basic bibliography in digital form, taking advantage of existing metadata in the online catalog whenever feasible to facilitate analysis of the collection in various ways (e.g., by year, place of publication, subject headings, classification), and to identify likely locations for each item. As library volumes are physically verified to be from Francis (or definitively ruled out), both the bibliography and online catalog would be updated to enable either serendipitous or purposeful discovery.

Transcription of the Manuscript Catalog and Identifying Likely Matches in the Online Catalog

The manuscript catalog of books given by Francis's family to Harvard Divinity School was jointly written by librarians Charles Noyes (A–L, W–Z) and Charles A. Cutter (M–V) in the summer of 1864, with additions recorded in October of the same year. The catalog is arranged alphabetically by author or title without contemporary notation of shelf marks, suggesting the books were also arranged physically in this manner. Users were directed to individual titles within 152 bound volumes of pamphlets through an assigned "tracts" number, suggesting that bound pamphlets were a distinct subcollection of the Francis Library. While the manuscript catalog surely served as a useful tool for navigating the collection in the nineteenth century, the ability to analyze it and reuse its contents today is limited by its analog nature.

Because it was assumed that, due to loss over the past hundred years, not every book with a citation in the manuscript catalog could be located, adding notes about Francis's ownership in the online catalog alone would be insufficient to represent the bibliographical details of the gift. Therefore, a spreadsheet for the complete bequest (or as complete as is possible) would serve as the primary clearinghouse for citations, shelf locations, and any other notes. Microsoft Excel was chosen for simplicity and ubiquity, with the expectation that the data could be transformed into a database or to other formats in the future.

Photographs of the manuscript catalog were taken to make remote work possible. Tedious at first, transcription speed increased as familiarity with the handwriting of Noyes and Cutter grew. Typical entries in the catalog include author, title, number of volumes, edition, place of publication, date, format (size), and tracts number (if applicable). To facilitate its use, the librarians employed cross references from alternate forms of names and between certain titles and authors. In some cases, entries had been made for individual volumes within larger multipart works, or for individual (but substantial) sections of single-volume books, with references directing the user to the location of the host item. In the interest of completeness and for potential use in future problem-solving, the cross references were also transcribed.

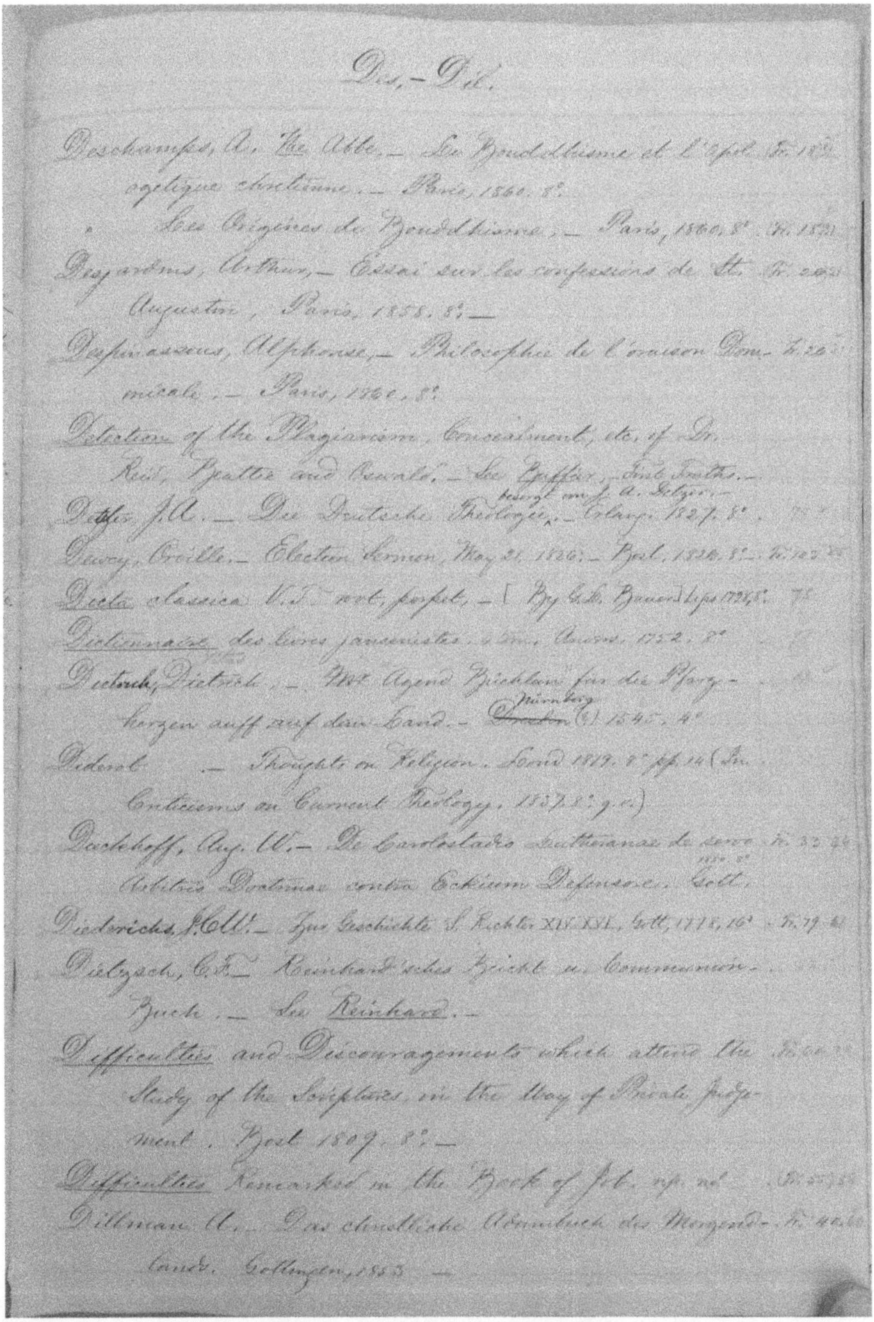

Image 1: Page from the *Catalogue of the Francis Library* (1864)
(Andover-Harvard Theological Library Special Collections).

The catalog was written in attractive, nineteenth-century hand, but, unfortunately, Noyes and Cutter liberally employed abbreviations for names, places, and common theological terms. Early in the project, it became clear that exact transcription of the manuscript would not be practical for the sake of time; the abbreviations in German proved particularly difficult for the transcriber. Instead, the initial transcription in Excel became a tool primarily for identifying books in the online catalog. More detailed review of each entry would be deferred until later, ideally with book in hand.

Later librarian annotations were also recorded. These include notes correcting original entries, as well as those indicating books known to have been lost or withdrawn. (In scattered places an ink stamp appears over entries marking "Duplicate Sold.") Almost all entries include a later shelf location, presumably added during or after the integration of the Francis Library into the larger divinity collection. In fact, the spreadsheet could be sorted by shelf marks to arrange the books "virtually" as they would have been on shelves in the early 1900s.

The next step was searching for titles in Harvard's online catalog—HOLLIS—and appending the spreadsheet with current system numbers and current shelf locations. Here the abbreviations used by Noyes and Cutter, pragmatic and sufficient for the pre-electronic era, became a challenge. For example, the librarians routinely recorded only the first initial with an author's last name. These conventions would have presented no problems for the manuscript catalog's first users, but they cause frustration for someone keyword searching across an expansive online database. For the majority of entries, however, a few keywords with the year of publication were adequate to reveal obvious or very likely matches.

Even in cases where a bibliographic match was found in HOLLIS but without a current location at AHTL, the system number was recorded for the ease of retrieving bibliographic details. When no good matches were found, WorldCat was consulted to identify errors made by Noyes and Cutter or during transcription from manuscript to spreadsheet. In cases where no good match presented itself in HOLLIS, but for which there was a record in WorldCat, this was noted so that metadata could be recorded from that source later. Also during this stage, if a matching title was found to have a link to Google Books, the digitized copy was reviewed to see if it was an obvious Francis book and the entry was marked for future review.

Next, the system numbers were fed into the reporting tool that is part of Harvard's integrated library system, Alma. Metadata was extracted from relevant catalog fields to supplement the roughly transcribed data with regularized, more complete, and other available information, including subject metadata. As online catalog records are updated to include the Francis provenance, researchers should be able to return this sort of metadata directly from the public HOLLIS interface, though the results will exclude any titles lost, withdrawn, or not yet identified. Finally, another report supplied hyperlinks to the Google Books scans of Francis's books, as identified earlier.

Initial Analysis of Bibliographic Data

In all, 3,184 entries were transcribed to the Excel spreadsheet. Of these, 482 lines were categorized as cross references and 15 as duplicate entries. Of the 2,687 unique entries in the manuscript catalog, matches in HOLLIS were made for 2,606 entries, and an additional 58 entries not matched with an existing HOLLIS record were identified in WorldCat. For those entries with matching records in HOLLIS, 169 bibliographic records indicated their only possible locations were at Harvard libraries other than AHTL. Remarkably, only 23 entries had data too incomplete (or in error) to match with an existing record in HOLLIS or Worldcat. The number of unique entries represents titles as opposed to volumes; some titles are in multiple parts, and about 900 titles are contained within 152 bound tracts volumes.

The associated bibliographic metadata pulled from Harvard's integrated library system included country/state of publication, language, publication year(s), author, title, edition, imprint statement, physical description, Library of Congress classification, and subjects. Once the metadata was appended to the spreadsheet, Excel pivot tables could easily be used to generate statistics related to the content of the Francis Library.

Here it is important to note a caveat about using catalog data for such analysis. The data available will only be as good as the catalog records, which can be inconsistent both in quality and completeness. To illustrate this point, fewer than half of the associated bibliographic records contain Library of Congress classification data, and more than two hundred records have no subject headings. The language metadata retrieved in this initial report represents only the primary language of the item. However, additional data to identify multilanguage works and translations could be retrieved for future studies. Ideally, all data would be verified as books are reviewed physically.

Based on this initial analysis, the international nature of the collection is apparent. In terms of primary language, about 36 percent of the collection is in English, but almost the same number of books are in German (32 percent), followed by French (19 percent), and Latin (12 percent). About 80 percent were printed abroad and, in fact, more than one-third was published in Germany alone. These statistics attest to Francis's strength in multiple languages, interest in Continental scholarship, and perhaps some familiarity with the international book trade.

Was Francis collecting modern books or acquiring antiquarian volumes? About 31 percent of the titles in the Francis Library were published between 1841 and 1863, during Francis's career as a Harvard professor, though roughly 25 percent were printed before 1800. These calculations on language, place of publication, and dates are simple examples; data points could be combined to support more complex analyses.

Analyzing the collection based on subject metadata proved difficult because so many records lack this information. An analysis of the records that do contain subject data suggests philosophy is a predominant topic in the Francis Library. Apart from the subject metadata, a simple scan of the catalog entries reveals a library of diverse topics. In addition to the expected printed sermons and abolitionist tracts, his collection contains works on Buddhism, Islam, Hinduism, Zoroastrianism, and pantheism, and works by Kant, Schleiermacher, Swedenborg, Maimonides, Confucius, and Plato.

Francis clearly owned books on non-Christian religions, but did he read them? Several books were recalled from storage and reviewed, including Francis's copy of Godfrey Higgins's 1829 work, *An Apology for the Life & Character of the Celebrated Prophet of Arabia, Called Mohamed*, located in Tracts 53. The volume, containing three titles on disparate subjects, was purchased by Francis in 1837 "at the sale of Dr. Prince's library." Within his copy of *An Apology*, which is an assertive defense by a British non-Muslim against Western critics of Mohammed, there are abundant marks in the margins (lines, *X*s, *N*s, etc.) and scattered annotations. While one must exercise caution in attributing marginalia to a particular past owner, especially when a book has been part of a circulating library or known to have belonged to more than one individual, the markings here appear consistent with those found in other books from Francis (see "Initial Analysis Using Scans of Francis Library Books," below). In one instance, responding to the author's description of a narrative from the Qur'an, Francis has noted, "There is no such account." In another place, the author notes a Qur'anic source in a footnote which Francis brackets with his note, "Misquotation." In other places, Francis has countered or supplemented the author's arguments with references to other works. If these marks indeed are by Francis, they demonstrate his engagement with this text beyond simple reading. As just one example, this volume affirms the potential research value of the Francis Library.

A scan of the catalog entries also reveals that the works by German scholars of the Tübingen School (a Protestant movement of the early to mid-1800s inspired by Georg W. F. Hegel and led by Ferdinand Christian Baur) noted as "conspicuously absent" from the Francis/Child auction catalog had, in fact, been donated to the divinity school (Pochmann 1957, 581 n. 685). At least two dozen titles by Baur, David Strauss, Eduard Zeller, and Adolf Hilgenfeld were included in the bequest.

Other curious titles reflect Francis's wide-ranging interests. These include an 1833 account of a cross-country journey to Oregon, a book of early life science from 1770, at least two books on phrenology, and even a 1732 tract on vampires. Undoubtedly, some of these unexpected titles have remained at AHTL because they were bound together with other works.

Identification of Francis Library Volumes via Google Books

Once the manuscript catalog was transcribed with the most likely shelf location for each, the obvious next step was to order the list by call number and begin to examine books physically to confirm their provenance. Unfortunately, due to ongoing building renovations during 2018–21, almost all materials were being stored offsite. The COVID-19 pandemic further reduced opportunities to request materials from storage. Would there be a way to continue the project remotely?

Here the work was aided by Harvard's participation in the 2008 Google Books scanning project. Any book out of copyright then in the circulating collection and in stable condition was scanned, with a link added in the online catalog. (Since the scanning project, many of these books have been transferred into Special Collections based on their age.) As a result, several hundred books from the original Francis Library can easily be verified through bookplate or inscription and examined for annotations without recalling them from storage. Interestingly, when following the links to scans from HOLLIS, twenty-six items from the Francis Library were found now to be part of the collections of other Harvard libraries.

Initial Analysis Using Scans of Francis Library Books

For a preliminary exploration of the evidence of use left by Francis in his books, one hundred of the roughly three hundred Francis Library titles verified via Google Books were reviewed for inscription and other data. Some examples of notes inscribed by Francis are given below to entice future researchers.

The review of scans confirmed that Francis routinely recorded his name and the year in his books (86 percent). Unfortunately, the review also confirmed that some inscriptions may already have been lost: Nine books in the survey appear to have been rebound with endpapers (where Francis routinely left his inscriptions) replaced. When present, the date accompanying Francis's signature was included in the spreadsheet to support future analysis of acquisition dates of the books.

Overall, 33 percent of the scans reviewed show some kind of inscription apart from his name—almost all initialed "C. F." when present. Seven percent include notes about the provenance of the item such as where the book was purchased, previous owners of the book, or from whom the book was acquired (e.g., "Bought at the sale of Rev. George Ripley's Library"; "From the library of Dr. Gesenius, purchased for me, at the sale of his books, through Mr. Radde, bookseller in N. York"; "bought in Baltimore").

Some 6 percent include notes on authorship or publication history (e.g., "The author of this account of Vanini, as I learn from Oettinger, *Bibliographie Biographique*, was Wilhelm David Fuhrmann"; "this 2d vol. was first published as a separate work in 1805 at Paris").

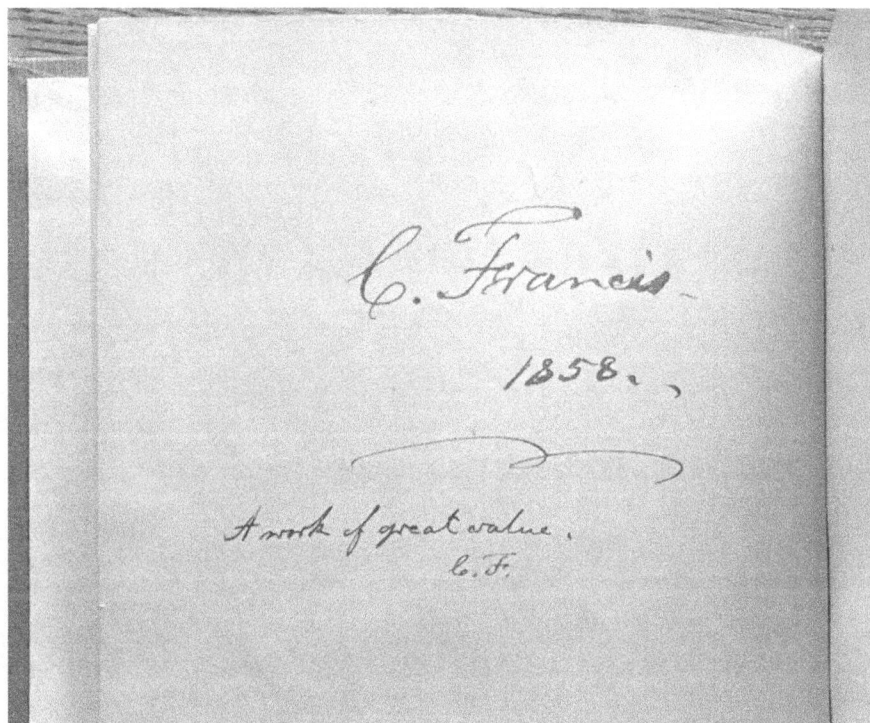

Image 2: Autograph inscription with date and comment. (Andover-Harvard Theological Library Special Collections 17 Carriere, M. Carriere, *Die philosophische Weltanschauung der Reformationszeit, in ihren Beziehungen zur Gegenwart*, 1847.)

Many inscriptions could be roughly categorized as referencing or quoting published reviews of the book (e.g., "The *North British Review* says, 'We recommend this work emphatically to the attention of our philosophical readers.' And the *Literary Gazette* calls it 'a masterly treatise'"), the comments of other scholars about the author at hand ("Dr. Parr (& who shall venture to question Dr. Parr's dictum?) declares that this book 'abounds with deep erudition & masterly reasoning'"), quotations or references from related works, and the occasional direct evaluation by Francis himself ("A work of great value").

Reviewing scans for annotations or other markings can be challenging. Still, even cursory skimming revealed that at least 62 percent of the sample set contain some kind of marking of text. The most common marks are *X*s, *N*s, and simple single vertical lines in the margins. At least fourteen titles were observed to have notes on rear endpapers or other annotations to the text, including the occasional correction of an author's Latin. These initial findings suggest that researchers may indeed wish to conduct a more thorough evaluation.

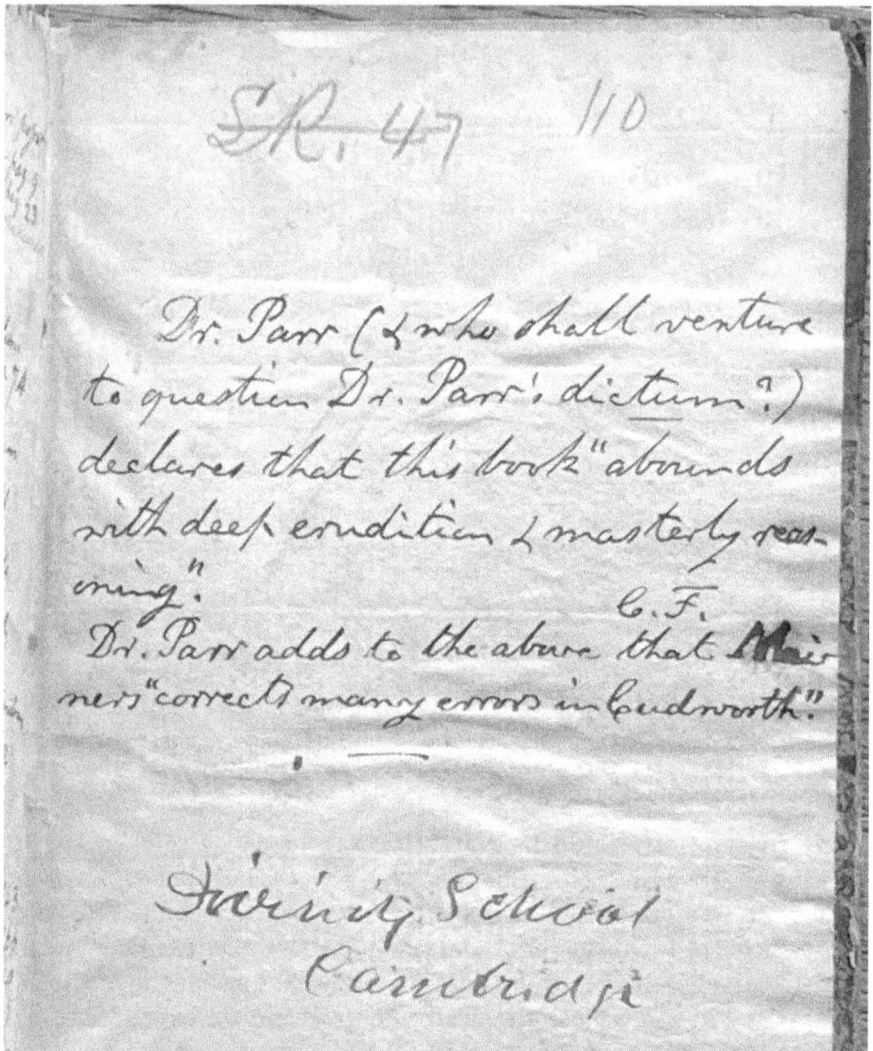

Image 3: Inscription referencing the opinion of English minister (and book collector) Samuel Parr. (Andover-Harvard Theological Library Special Collections 110 Meiners, Meiners, C. *Historia doctrinae de vero Deo omnium rerum auctore atque rectore*, 1780.)

It is important to note that, though some annotations can be readily identified by comparing them with Francis's signed inscriptions, other markings are more ambiguous. Further careful, in-person examination is warranted.

In an attempt to record binding information based on the digital surrogates, it was found that as many as one-third of the scans reviewed appear to indicate later rebinds. In one instance, Francis

Preserving the Past & Engaging the Future

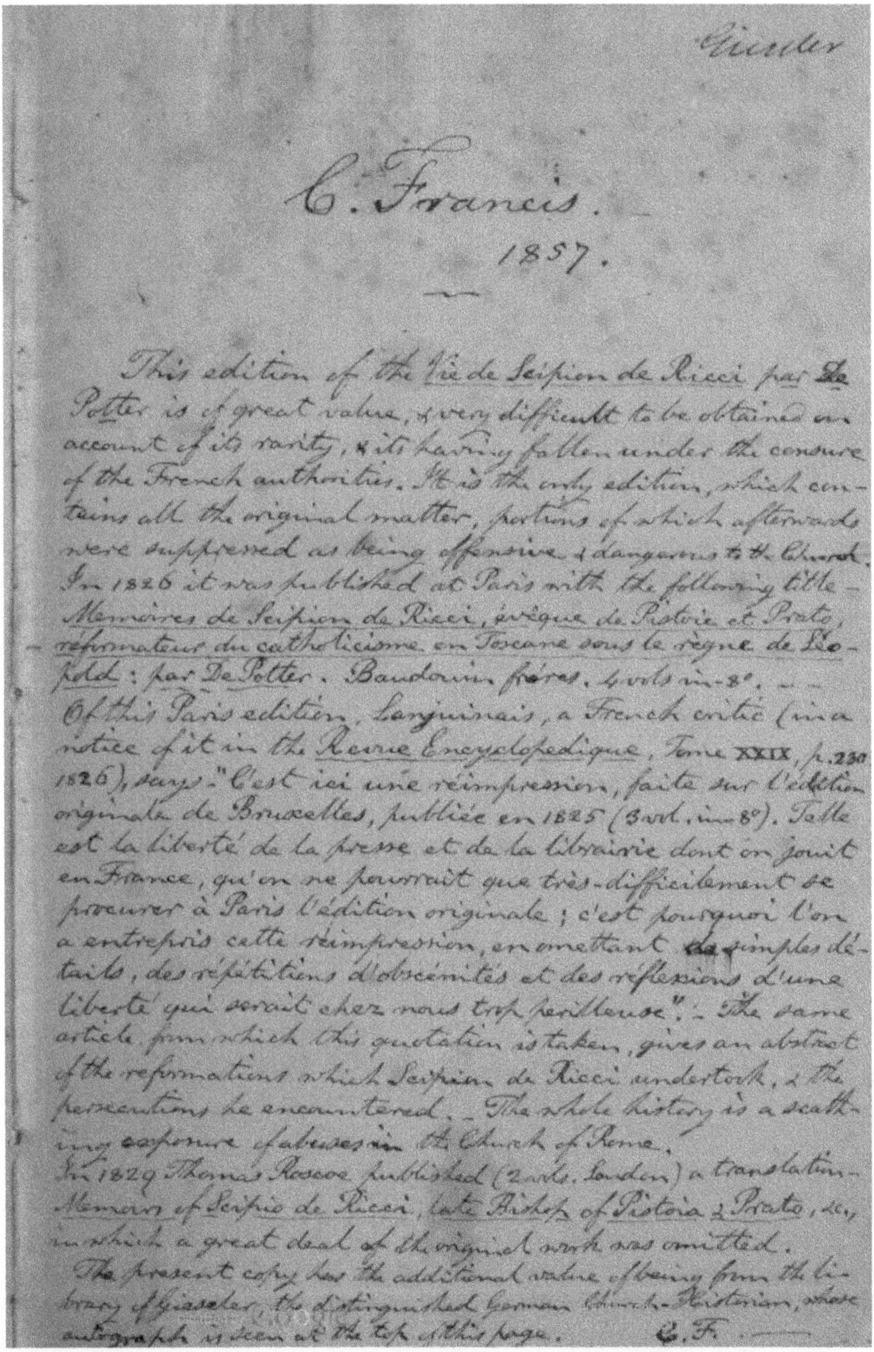

Gieseler

C. Francis.

1857.

This edition of the *Vie de Scipion de Ricci par de Potter* is of great value, & very difficult to be obtained on account of its rarity, & its having fallen under the censure of the French authorities. It is the only edition, which contains all the original matter, portions of which afterwards were suppressed as being offensive & dangerous to the Church. In 1826 it was published at Paris with the following title — *Mémoires de Scipion de Ricci, évêque de Pistoie et Prato, réformateur du catholicisme en Toscane sous le règne de Léopold: par De Potter. Baudouin frères. 4 vols in 8°.* — Of this Paris edition, Lanjuinais, a French critic (in a notice of it in the *Revue Encyclopédique*, Tome XXIX, p. 230 1826), says: "C'est ici une réimpression, faite sur l'édition originale de Bruxelles, publiée en 1825 (3 vol. in 8°). Telle est la liberté de la presse et de la librairie dont on jouit en France, qu'on ne pourrait que très-difficilement se procurer à Paris l'édition originale; c'est pourquoi l'on a entrepris cette réimpression, en omettant de simples détails, des répétitions d'obscénités et des réflexions d'une liberté qui serait chez nous trop périlleuse". — The same article from which this quotation is taken, gives an abstract of the reformations which Scipion de Ricci undertook, & the persecutions he encountered. — The whole history is a scathing exposure of abuses in the Church of Rome. In 1829 Thomas Roscoe published (2 vols. London) a translation — *Memoirs of Scipio de Ricci, late Bishop of Pistoia & Prato*, &c., in which a great deal of the original work was omitted. The present copy has the additional value of being from the library of Gieseler, the distinguished German Church Historian, whose autograph is seen at the top of this page.   C. F. ———

Image 4: Inscription detailing the book's rarity, publication history, history of censorship, reviews, and with note on the book's previous owner. (Andover-Harvard Theological Library Old Div C Ricci v. 1, L. De Potter, *Vie de Scipion de Ricci, évêque de Pistoie e Prato, et réformateur du catholicisme en Toscane, sous le règne de Léopold*, 1825. Google Books image via HathiTrust: *https://hdl.handle.net/2027/hvd.32044029913894.*)

notes that his book containing two titles was bound in 1853 but, alas, the book now lives within nondescript black buckram covers. Further study of physical items might reveal Francis's binding preferences as either typical or atypical for his time and location, though it seems likely that much evidence may already have been lost.

Next Steps and Project Conclusions

The spreadsheet with transcription of the manuscript catalog data, supplemented with likely shelf locations and metadata from the current online catalog, provides a solid starting point for future research on the Francis Library. The file can be updated with additional information (confirmed location, presence of annotations, inscriptions, markings, bindings, etc.) as Francis books are identified during other routine library activities. Ideally, the transcription of the manuscript (having been created in some haste) would be reviewed and corrected at the same time. Though cost constraints prevent a systematic search for Francis volumes at this time, the library can provide interested researchers with the spreadsheet data in progress and accept new evidence from researchers when available.

In addition to gradually updating the spreadsheet of citations, records in the online catalog should also be updated to include entries for Convers Francis as the former owner. A collection-level record can provide a place to describe the Francis Library at AHTL, its context, and biographical information about Convers Francis, while also providing guidance to users on ways to find the books in the online catalog (or elsewhere) (Nicholson 2014, 32, 39).

A practical question that arose during the project is whether the identified Francis books in the circulating collections should be transferred into Special Collections. It was decided that the books would be evaluated for transfer on a case-by-case basis, prioritizing books with inscriptions or annotations. Some books might be allowed to continue circulating, or perhaps be restricted to in-library use.

This project affirmed suspicions that the Francis Library has deep potential for research in Unitarian history, the history of the study of religion in America, Transcendentalist thought, and nineteenth-century book history. Even though the Francis Library is but one part of the larger reading life of Convers Francis, the collection of more than two thousand titles represents a significant portion for analysis. Even before all the books can be physically examined, the creation of a digital file to facilitate analysis represents a significant step towards the goal to "reconstruct" the library of Convers Francis.

The Legacy of the Francis Library: An Enlightened Ministry

Shortly after Francis began his new role as professor at Harvard Divinity School, his good friend Theodore Parker wrote him: "the School already wears a new aspect, as it has a new soul; that you stimulate the dull and correct the erratic and set right such as have prejudices inclining to narrowness if not bigotry" (Weiss 1863, 39). Mark Harris argues that Francis's teaching brought a transition in Unitarian thought "from a rational liberal Christian revelation to a broader pluralism" (Harris 2017, 135). In his memoir of Francis, William Newell writes, "Without accepting their views and conclusions, he was ready to give a hearing to the thinkers and scholars of other lands, and to receive whatever truth, new or old, they had to offer; to prove all things, and to hold fast the good" (Newell 1866, 12).

The initial analysis of the Francis Library demonstrates the multilingual and multifaith nature of his collection and confirms Francis's role as an advocate of this "broader pluralism"—the broadening of theological dialogue in New England beyond the English-speaking world, the broadening of dialogue within Unitarianism, and broader engagement with non-Christian ideas. One imagines Francis would be pleased with how AHTL collections have evolved over time, maintaining historic strength in Protestant theology (with a particular strength in Unitarian Universalism) but expanding to include diverse faith traditions, reflecting Harvard Divinity School's guiding principles that "Scholars of religion should employ critical analysis, multiple disciplines and be reflective about their own positionality and that of others" and "should have a deep and broad understanding of more than a single religious tradition" (Harvard Divinity School, n.d.). Thus the Francis Library represents a contribution to the liberal tradition of Harvard Divinity School—a tradition of scholarship not confined by boundaries of language and creed. Convers Francis stood firmly in this tradition of learning and scholarship.

In 1815, shortly before Francis began his ministerial studies, William Ellery Channing wrote a pamphlet soliciting funds to establish what soon became Harvard Divinity School. In it, he argued that "an enlightened age requires an enlightened ministry" and that an enlightened ministry "is the only barrier against fanaticism" (Channing 1815, 6–7). Though not a household name like his friend Ralph Waldo Emerson, it is clear that Convers Francis was influential as a teacher and colleague, exemplifying the educated minister sought by the School's founders.

His friend and colleague John Weiss wrote of Francis, "His favorite seal displayed a book underneath the motto, *Qui studet orat* (He prays who studies)" (Weiss 1863, 52)—a fitting maxim that captures the love for books and learning and the "enlightened ministry" he sought to practice.

References

Algaier, Ermine L. 2020. *Reconstructing the Personal Library of William James: Markings and Marginalia from the Harvard Library Collection*. Lanham: Lexington Books.

Cadbury, Henry J. 1951. "Religious Books at Harvard." *Harvard Library Bulletin* 2 (Spring): 159–80. *https://nrs.harvard.edu/URN-3:HUL.INSTREPOS:37363583*.

Catalogue of a portion of the libraries of the late Rev. Convers Francis, and his sister, Lydia M. Child, of Cambridge . . . . (1887) 1970. Boston: Charles F. Libbie, Jr. Reprint, *American Transcendental Quarterly* 6, pt. 2 (2nd quarter). Citations refer to the reprint.

Channing, William Ellery. 1815. *Observations on the Proposition for Increasing the Means of Theological Education at the University in Cambridge*. Cambridge: Hilliard and Metcalf. *https://hdl.handle.net/2027/umn.31951002167553e*.

Child, Lydia Maria. 1982. *Lydia Maria Child, Selected Letters, 1817–1880*, edited by Milton Meltzer and Patricia G. Holland. Amherst: University of Massachusetts Press.

Davis, George S. 1890. *Catalogue of the Private Library of Mr. George S. Davis*. Detroit. *https://hdl.handle.net/2027/uiug.30112109604832*.

Goodwin, Joan. 2001. "Lydia Maria Child." In *Dictionary of Unitarian and Universalist Biography: An On-line Resource of the Unitarian Universalist History & Heritage Society*. Unitarian Universalist History & Heritage Society. *https://uudb.org/articles/lydiamaria-child.html*.

Grady, Charles. 2000. "Frederic Henry Hedge." In *Dictionary of Unitarian and Universalist Biography: An On-Line Resource of the Unitarian Universalist History & Heritage Society*. Unitarian Universalist History & Heritage Society. *https://uudb.org/articles/frederichenryhedge.html*.

Harris, Mark W. 2017. "Convers Francis and the Creation of an Inclusive Unitarianism." *Journal of Unitarian Universalist History* 41 (January): 119–37.

Harris, Mark W. 2011. "From Revelation to Reason to Intuition: The Development of Unitarianism in America – A Local Perspective." *https://fpwsermons.wordpress.com/2011/09/19/from-revelation-to-reason*.

Harvard College. 1865. *Annual Reports of the President and Treasurer of Harvard College: 1863–64*. Cambridge: Welch, Bigelow, and Company. *https://hdl.handle.net/2027/uiug.30112074971257*.

Harvard Divinity School. n.d. "History and mission." Accessed January 18, 2021. *https://hds.harvard.edu/about/history-and-mission*.

List of Books Bequeathed to Harvard College Library by Convers Francis. 1886. Harvard University Archives, Harvard University.

Myerson, Joel. 1978. "Convers Francis and Emerson." *American Literature* 50, no. 1 (March): 17–36.

Newell, William. 1866. *Memoir of the Rev. Convers Francis, D.D.* Cambridge: John Wilson and Sons. *https://hdl.handle.net/2027/hvd.hnqmqz*.

Nicholson, Joseph. 2014. "Cataloging Writers' Private Libraries." In *Collecting, Curating, and Researching Writers' Libraries*, edited by Richard W. Oram with Joseph Nicholson, 29–51. Lanham: Rowman & Littlefield.

Pearson, David. 1998. *Provenance Research in Book History: A Handbook*. The British Library Studies in the History of the Book. London: The British Library.

Pochmann, Henry A. 1957. *German Culture in America: Philosophical and Literary Influences, 1600–1900*. Madison: University of Wisconsin Press. *https://hdl.handle.net/2027/mdp.39015008879374*.

Teets-Parzynski, Catherine. 2000. "Child, Lydia Maria Francis (1802–1880), Author and Abolitionist." In *American National Biography Online*. New York: Oxford University Press.

Vaughan, Mosetta I. 1944. *Sketch of the Life and Work of Convers Francis, D.D.* Watertown: Historical Society of Watertown.

Weiss, John. 1863. *Discourse Occasioned by the Death of Convers Francis, D.D.* Cambridge: Welch, Bigelow, & Co. *https://hdl.handle.net/2027/hvd.32044029889276*.

Woodall, Guy R., ed. 1981. "The Journals of Convers Francis (Part One)." *Studies in the American Renaissance*: 265–343.

———, ed. 1982. "The Journals of Convers Francis (Part Two)." *Studies in the American Renaissance*: 227–84.

———. 1993. "Convers Francis and the Concordians: Emerson, Alcott, and Others." *The Concord Saunterer* 1, no. 1 (Fall): 22–58.

———. 2000. "Francis, Convers (1795–1863), Unitarian Clergyman and University Professor." In *American National Biography Online*. New York: Oxford University Press.

CHAPTER 4

Hogwarts in Minnesota

The History, Description, and Impact of Special Collections at Luther Seminary

BRUCE ELDEVIK & MARY ANN TESKE

A soft knock sounds on the door of the special collections room on the upper floor of Gullixson Hall—the 1950s-era limestone building that houses Luther Seminary's library, archives, classrooms, and faculty offices. Today, the visitors are a confirmation class of middle school-age young people along with their youth pastor and a seminary campus guide. The door opens and the gaggle of kids begins filing in, a few still laughing from conversations begun on the stairs outside. A few paces into the room, however, the group quickly grows quiet, as they survey the floor-to-ceiling bookcases lining three sides and the angled rolling ladders for access to the topmost shelves, the triad of stained glass windows at the far end, and, along one side, the gothic arches and pillars. Suddenly, the eyes of a girl at the front of the group light up and her face breaks into a broad smile. "Hogwarts!" she exclaims.

Luther Seminary Library is fortunate to have a space that creates a magical, step-back-in-time ambience in which to house and showcase its special collections. The room reflects its contents. Its visual appeal has made it a fixture on the campus tour circuit, opening its door to visitors of all ages, and so the "Rare Book Room" is itself an important part of the story of special collections at the seminary. Therefore, this room is where we begin to relate the history, contents, and impact of special collections at Luther Seminary.

Background

Luther Seminary is the product of numerous mergers of immigrant Midwestern church bodies, all rooted in northern European Lutheranism. In 1917, three Norwegian Lutheran denominations merged and established Luther Theological Seminary in a stately brick building on its leafy campus in a quiet corner of Saint Paul, Minnesota. As the seminary grew, a second building opened in 1950 to accommodate classrooms, faculty offices, and the new seminary library. This new building was subsequently named Gullixson Hall to honor Thaddeus F. Gullixson, seminary president from 1930–54.

The modern library at Luther Seminary can be traced back to 1943 when the first professional librarian was hired to catalog and organize a collection of around three thousand books. Before mid-century, the library played only a marginal role in the theological education and formation of its male students. Prior to this time, books and journals were largely collected by individual faculty members in the course of their research, teaching, and travel. The faculty then made them available for loan to their students. Many of these books were standard, foundational texts of the Christian tradition and its Lutheran expression. Most were in Latin, German, Dano-Norwegian, Swedish, and a smattering of other European languages. Between the wars, as the transition to English took hold, they received declining use beyond the professors who owned them. As these faculty retired, many of these texts remained at the seminary, tucked away in various places. Later, they would become the core of Luther's special collections.

History of the Rare Book Room

The top floor of Gullixson Hall is a mix of small classrooms and faculty offices, but in a corner just off the main stairway is a room originally designed as a meditation chapel and preaching laboratory. For a time, it was outfitted with broadcast equipment and served as an ad hoc, low-wattage radio station where students could practice conducting worship services over the airwaves. With the hiring of two professors from Latvia, this studio was also used to broadcast worship services in Latvian to the surrounding neighborhood, where a small community of Latvian Lutheran families, displaced as a result of World War II, had settled.

Since the chapel/classroom/studio was used only intermittently, when Norman G. Wente arrived as librarian in 1968, a vision began to take shape to transform the room into a space resembling a medieval scriptorium, where the library's oldest books could be shelved, consulted, and displayed appropriately. Eleven years later, this vision became a reality.

Until this time, these books, as well as some medieval manuscripts and codex facsimiles, had been shelved in various closets and locked-stack areas without proper environmental controls. Consequently, many of the books had begun to deteriorate and needed a "new home."

The development that provided this "new home" was the project to enlarge and remodel Gullixson Hall to make room for the merged library collections of Luther and Northwestern Lutheran theological seminaries, for it was during this major renovation that Librarian Wente undertook the work of creating the space necessary to bring the oldest books together in one place. He worked with architects, builders, wood craftsmen and stained glass artisans, seminary administrators and maintenance workers, and a donor to create the new Rare Book Room.

With a significant gift from Jeanne Preus Rost in honor of her parents—Dr. and Mrs. J. C. K. Preus—the Rare Book Room was dedicated on January 3, 1979 and became the home for the print special collections of the Luther Seminary Library.

In the Rare Book Room are Gothic arches, Celtic pillars, gargoyles, and floor-to-ceiling shelves (image 1). The angled rolling ladders that so intrigue visitors are the original ones used in the first seminary library. A large study desk with seating for four and drawers for flat

Image 1: Rare Book Room showing arch, ladder, etc.

storage was crafted by a seminary woodworker. An immigrant trunk and a hand-carved wooden chair with figures of lions on the back and arms are housed here. There are smaller items, too, which add to the room's ambience and represent the seminary's heritage: a model of an early hand-press, a ninth-century Norwegian wedding cup, and tall, ornamental candlesticks formerly used in the seminary chapel.

There is much about this room that draws the eye, but the focal point, which adds color and historical information, is the stained glass windows set in three lancet arches (image 2). The Rev. Wente consulted with Dr. Howard W. Winger, professor in the University of Chicago's Graduate Library School, to select five prominent early Reformation printers and one eighteenth-century Lutheran printer and use their printer's marks as designs for the windows. The designs are in the medieval manner, use antique English cathedral glass, and were crafted by John Salisbury of Gaytee Stained Glass Inc. (Minneapolis, Minnesota). The printer's devices of Jacob Van Liesveldt, Johann Petreius, Bartholomew Ziegenbalg, Crafft Muller, Philip Ulhart the Elder, and Hans Lufft are depicted in circle medallions surrounding the central "master printer and his apprentice" scene (image 3).

Pre-1800 Collection

Luther Seminary Library has several named special collections honoring donors who collected in specific areas, but its largest special collection is often simply referred to as the "pre-1800 collection." The four to five thousand volumes in this collection came to the library over many decades and in various ways. The most common paths have been: 1) former faculty who gave their books to the seminary or simply left them behind when they retired, 2) Lutheran clergy or laypersons with ties to the institution, and 3) area families who donated books passed down from a pastor in the family. Books from these three sources that reflect the Christian heritage and were published prior to 1800 are placed in this collection. As a Protestant Lutheran seminary, most of these pre-1800 books document the Lutheran tradition, from its initial publishing frenzy in the form of pamphlets (primarily sermons and polemical tracts) to later and more expansive works of translation, biblical commentary, and theological explanation. The largest single source of books in this group are from the library of F. A. Schmidt.

Image 2: Printers' windows.

Image 3: Master printer and apprentice (detail).

Dr. F. A. (Friedrich Augustus) Schmidt (1837–1928) taught at Luther Theological Seminary from 1890 to 1912. Even for that pioneering era in Lutheran education, Prof. Schmidt had an interesting career path. He was a product of a system of theological education grounded in the knowledge of ancient languages: Hebrew, Greek, and Latin. German was his native language, and he learned English when he arrived in St. Louis, Missouri at age four. He acquired Norwegian as a student at Concordia Seminary, when he was asked to proofread issues of *Kirkelig Tidende*, a Norwegian-Lutheran church newspaper published in St. Louis. Familiarity with Norwegian likely contributed to his being offered a teaching position at Luther College (Decorah, Iowa) in 1861. As one of only two faculty members, he taught "religion, Greek, Latin, German, mathematics, English, penmanship, music, logic, and U.S. history." His obituary in the *Lutheran Church Herald* notes that his chief interest remained theological studies and that, even in the early years of his career, he had acquired a large library ("Dr. Friedrich Augustus Schmidt" 1928, 679). In short, Prof. Schmidt was also a bibliophile.

Dozens of sixteenth- to eighteenth-century volumes from Schmidt's library attest the contours of Lutheran theological education in the nineteenth century. As a professor of dogmatics, representatives of the systematizing movement known as Lutheran orthodoxy (e.g., scholastic theologians the likes of Johann Gerhard [1582–1637], Abraham Calov [1612–86], and Johannes Andreas Quenstedt [1617–88]) figure prominently in this collection. It should be noted, however, that Pietism—the counterpoint movement that arose in the century following the early reformers and advocated most notably in works by Johann Arndt (1555–1621) and Philipp Jakob Spener (1635–1705)—is also included. Thus, faith both of head and heart co-exist on the shelves, providing a representative picture of the Lutheran polarities that influenced doctrine and practice in the succeeding centuries.

Perhaps the most surprising part of Schmidt's biblio-legacy is his collection of 187 parchment-bound volumes of seventeenth- and eighteenth-century dissertations from scores of German universities. Where and how Schmidt acquired such a large quantity of dissertations is not known. Presumably, his interest in academic theology and his passion for collecting led him in this direction. Most are less than a hundred pages, so that each bound volume contains between fifteen and thirty dissertations. In an interesting study of German dissertations from this era, Armin Siedlecki (2005, 104) of Pitts Theology Library, Emory University, has pointed out that, unlike the dissertations produced today, the professor/advisor was the author of the content of the dissertation, while the student had the role of the respondent. While such materials are not often used by scholars today, they are valuable for tracing the course of scholarship over several centuries—a method that Schmidt himself likely used. At this writing, only about fifteen percent of the dissertation collection has been cataloged.

From 1987 to 2000, Terrance Dinovo served as curator of the library's special collections. Through Terry's efforts, financial support for the collections increased substantially. In particular, Terry was able to interest former Minnesota governor Elmer L. Anderson, a book collector in his own right, in underwriting the purchase of several items from the early decades of Lutheranism. Chief among them was the acquisition of a complete Luther Bible, printed in 1556 by Hans Lufft. With striking woodcut illustrations by Hans Brosamer and Georg Lemberger, it is one of the jewels of the collection. It is permanently displayed and always attracts strong interest among visitors.

Addressing the issue of environmental controls, in the mid-1990s Terry facilitated the purchase and installation of a modern HVAC system dedicated to the Rare Book Room. He also began outsourcing higher-profile items that required expert attention to professional conservators in the Twin Cities—a practice that has continued as funds allow. Nevertheless, there are many books in the collection that need some level of repair, but there is limited staff time to attend to them. As time permits, phase boxes are made in-house to stabilize books that are in the most serious state of disrepair.

Governor Anderson's generosity also made it possible to purchase a small collection of pamphlets written by Martin Luther. These are from the quarter-century following the posting of the Ninety-five Theses and represent genres typically employed by Luther (sermon, open letter, theological polemic, biblical exposition, etc.), as well as the work of prolific printers such as Melchior Lotter, Georg Rhau, Adam Petri, Johann Rhau-Grunenberg, and Friedrich Peypus. Finally, Governor Anderson made it possible to acquire a rare official edition of the *Confessio Augustana* and the *Apology*, written by Philipp Melanchthon (Wittenberg: Georg Rhau, 1531). The Augsburg Confession is a foundational document of Lutheranism—the first in the collection of confessions known as the Book of Concord. The title page indicates the text is in both German and Latin ("beide Deudsch vnd Latinisch"), but only the Latin is present in the volume, perhaps because the German translation by Justus Jonas was not yet ready at the time of publication (Richard 1907, 486).

The special collections also include two items printed before 1500. The oldest is a Bible handbook, *Mammotrectus super Bibliam* (roughly "mother's milk on the Bible" or "Bible nourishment"), written by Franciscan John Marchesinus at the end of the thirteenth century (Venice: Franciscus Renner, de Heilbronn, and Petrus de Bartus, 1478). It is a fine example of the gradual transition from manuscript to print publishing. Typical of a manuscript, it is without a title page, and the text is printed in gothic type emulating script, with hand-drawn initial letters in blue and red marking the start of new sections. Its first page is illuminated with gold, blue, green, and red inks (image 4). *Mammotrectus* most likely served as a reference book, surveying the Bible and the four liturgical seasons, explaining difficult words and grammatical constructions, and providing an alphabetical index.

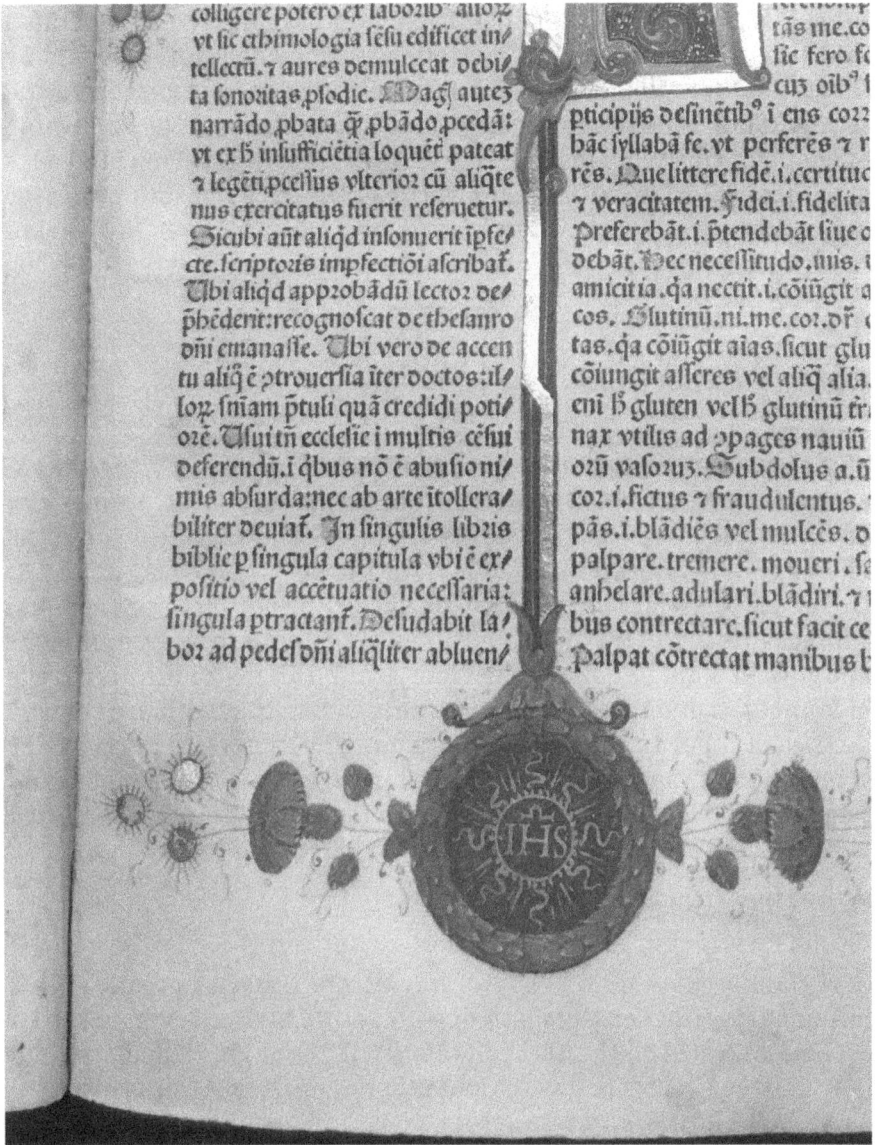

Image 4: *Mammotrectus super Bibliam* (detail).

    The library's second incunable is a Latin Vulgate, *Biblia integra* (Basel: Johann Froben, 1495). Known as the "poor man's Bible," it represents one of the first efforts to create a portable, almost pocket-sized Bible. To accomplish this, Froben used an extremely small rotunda type, newly created and used primarily for Italian humanist texts. Froben's first edition was produced in 1491, but Luther Seminary's second edition has the distinction of being the first printed Bible to include a woodcut illustration—a copy of a 1492 woodcut by Albrecht Dürer depicting Saint Jerome removing a thorn from the paw of a lion. The library's copy shows the indents at the beginning of chapters that were to have been drawn in by hand. This Bible was a gift from O. M. (Olaf Morgan) Norlie (1876–1962), pastor, professor, and collector of Bibles and many books by and about Norwegian Americans.

Named Collections

There are four named collections in Luther Seminary's special collections: the Carl Døving Hymnal Collection, the Jacob Tanner Catechism Collection, the Olaf Storaasli Manuscript Collection, and the Edward Sovik Collection.

As the Rev. Carl Døving and Dr. Jacob Tanner were friends and supported each other in their "hobbies" of collecting hymn books and Luther's *Small Catechisms* from around the world in hundreds of languages and dialects, it seems only fitting that both are shelved near each other in the Rare Book Room. The men were born in Norway and emigrated to the United States, where they became pastors, scholars, and leaders in the Norwegian Lutheran Church of America.

The Carl Døving Hymnal Collection

Carl Døving (1867–1937) left Norway at age sixteen to work with a missionary—the Rev. Nils Astrup—in South Africa. Seven years later, he emigrated to the United States, where he graduated from Luther College (Decorah, Iowa) and Luther Seminary. After ordination, he served churches in Minnesota, New York, and Illinois. The Rev. Døving "became especially interested in hymns and started collecting them in different languages in 1910, when he became a member of the hymn book committee of the Norwegian Lutheran Church" (Miller 1936, 12). For the next twenty years, he was in contact with missionaries around the world, asking them for hymn books in use in their respective mission outposts to supplement his collection. Therefore, his holdings are strong in hymnody as it developed in overseas missions, particularly in the nineteenth and twentieth centuries. Lutheranism is especially well-represented, as illustrated in the publications of its world mission societies, but other denominational mission activities are also included. In January 1934, when the Rev. Døving donated his remarkable collection to Luther College, it totaled approximately 1,400 volumes in 325 different languages and dialects. In 1951, the Døving Hymnal Collection came to Luther Theological Seminary on an indefinite loan and, in 1997, it was transferred formally to Luther Seminary.

In 1936, Døving was interviewed by Luther College student Frank R. Miller, who wrote, "In speaking about his hymns, Mr. Doving's face lights up with joy. He says it is a great thrill to find a hymn and unheard of dialect and search through it diligently until he is able to recognize some familiar words or signs that will enable him to identify it" (Miller 1936, 12).

The Jacob Tanner Catechism Collection

Jacob Tanner (1865–1964) was a professor at Concordia College (Moorhead, Minnesota) and a professor of dogmatics for thirteen years at Luther Seminary before retiring and then being called back into service to teach at Waldorf College (Forest City, Iowa) until age 97. Over a thirty-year period, Dr. Tanner assembled a collection of Martin Luther's *Small Catechism* with the assistance of the Rev. Carl Døving. "It was the intensive research work and the extensive correspondence carried on with every nook and corner of the globe in connection with the hymnal enterprise that made possible the marvelous collection of catechism-translations owned by Dr. Jacob Tanner of the Lutheran Theological Seminary, St. Paul, Minn" (Hoppe 1933, 638).

In 1933, Tanner's collection of Luther's *Small Catechism*, translated into 121 languages and dialects, was exhibited in the Lutheran section of the Hall of Religion at Chicago's Century of Progress, also known as the Chicago World's Fair. By the time Dr. Tanner donated his collection to the Luther Theological Seminary Library in 1955, it had grown to include translations in 146 languages. This original collection included forty-one European translations, thirty-three from Asia, fifty-three from Africa, eight from the Americas, four from Australia, and seven from New Guinea. The *Small Catechism* was the first printed book published in a language native to what is now the United States—Algonquian—in 1648. The Tanner Collection includes a facsimile edition of the 1696 printing of that catechism. Many catechisms were not printed separately but were combined with a hymnal to form a single volume. Some catechisms were printed as schoolbooks. Those from China in this collection are not in book form at all but consist of individually-printed sheets tied along one side with string (image 5).

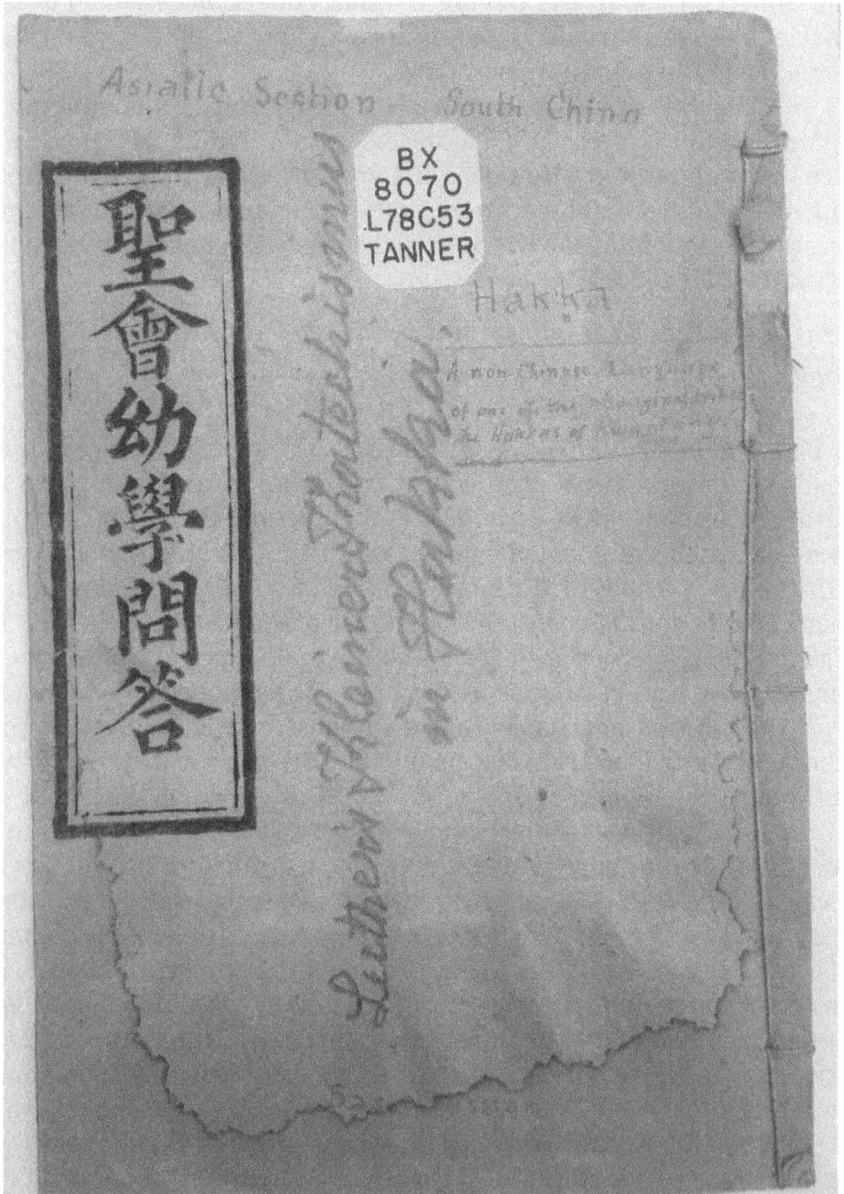

Image 5: Tanner Collection catechism from China.

Preserving the Past & Engaging the Future

Why did Dr. Tanner collect Luther's *Small Catechism*? Perhaps because he was a "catechism" theologian "and feared that Seminary dogmatics had become more concerned with what other theologians of all denominations today were teaching, than what Lutheran dogmaticians meant by their historic statements" (Storaasli 1974, 45).

The Olaf Storaasli Manuscript Collection

Olaf K. Storaasli (1915–2006) was a New Testament professor at Luther Seminary. Dating from his time in graduate school at Princeton and Temple universities, he began collecting leaves from late medieval manuscripts and early printed books. Following his retirement in 1996, he gave his collection to the library. Approximately three-fourths of the 107 items in this collection are manuscript leaves representing books of hours, missals, antiphonaries, breviaries, Bibles, and psalters. Most are written on vellum, and a few are illuminated with decorative foliate borders in gold and color along the outer margins (image 6).

Of the printed leaves, several are from incunabula, two of the earliest being from a 1475 Bible (Augsburg: Günther Zainer) and from the *Summa confessorum* of Johannes Freiburger (Ulm: Konrad Dinckmut, 1484). The collection also includes several leaves from the well-known *Liber chronicarum* (Nuremberg Chronicle) printed in 1493 by Anton Koberger. These manuscript and printed leaves have been featured in several displays, the first in 1997 at a reception thanking Olaf and Lila Storaasli for their gift.

Image 6: Storaasli Collection manuscript leaf.

The Edward Sovik Collection

Edward "Ed" Sovik (1918–2014) was born in China to Lutheran missionary parents, graduated from St. Olaf College (Northfield, Minnesota) and attended Luther Theological Seminary before choosing a career in architecture. He was the founder and principal of Sovik, Mathre & Madson (now SMSQ Architects), based in Northfield, Minnesota. The firm specialized in church building projects, and Ed himself had both a professional and personal interest in the career of Sir Christopher Wren. In 2008, Ed gave his substantial library of books on church architecture to Luther Seminary, among which was a collection of books about seventeenth- and eighteenth-century English ecclesiastical architecture with particular emphasis on the works and influence of Wren.

Of notable interest in this collection are a history of St. Paul's Cathedral by Sir William Dugdale, published in 1716, and an elephant folio volume (76 x 57 cm), *The Works of Christopher Wren: the dimensions, plans, elevations, and sections of the parochial churches of Sir Christopher Wren: erected in the cities of London & Westminster* by John Clayton. Clayton spent ten years making measured drawings of all of Wren's city churches and published them in this expansive volume in 1848. Both were featured in a special exhibit of items from this collection in 2009.

Impact of Special Collections

Special collections exist within the library's participation in the mission of Luther Seminary to educate leaders for Christian communities. In its role as an educational partner, the library enables research and scholarship at all levels and stewards physical and digital collections, space, and services. The curation, organization, and preservation of its oldest and most historically significant materials have always been leading functions of special collections. More recently, however, their interpretation and integration with the curriculum have received increased attention. Thus, special collections at the library have contributed to the institutional life of Luther Seminary through their connection to students' academic coursework and to the wider seminary constituency via campus tours, special displays, and an offering in the seminary's Lay School of Theology program.

Programmatically, special collections have been driven primarily by the library staff, although they have benefited greatly by allies in the administration and on the faculty. When the transformation of the chapel/classroom/lab into today's Rare Book Room was proposed, the support of the presidents of Luther Theological Seminary and Northwestern Lutheran Theological Seminary (the two institutions had not yet merged) was vital and was generously provided. Individual faculty in Bible and Church history have been very receptive to holding class sessions in the Rare Book Room and, in the process, have stretched the library staff to discover more about the items in its care. The partnership between the library and Seminary Relations has been very fruitful with respect to scheduling and hosting tour groups—an activity that has remained consistently popular. The Center for Lifelong Learning initially approached the library about offering a course in the Lay School of Theology, opening a new avenue for special collections to be showcased for interested community members.

Coursework

The library's collection of facsimile editions of important biblical manuscripts has occasioned regular visits by Hebrew Bible and New Testament faculty and their students. The opportunity to see exact replicas of these manuscripts, either in photographic or typeset editions, has provided students a more complete understanding of the textual history of the Bible. Hebrew Bible classes will typically examine the tenth- and eleventh-century Aleppo and Leningrad codices, aided by seeing alongside both the library's eighteenth-century Esther Scroll and sixteenth-century Syriac liturgical codex. The instructor and the librarian discuss the evolution and use of scrolls and codices in the ancient world, the various writing surfaces employed, and the scribal traditions used in copying sacred texts. In terms of the practice of book-making, the Esther Scroll clearly displays how the panels of goatskin have been stitched together and how the skin has been ruled with a knife (image 7). The Syriac codex shows the paper leaves tied together with thick string and bound by wooden boards covered with a fabric resembling burlap (image 8).

Image 7: Esther scroll.

Image 8: Syriac codex.

New Testament classes often schedule visits to view facsimile editions of the great fourth- and fifth-century codices: Sinaiticus, Vaticanus, Alexandrinus, and Washingtonianus. Displaying them side-by-side allows their similarities and differences to be seen at a glance, particularly their use of continuous script with no breaks between words and sentences. In the case of Sinaiticus, which is a full-size photographic edition, some of the insertions in the text and the margins by different scribal hands can be pointed out. The library's copy of Codex Alexandrinus is a relative rarity. Just 450 copies were printed in London by John Nichols in 1786, financed by the British Museum, which holds the manuscript. For this typeset folio edition, Nichols used a "noble" font designed by Joseph Jackson, a designer who specialized in oriental fonts. This manuscript uniquely places an enlarged initial letter of the first complete line of a paragraph into the margin. A smile of recognition typically crosses the faces of students who have studied Greek at picking out the run of the letter K, beginning the Greek word *kai* (and) indicating the breathless, urgent nature of Mark's narrative.

Campus Tours

Since the Rare Book Room is recognized as one of the most beautiful and classic spaces on campus, an in-person stop here is nearly always included for campus visitors, whether prospective students or donors, confirmation classes, senior groups, seminary board members, visiting lecturers, or other guests.

Although tailored somewhat for each group, a typical tour led by a library staff member would begin with the background of the room itself and then move to the stained glass "printers" windows with comments on the confluence of the relatively new occupation of printing that enabled the rapid spread of the ideas coming from the pens of Martin Luther and others, together fueling the movement for the reform of the church. On display below the windows is the 1556 Bible in Luther's German translation. The librarian would discuss the monumental event that was the 1522 publication of the New Testament, essentially opening the Bible to ordinary literate Germans unschooled in Latin. The complete Bible, finally available in 1534, led to another surge in demand met by a succession of printings. The Wittenberg printer, Hans Lufft, favored by Luther because of his careful work, was responsible for many of these, including the library's copy. His printer's device or logo—the upraised sword piercing the heart and driving out sin, represented by snakes—would be pointed out on the window (image 9). The increasingly popular use of woodcut illustrations to add visual interest would be shown in this Bible by the dramatic full-page woodcut of Eve being drawn out from Adam's side (image 10).

Image 9: Luther Bible with printer's device of Hans Lufft.

Image 10: Luther Bible full-page woodcut.

Attention might then shift to the other end of the bookcase, where the Esther Scroll is displayed. The tour leader would ask the group if they thought what they see is a book, which—following a scattering of yes or no answers—would lead to a discussion of the scroll versus the codex as differing formats for a book. Examining the scroll in more detail, the leader would explain that the interior or smooth side of the skin was the writing side. Flipping the scroll to its underside, the group could easily see the roughness of the exterior or hair side of the skin, unsuitable for writing. Looking at the text itself shows how the surface has been scored with a knife and how the letters run from right to left and hang from the line rather than rest upon it. Particularly for confirmation-age groups, the connection between the book of Esther and the Jewish festival of Purim would be highlighted—that the entire book is read or chanted, the heroes cheered and the villains scorned.

Typically a few minutes are reserved for questions. By far the most frequently asked is "What's your oldest book?" This prompts pulling the 1478 *Mammotrectus super Bibliam* from the shelf, commenting that, in the first few decades after Gutenberg, there was the desire in many cases to make printed books resemble the manuscripts their readers would have expected and been familiar with. The colorfully hand-decorated and illuminated initial page of the *Mammotrectus* is a delightful example of this period of transition from manuscript to print.

Displays

In recent years, the library staff has hosted at least two open houses during the academic year. One takes place on or around Reformation Day (October 31st), when Lutherans commemorate Martin Luther's nailing of the Ninety-five Theses on the door of the castle church in Wittenberg. The other open house is during commencement weekend, when the library welcomes graduates and their families and friends on their self-guided campus tours.

During both of these open houses, a themed display of books and accompanying information provides visitors with a glimpse into the collections. Displays have also been mounted for other events or groups upon request. Topics showcasing items from the collection in these displays have included:

- Pamphlet literature in Reformation history

- Sixteenth-century printers as known by their printer's marks

- Early English Bibles (400th anniversary of the King James Bible)

- Music and hymnals of the Reformation

- Christopher Wren and English ecclesiastical architecture

- Family Bibles in America

- The medieval scribal tradition

- The Nuremberg Chronicle

Brainstorming ideas for future displays has recently begun again in anticipation of students and visitors returning to campus post-pandemic. One idea that has come to the forefront is a new display highlighting Bible "firsts" in the century following Gutenberg. In such a display, the library's folio of the first complete Bible in Danish—*Biblia, Det er den gantske Hellige Scrifft* (Copenhagen: L. Dietz, 1550)—and the first Bible in a Swiss low-German vernacular translation by Huldrych Zwingli and Leo Jud—*Die gantze Bibel das ist alle bücher alts vnnds neüws Testaments, den vrsprünglichen sprachen nach, auffs aller treüwlichest verteütschet* (Zurich: C. Froschauer, 1545)—would be included. The first printing of the Zwingli/Jud translation (1531) contained a map, thought to be the first printed Bible to do so. Also, the previously mentioned Vulgate (1495), the first Bible to incorporate a woodcut illustration, would naturally have a place in the display. Since the 500th anniversary of Luther's "September Testament" is drawing near (1522), the library's facsimile copy, edited by Kenneth Strand (Ann Arbor: Ann Arbor Publishers, 1972), would be featured as well. Luther's is the first translation of the New Testament into German based upon the original Greek.

Beyond its campus, in 2016–17 the library had the opportunity to collaborate with two large-scale exhibits marking the 500th anniversary of the start of the Protestant Reformation by contributing items from its special collections to the Minneapolis Institute of Art for its "Martin Luther: Art and the Reformation" exhibit and the University of Minnesota Libraries' exhibit, "Luther and the World Turned Upside Down" (image 11).

Image 11: Reformation anniversary exhibit – University of Minnesota.

Lay School of Theology Course

On several occasions, the library featured its special collections through a five-session course offered through Luther Seminary's Lay School of Theology program. The course was entitled, *"Ad Fontes*: the History of the Bible as a Book,"* and aimed to demonstrate the many format changes of the Bible through its history as a physical object, from fragments of papyrus or parchment—as evidenced by the Dead Sea Scrolls—to the handy, compact codex between plain or fancy covers so familiar today. The course typically discussed: the Bible in Bible times and the great Bible codices, St. Jerome and the Latin Bible, medieval Bibles, Gutenberg and the printing revolution, Martin Luther and the German Bible, William Tyndale and the English Bible, the Bible in America, and the Saint John's Bible. For each session, pertinent items from special collections were displayed. The excellent *The Book: a History of the Bible* by Christopher de Hamel (London: Phaidon, 2001) was foundational for course content.

Summary: Special Collections as Touchstone

Special collections in theological libraries, in tandem with institutional archives, have the ability to foster a greater understanding and appreciation among students, donors, and others of the history of the school that has preserved and cared for them and the denominational tradition out of which they have come. The parchment-bound volumes lining the shelves of the Rare Book Room, most written in German or Latin, speak to the northern European origins of Lutheranism. In a corner of the room, the wooden steamship trunk decorated with an embossed metal acorn motif (image 12) points to the immigrant experience and how many of these books may have arrived in Minnesota with their pastor or professor owners. Seeing the carefully hand-lettered titles or title transcriptions by Carl Døving and Jacob Tanner of hymnals and *Small Catechisms* in languages and dialects from around the world gives evidence of the mission impulse among Lutheran churches.

The ability to personally view artifacts contemporaneous with ground-breaking ideas, movements, and figures within Christian history creates a deeper connection to that history. When students see Luther's marginal notes to the text of his Bible translation or are shown his reordering of the books of the New Testament (including his disinclination to even assign numbers to the books of Hebrews, James, Jude, and Revelation), a more immediate sense of who Luther was and of the Reformation era in general is often the result (image 13).

Image 12: Steamship trunk.

Finally, there is the feeling of wonder and delight that special collections can create in the experience of the viewer. Historian Abby

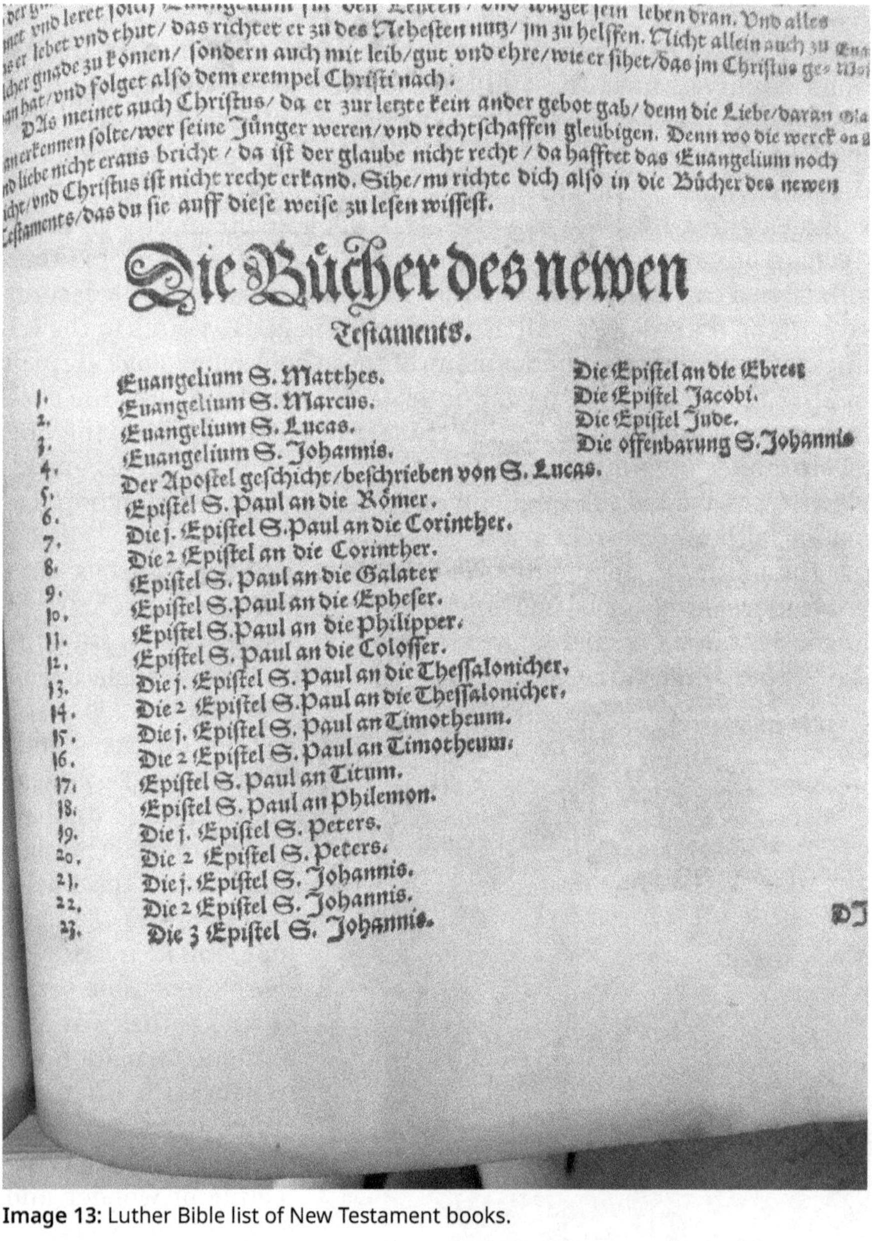

der gut vnd leret folch) Euangelium [in den zeiten] vnd waget sein leben dran. Vnd alles
was er lebet vnd thut/ das richtet er zu des Nehesten nutz/ jm zu helffen. Nicht allein auch zu Eu
lcher gnade zu komen/ sondern auch mit leib/gut vnd ehre/wie er sihet/das jm Christus ge= Wol
an hat/vnd folget also dem exempel Christi nach.

DAs meinet auch Christus/ da er zur letzte kein ander gebot gab/ denn die Liebe/daran Gla
an erkennen solte/wer seine Jünger weren/vnd rechtschaffen gleubigen. Denn wo die werck on g
nd liebe nicht eraus bricht / da ist der glaube nicht recht / da hafftet das Euangelium noch
icht/vnd Christus ist nicht recht erkand. Sihe/nu richte dich also in die Bücher des newen
Testaments/das du sie auff diese weise zu lesen wissest.

Die Bücher des newen
Testaments.

1.	Euangelium S. Matthes.	Die Epistel an die Ebreer
2.	Euangelium S. Marcus.	Die Epistel Jacobi.
3.	Euangelium S. Lucas.	Die Epistel Jude.
4.	Euangelium S. Johannis.	Die offenbarung S. Johannis
5.	Der Apostel geschicht/beschrieben von S. Lucas.	
6.	Epistel S. Paul an die Römer.	
7.	Die j. Epistel S. Paul an die Corinther.	
8.	Die 2 Epistel an die Corinther.	
9.	Epistel S. paul an die Galater	
10.	Epistel S. Paul an die Epheser.	
11.	Epistel S. Paul an die philipper.	
12.	Epistel S. Paul an die Colosser.	
13.	Die j. Epistel S. Paul an die Thessalonicher.	
14.	Die 2 Epistel S. Paul an die Thessalonicher.	
15.	Die j. Epistel S. Paul an Timotheum.	
16.	Die 2 Epistel S. Paul an Timotheum.	
17.	Epistel S. Paul an Titum.	
18.	Epistel S. Paul an philemon.	
19.	Die j. Epistel S. Peters.	
20.	Die 2 Epistel S. Peters.	
21.	Die j. Epistel S. Johannis.	
22.	Die 2 Epistel S. Johannis.	
23.	Die 3 Epistel S. Johannis.	

DI

Image 13: Luther Bible list of New Testament books.

Smith states, "[T]here is something irreducible about an encounter with the real thing" (Smith 2003, 174). This subjective experience is perhaps more significant than is often recognized and could plant a seed that may later influence a career decision or a desire to support the library or the institution. Mark Dimunation, the director of the Rare Book and Special Collections Division at the Library of Congress, writes, "In the end, the real measure of our own work will be what we have done to further the knowledge and appreciation of the collections that we have the great privilege to build and administer" (Dimunation 2006, 74). By building special collections and creating an enchanting space (but perhaps not quite so much as Hogwarts), where centuries-old books, manuscript leaves, and furnishings are interpreted by classroom sessions, tours, and displays, Luther Seminary has tried to do just this, advancing the knowledge and appreciation of the school's institutional heritage and the Christian tradition, as well as fostering a sense of joy at seeing the past still alive in the present.

References

Dimunation, Mark. 2006. "Red Wine and White Carpets: What We Didn't Learn in Library School, or When the Dog and Pony Goes Bad." *RBM: A Journal of Rare Books, Manuscripts, and Cultural Heritage* 7, no. 1 (Spring): 73–84.

"Dr. Friedrich Augustus Schmidt." 1928. *Lutheran Church Herald* 12, no. 22 (May 29, 1928): 679.

Hoppe, Anna. 1933. "The Dr Jacob Tanner Catechism Collection." *Lutheran Herald* 17, no. 28 (July 11, 1933): 638.

Miller, Frank R. 1936. "The Doving Hymn Collection." *The Friend: A Family Magazine* 13, no. 2 (February): 12–13.

Richard, J. W. 1907. "The Melanchthon Editions of the Augsburg Confession." *Lutheran Quarterly* 37 (October): 481–507.

Siedlecki, Armin. 2005. "Dissertations of the Past: The Production of Academic Theses in European Universities in the 17th and 18th Centuries." In *ATLA Summary of Proceedings* 59: 102–22.

Smith, Abby. 2003. "Authenticity and Affect: When Is a Watch Not a Watch?" *Library Trends* 52, no. 1 (Summer): 172–82.

Storaasli, Olaf K. 1974. "Centennial Article: Jacob Tanner (1865–1964)." *Luther Theological Seminary Review* 13, no. 1 (Spring): 40–8.

Special Collections at Work in Teaching & Research

CHAPTER 5

Gifts of Great Libraries

Teaching with Special Collections at the Burke Library at Union Theological Seminary

MATTHEW BAKER

*T*he special collections of the Burke Library began with the 1836 founding of Union Theological Seminary.[1] As with many historic collections in the United States and elsewhere, its earliest stages of growth occurred through a combination of accident, gifts, and purposeful acquisition, and often some combination of these. The history of the Burke from its founding until the 1980s has been ably detailed in Thomas Slavens's *A Great Library Through Gifts* (1986). Slavens draws on the several works about the history of Union and its library written in the nineteenth and twentieth centuries, as well as his own extensive research in Union's administrative records (Prentiss 1889, 1899; Handy 1986). The years since Slavens wrote have been marked by important changes in the Burke's collections in general and particularly by its work in building and sharing special collections. The use of special collections for teaching has become a cornerstone of the library's overall mission, touching every facet of collection development, management, and planning.

A few highlights from the history of the Burke's collections will provide some background to the examples and discussion below. The celebrated Leander van Ess Collection illustrates the first of these factors noted above—accident—not unusual among nineteenth-century libraries. Founding faculty member Edward Robinson, traveling in Europe on his way to the Near East to conduct the geographical research for which he is most remembered, became aware that the aging Van Ess, a former Benedictine monk, was interested in selling his large, important, and well-preserved collection of manuscripts and early printed editions (Gatch 1996).[2] Robinson persuaded the fledgling seminary to provide what was then the considerable sum of $5,000 to acquire it. It was a risk and would constitute a financial burden to the seminary for several decades. It also indicates the importance, from the outset, of its library for the seminary's educational mission. The Van Ess materials remain among the most celebrated of their kind, especially because many preserve unique material evidence in original bindings, which has too often been lost or destroyed due to "preservation" work done by past owners or collectors wanting to repair or otherwise rebind them.

It is also a noteworthy irony that a Roman Catholic monastery would be the foundational source for a liberal Protestant seminary, and that within the Van Ess Collection were many pamphlets and books by early Protestant Reformers such as Luther, Melanchton, and Zwingli. Less surprising, perhaps, were the scores of medieval manuscript Bibles and liturgical and theological works that form the core of the Burke's western manuscript collection, as well as hundreds of incunabula.[3]

A second foundation story can be told about the Burke's McAlpin Collection of British History and Theology—a combination of gift and purposeful acquisition. Funded in large part by Union board member David Hunter McAlpin—a real estate and tobacco magnate—several early librarians (notably Charles Briggs—famously tried for heresy in 1892 and co-editor of the Hebrew lexicon—and Ezra Hall Gillett) were able to acquire the thousands of sixteenth- and seventeenth-century British printed editions in the collection bearing McAlpin's name (Gillett 1927–30; Slavens 1986, 118). This collection includes many important works of early English Deism, Protestantism, and Civil War pamphlet literature, of a scope arguably unmatched this side of the Atlantic, apart perhaps from the Folger Library.

A third collection further illustrates a confluence of the accidental and the purposeful, and how the nature of special collections' growth, use, and significance can change quite dramatically over time. The Missionary Research Library (MRL) was founded following the 1911 Edinburgh World Missionary Conference (Dictionary Catalog 1968). Over the course of the twentieth century, a veritable avalanche of archives, books, pamphlets, reports, maps, and other genres poured in from around the world, even as the very meaning of "missions" changed dramatically, and the economic and cultural power of the mainline denominations supporting the enterprise began to wane (Hollinger 2017). By the 1970s, the MRL had run out of resources, and its collections became part of the Burke Library. Although it was conceived and developed to further Christian proselytization, in recent decades it is understood and used as a unique body of global primary sources sought out by historians, anthropologists, linguists, and others (interestingly, by scholars often not specifically studying religious history or theology per se).

Other such stories of bibliographic adventurism, philanthropy, and fortuitous accident could be told by other libraries. The crucial event in the recent history of the Burke Library is its having joined the Columbia University Libraries (CUL) system in 2004. In addition to Columbia, Morningside Heights in Manhattan is also home, within approximately ten city blocks, to Union Theological Seminary, the Jewish Theological Seminary, the Manhattan School of Music, Barnard College, Columbia's Teachers College, the Bank Street School of Education, the Riverside Church, and the ecumenical Interchurch Center. There is a long history of formal and informal relationships among these institutions, including cross-registration and dual-appointed faculty. The change in the Burke's institutional context opened many new opportunities for using collections for learning and research, particularly at Columbia and Barnard Colleges, with their rich humanities and social sciences curricula, including the fields of religion, history, classics, and global studies. Unique among peer theology and religion libraries, the Burke is a member of a large research library system while being located within and continuing to serve the administratively independent Union Theological Seminary. As part of CUL, the Burke Library's mission is also shaped by consortial relationships in metropolitan New York as well as by broad inter-institutional contexts such as Ivy Plus and ReCAP.[4]

These collections are now central to its special collections. They are foundational to nearly every aspect of its ongoing work, from new collecting to digitization to instructional efforts. The following discussion will address how the Burke's librarians have worked to integrate special collections into primarily undergraduate and master's level courses to foster an embodied, immersive, and contextually attuned approach to learning.

Working Collections

Since special collections are at the heart of the Burke's services, they are very much developed and managed as "working collections." In some fashion, this has always been the case, with rare books, archives, and ephemera accessible by appointment and available for consultation by faculty, students, and visiting researchers. Generally, this approach has best served specialists: advanced scholars trained to use resources like union catalogs, complex databases, and domain-specific tools. In the past decade in particular, the work of integrating collections into courses and getting them into the hands of undergraduate and master's degree students has been a consistent focus and goal, shaping every facet of our mission, staffing, and planning. The Burke staff are actively exploring ways to connect students with special collections and to creatively and holistically integrate them into the curricula of the departments it supports. Simply put, teaching with special collections is the core of the Burke Library's mission. This constitutes both a deep connection with its history (noted above) and an energetic and careful engagement with present and future new directions.

The embodied, tactile qualities of special collections are integral to their meaning and therefore essential to their uses for teaching. The more abstract, two-dimensional realm of the digital, with accompanying perceptions and expectations of ubiquitous and perpetual availability, is contextualized and challenged by the immediacy, irreplaceability, and fragility of physical objects. As librarians well know, there are so many strands of human knowledge and culture that have vanished, never to be recovered. With students of theology or religion, for example, the focus may often be on ideas and concepts. Important though these are, it is also important to study the material forms in which these ideas have been recorded, transmitted, and preserved, as essential aspects of their ongoing value and meaning. John Dewey once famously critiqued those who "seem to accept a dogma of immaculate conception of philosophical systems" (quoted in McGilchrist 2009, 385). The same dogma can sometimes be assumed about theological or other theoretical systems, and special collections serve as an important reminder of their corporeal origins.

Despite having many museum-caliber holdings, the Burke Library is not a museum. What may be behind glass at the Met is available for use and study at the Burke. To enable this, training in proper handling is a crucial initial step, and the expertise of Columbia's conservation team is therefore indispensable. We want the materials to be experienced safely, with appropriate care and also without undue intimidation. Such training and support, with all the instruction and practice required to become responsible "users" of special material, is integral to the process. To some extent, it involves passing on the ethos of librarians, curators, and conservators—stewardship, care, and a longer view of our place in the materials' story—that is itself a perennial learning outcome. The goal is not necessarily to make more librarians or archivists (though that has happened and is a wonderful result!) but to establish a shared understanding of responsibility and appreciation. Neither is the goal necessarily to create more advanced graduate students, but the seemingly paradoxical aim of both demystifying and creating an appropriate sense of reverence for what has (and, by implication, what has not) made it through the vicissitudes of history to our own time. Creating trained confidence in how to safely approach and handle such materials involves our users in better understanding and supporting the stewardship responsibilities of libraries—the planning, knowledge, and labor involved in keeping historical sources (all of them ephemeral by nature) available for study, criticism, and inspiration.

A Teaching Library

The fact that the Burke serves several kinds of academic community—a theological seminary, graduate programs in the humanities and social sciences, undergraduates at Columbia and Barnard—offers opportunities for staff to explore a variety of approaches to teaching with special collections. I will summarize a number of examples, focusing primarily on undergraduate and master's degree levels, as well as some examples beyond primary institutional affiliations. In closing, I will offer some observations and commentary on what we have learned so far.

Columbia's Core Curriculum

Since joining the Columbia University Libraries system, an important area of growth for the Burke's special collections services has been to support Columbia's undergraduate Core Curriculum, a required sequence of undergraduate courses engaging literature, history, philosophy, science, and the arts from the ancient through the modern worlds. Often, this takes a familiar form of hosting one or two course meetings per semester, where librarians offer a presentation of materials to complement or illustrate the modern editions of course texts. There have, however, also been other important opportunities to offer more sustained support and invite students to learn with collections beyond this more conventional (though still important and helpful) approach.

One Core course—The Global History of the Book, designed and taught by classics professor Joseph Howley—worked closely with all Columbia's special collections libraries over the course of the semester, as well as the conservation and digitization labs, and it included a visit to ReCAP. Students experienced a holistic, semester-long exploration of the process of manuscript production, early and modern printing, and the impact of modern technologies on the creation, development, and dissemination of knowledge, as well as on current technical processes, such as digitization and metadata creation. Special collections were deeply embedded throughout the design and structure of the course, and students experienced how a range of original objects have been created and used across space and time, as well as gaining a "nuts and bolts" exposure to how surrogates are created and the many infrastructural and ethical questions related to providing access and use.

A second example, which will be familiar to seminary and divinity libraries, involves teaching the history of format: from papyrus to scroll, parchment to paper, and medieval codex to early printed book. For a range of courses on the Bible (and its influences) and religious history, this brings into focus the means of transmission, showing the many ways by which texts and ideas have been preserved and transmitted and are inseparable from their meaning and significance. This can take many forms and be incorporated at many stages in a course: the propagandistic role of the pamphlet or the image in the Protestant Reformation, the way printers and scholars collaborated in the early modern period to establish and disseminate authoritative editions of biblical or scientific texts and accompanying paratextual tools, the ways in which serial literature's explosion in the nineteenth century was a scholarly tool and a tangible expression of mass culture and consumerism. Not surprisingly for a Western, theologically-rooted library, the medieval and early modern periods are particular strengths, as well as the nineteenth-century Protestant global missionary movement. Since the last of these has informed so many subsequent developments—imperialism and colonialism, the history of the study of world religions, the emergence of the current approaches to the study of history and the social sciences, the development of modern education and healthcare, among others—they offer a rich source of reflection for a range of courses. Burke librarian Jeffrey Wayno has worked with special collections staff across CUL in developing a faculty-facing "menu" of offerings to engage faculty and support them in course design and planning. A frequent and welcome result is the chance to connect with individual students, learn about their particular interests and projects, and assist in scheduling additional consultations and appointments.

Religion in the Archive

The Barnard College Religion Department has twice offered an undergraduate course—Religion in the Archive. It was designed by Professor Gale Kenny from its inception with sustained engagement with archival collections at its very center. Focusing on the papers of Mathilda Calder Thurston—an American missionary to China and founder of Ginling College (the first four-year women's college in China)—the course requires students to work in the library, individually and in groups, with the physical collection throughout the semester ("View from Ginling" n.d.). Students explore questions of colonial power and gender, for example, in working closely and carefully through the archival papers, as well as in addressing theoretical and historical aspects of archival history and practice. As final projects, they create and curate a series of interconnected Web exhibits, including mapping and data visualization, and consider the ethical, legal, and intellectual issues related to digital humanities. Students participate in the full gamut of activities needed to digitize archival materials, including creation and management of their own research and image database systems, annotation and metadata creation, site design, project management, and rights assessment. One assignment asks students to draft a grant proposal to support conducting archival research at a repository of their choice. Professor Kenny's course is a model of collaborative engagement with special collections in the classroom, from basic physical access issues through the research process to sophisticated presentations of course outcomes through the media of digital humanities.

Religion Lab

Barnard College religion majors are required to take Religion Lab, which introduces them to a range of research methods into primary sources—from museum studies to fieldwork to visual culture to oral history and, of course, archival research. The Burke plays a central role in supporting hands-on work with archives: what they might contain, how and why they are collected and described as they are, and their responsible use. Supported by the Burke's outreach archivist[5] Leah Edelman, this experience in the archives encourages an inductive approach to the collections, moving from the broader finding aid perspective to closer examination of particular portions of larger collections to explore their detailed contents, as well as how their structure as archives inevitably shapes how they are understood and used. One of the several assignments for the course requires students to analyze questions of archival provenance, arrangement, and access. As with the Core and elsewhere, students are offered an opportunity to reflect together on the "how" as well as the "what" of special collections.

Queering Ethics

In the seminary context, an example of deep engagement with special collections has been Union's Queering Ethics course. MDiv and MA students worked with Union's administrative and faculty archives and with the Archives of Women in Theological Scholarship (AWTS) to examine questions of gender, ethics, justice, and identity in the social, theological, and educational milieus of the United States. Students were assigned readings on the history, theory, and practice of archives, working with Burke librarian Caro Bratnober to engage institutional and personal archival papers and address key critical, practical, and historical questions concerning them (e.g., Manoff 2004). Students were invited to consider what kinds of documentation is and is not included in archives, explicit and implicit meaning, and how factors like selection and archival arrangement impact meaning. Significantly, students were offered the opportunity to complete an archives-based project in lieu of a final exam, and many opted to do so. These projects entailed making multiple appointments in the archives and working closely with an archival collection of their choice and with library staff, and their projects were presented in the library at the end of the semester. Central to the course was examining how the practices of archival collecting and organization can evolve to better reflect and collect silenced or marginalized voices and perspectives—an urgent concern for every special collection (Bratnober 2019).

Tracing the Sources

The Burke has also explored some approaches to teaching with special collections instruction that can be adapted to various occasions. Former Burke librarian Elizabeth Call co-organized a conference on the Student Interracial Ministry (SIM), which originated at Union in the 1960s and whose archives are held at the Burke (Cline 2017). In conjunction with the conference were "pop-up" archives exhibits from the SIM collection for students and alumni and sessions in a Union course studying the SIM. One very helpful exercise related to David Cline's history of the SIM movement (Cline 2016). Students were asked to read short sections of Cline's monograph and then consulted the sections of the SIM archives Cline had cited. Guided by a series of questions, they discussed how the sources had been integrated into the narrative or argument, what information was contained in the collection itself and what from broader knowledge of other sources, and whether they had any questions or critiques of the author's use of the source material. It was a small-scale and impactful attempt to look "under the hood" at how historians use original primary sources in constructing a narrative or analyzing complex events.

Many undergraduates and master's students work with secondary sources—the monographs, chapters, and articles resulting from scholars' use of primary materials that are the "end products" of advanced research with primary sources. This exercise can have a formative impact, whether or not the student plans to pursue more advanced study. Having been through the process with one collection or part of a collection, the insights can be borne in mind as showing the critical and imaginative processes by which arguments are made and articles and books are written. Just following one citation, seeing its original location in a letter, for example, or report or meeting minutes, illustrates its embeddedness in the context of a document, collection, institution, or occasion. Particularly for undergraduate and master's students, it has been a fruitful exercise that reveals how sources inform the dialogical process of conducting original research.

Another set of archival teaching sessions related to the 2015 centenary of the Armenian Genocide and coincided with the completion of the MRL's Near East Relief papers. Not surprisingly, given the timing, there was considerable interest by researchers in this collection. More open-ended than the SIM sessions, students discussed the events of 1915 generally, looked at correspondence and other primary documents from the collection (e.g., letters, fundraising appeals, and contemporary accounts), and then shared what they found and how it informed their understanding of the events. With this, as with the examples noted so far, there is often an important element of peer learning that emerges organically. Getting involved in physically working with materials, whether based on an assignment or a set of tasks, students "sharing out" what they are finding has often led to a powerful experience of collaboration, with those more experienced with special collections taking the lead or assisting those newer to the process.

These are examples of putting students in extended contact with physical collections and asking them to consider a range of questions, anchored by the collections: On the basis of this document or set of papers, what conclusions can (or cannot) reasonably be drawn? What is missing? What might one wish were there, but isn't, and why might that be? What seems assumed but not explicitly stated, and on what grounds? Is that assumption discernable in the source itself or perhaps a function of the researcher, or some combination? A discussion that frequently and somewhat soberingly arises, when considering printed correspondence from the pre-digital era, is how much correspondence from more recent years has been and will be lost, even as libraries and others strive to find ways to collect and preserve email and other "born digital" content.

Another approach to teaching special collections addresses how they may relate to surrogate forms of access. For example, we ask students to consider the differences in meaning between an English Civil War pamphlet they hold in their hands and a digital version in Early English Books Online (EEBO). Both have a place, of course, but which needs and questions are best served by digital resources like EEBO, and which by an opportunity to experience the object? Or, if one is looking at, for example, the artistry of a woodcut or engraving, what is gained or lost by the different means of accessing it? A similar approach has been taken in comparing a physical manuscript codex and its (partial) surrogate in the Digital Scriptorium. Again, both have an important role for research, but taking time to experience and discuss the very palpable differences has proven to be an impactful approach, even (or especially) for those who might be encountering such materials for the first time. Taking a related approach, we have invited students to look at the quaintly old-fashioned format of microfiche—for many students, in fact, an unknown medium—and compare them with commercial databases containing some of the same texts and, in turn, with a physical copy of the same thing. Simultaneous consideration of the "many lives" of an item is a productive occasion to reckon with how the means by which we encounter and use a document often significantly impact our understanding of it. (And of course, as librarians know, many important sources from around the world remain accessible only in this format.)

History of Christianity

Not surprisingly, an important aspect of special collections teaching for the Burke and other theology libraries involves supporting courses in biblical studies and the history of Christianity. We continue to draw on time-tested methods: examining papyri (both to illustrate the nature of the earliest strata of textual evidence and the vagaries of scribal practice, as well as to try students' New Testament Greek skills on some difficult-to-decipher material), visiting Columbia's Rare Book and Manuscript Library to consult its collection of Graeco-Roman coins and consider the economic and imperial contexts of early Christianity, using medieval manuscripts to understand the preciousness of books before printing and the skill and labor involved making and preserving them, studying the pamphlet literature of the Reformation as a technological and mass media phenomenon to make clearer the sheer volume of polemic pouring off the early presses, and examining the proliferation of paratextual commentary that quickly emerged even among the "*sola scriptura*" Reformation traditions. Beyond these important and worthwhile approaches, a few examples illustrate attempts to draw on the material nature of unique special collections to open up new perspectives on course outcomes.

The Burke archives hold the papers of two of the three editors of the "BDB"—the *Hebrew and English Lexicon of the Old Testament*— Charles Briggs and Francis Brown. Both collections contain extensive research notes and files used in compiling the lexicon, amply illustrated close analysis of citations and usage, and meticulous hand annotations. They illustrate the long, painstaking, often unacknowledged work involved in lexicography and make clear the dynamic nature of language and diction that may seem more fixed on the pages of a reference work.[6] With a bit of experience learning biblical Hebrew under students' belts, spending some time with these collections offers awe-inspiring evidence of the long, slow, difficult work behind such powerful and helpful digital tools as Accordance, Logos, the TLG, and the Perseus Project—these tools also being reminders that the "digital humanities" have their roots in the ancient fields of biblical studies and classics.

Another approach creatively utilizing special collections for teaching was Prof. Jane Huber's church history survey course, in which students were offered the assignment of writing a "biography" of a manuscript or rare book from the collections. Combining the art of bibliography and the historical survey content of the course, students worked together with librarians to closely examine and describe a medieval or early modern biblical, theological, or liturgical work. Students made multiple appointments to work with librarians in the reading room to learn proper handling and waded into the domains of codicology and descriptive bibliography (i.e., measuring, collating, paleography/typography, bindings, decoration, and illustration) to approach texts in a methodical, physical way, not only as carriers of theological content but as embodied artifacts.

Broader Audiences

Special collections teaching has also played an important role in more public-facing work. Examples of this include an NEH Summer

Seminar on Researching Early Modern Manuscripts and Printed Books (sponsored by the CUNY Graduate Center), which brought faculty from around the country to work in NYC-area special collections. In this context, participating faculty worked on their own projects, as well as developing their teaching with special collections at their home institutions. Relatedly, each year, the Interfaith Center of New York, located at the nearby Interchurch Center, hosts the NEH-funded Religious Worlds of New York Summer Institute—a month-long program for K-12 teachers from around the US. In this program, a "combination of classroom and community-based education introduces teachers to American religious diversity, helps [participants] distinguish between academic and devotional approaches to the study of religion, and gives them the pedagogic tools they need to teach about contemporary lived religion" (Interfaith Center of New York, n.d.). Faculty from Columbia, Union, Barnard, CUNY, and elsewhere participate, and teachers visit religious sites around New York City with a view to developing their own teaching of religion. Because the participants are teaching elementary, middle, and high school students, special collections don't always play a role. However, one successful approach involved working with materials from the Council of Churches for the City of New York (CCCNY) archives—a large collection documenting institutional histories and charting denominational, organizational, and demographic changes—which fostered discussions of how the histories of diverse traditions and institutions throughout the city may or may not be captured, complementing the site visits and immersive focus of the program. It is also an invitation for the teachers to be reminded to utilize the special collections available in their own areas as resources for their teaching of religions.

In the World, Of the World

The examples here share a goal of putting students in touch with special collections in a sustained, contextually meaningful way that deepens their coursework and, it is hoped, their education overall. Having provided a survey of some experiences teaching with special collections, I want to conclude with a few reflections on lessons learned. Generally, it is clear that all are purposeful attempts to move beyond the "show and tell" model of special collections instruction (and therefore not unlike attempts in information literacy to move beyond the one-shot model, where possible). They all focus on physical experience with special collections, not simply as illustrative but as embodied human artifacts, and placing special collections at the heart of the learning process. Though every library will be distinctive because of the particular nature of its collections and the communities it supports, the examples above may serve as useful reports of experiments that have been successful.

All forms of library instruction aim to help students understand and use the wide variety of genres, formats, and tools available to further whatever work they may be undertaking. They help filter the "noise" that arises from information overload and may help ground and focus the thinking and learning process. What so often flits across our attention, in our personal and professional lives, are decontextualized words and images. Librarians teaching with special collections have an important role to play in reminding students (and ourselves!) that knowledge—however conceptual or theoretical—is also rooted in the physical world and embodied experience and that crucial insights are lost when that is forgotten.

Libraries know that context is essential to understanding. Close work with special collections confirms that knowledge and ideas are mediated through the material—our bodies (which create and perceive) and particular forms (from vellum to silicon) that carry and inevitably affect their meaning. The study of content cannot be separated from the media in which it is contained, and historical and cultural literacy includes the ability to understand the "how" as much as the "what" of what is being written, said, or shown (McGilchrist 2009, 31 et passim). The dialogical nature of learning and research is potently underscored by special collections, not only in terms of ideas and arguments but in terms of the students and the collections' placement in the physical world. We are, after all, embodied beings—a fact that many social, institutional, and technological forces may too easily allow us to overlook or forget.

We have also learned to pay better attention to what is missing from our collections, special or otherwise, and what stories they are not, or not yet, able to tell. The examples discussed here invite students to consider not only what is included in the collections but what is not, and why and which voices and perspectives cannot be heard and learned from as a result of both circumstance and deliberate exclusion. As we continue to build collections both retrospectively and prospectively, we are challenged to purposefully and energetically work to include such silenced, overlooked, or excluded voices and to do a better job ensuring they are collected, preserved, and shared.

Special collections—apart, perhaps, from the earth upon which we walk—are some of the oldest things that many of us encounter. Many are also completely unique—a very uncommon quality in societies dominated by mass-produced, interchangeable objects. For better or worse, many can only be seen or touched in a particular place—a library or a classroom. Their very nature requires us to slow down and focus for a period of time. They confront us with the distance of past times, places, and persons, and of works made by other hands for purposes similar, or perhaps inexplicably different from, our own. A large part of the Burke Library's mission is to care for and share its special collections with students. Whatever the specific goals for a course might be, in the humanities and social sciences at least (and certainly beyond these fields as well), special collections can keep the important realities of our histories and the embodied nature of all we undertake (even the seemingly most "virtual") as vital to learning.

Perhaps there is a helpful analogy—all the more poignant in a time of pandemic-induced isolation and distancing—between in-person conversations and interactions and working with special collections. It seems that relating to one another through screens (in spite of the ways that this has been a lifeline for our teaching and other work) in no way approaches the important and meaningful realities of being in one another's company, of having physical face-to-face conversations, of sharing the same places, of the engagement that can only happen through physical presence. Certainly the librarians, faculty, and students who regularly work with collections are missing those experiences in a tangible, powerful way. We hear this often from our communities. We realize both the value as well as the limitations of surrogates and other digital means of approach, as grateful as we may be that they afford at least some access and provide important support in a difficult time. Still, one could argue that this has further reaffirmed some of the important insights that those who work and teach with special collections have always known and tried to share: that knowledge, learning, growth, community—all the enlivening goals of education—need deep roots in the physical as well as the virtual, in the material as well as the conceptual, in bodies as well as minds.

References

Bratnober, Carolyn. 2019. "Queering the Archives at Union Theological Seminary." *Burke Library Blog,* March 18, 2019. *https://blogs.cul.columbia.edu/burke/2019/03/08/queering-the-archives-at-union-theological-seminary.*

Cline, David P. 2016. *From Reconciliation to Revolution: The Student Interracial Ministry, Liberal Christianity, and the Civil Rights Movement.* Chapel Hill: The University of North Carolina Press.

———. 2017. "Bringing the Church into the World: The Civil Rights Struggle & the Student Interracial Ministry." *Folklife Today,* March 9, 2017. *https://blogs.loc.gov/folklife/category/student-interracial-ministry.*

Dictionary Catalog of the Missionary Research Library, New York. 1968. 17 vols. Boston: G. K. Hall.

Gatch, Milton McC., ed. 1996. *'So Precious a Foundation': The Library of Leander Van Ess at the Burke Library of Union Theological Seminary in the City of New York.* New York: Union Theological Seminary and the Grolier Club.

Gillett, Charles Ripley, ed. 1927–30. *Catalogue of the McAlpin Collection of British History and Theology.* 5 vols. New York.

Handy, Robert T. 1987. *A History of Union Theological Seminary in New York.* New York: Columbia University Press.

Hollinger, David A. 2017. *Protestants Abroad: How Missionaries Tried to Change the World but Changed America.* Princeton: Princeton University Press.

Interfaith Center of New York. n.d. "About Our Work: Why Study Lived Religion?" Accessed January 26, 2021. *https://religiousworldsnyc.org/about.*

Manoff, Marlene. 2004. "Theories of Archives from Across the Disciplines." *portal: Libraries and the Academy* 4, no. 1: 9–25.

https://dspace.mit.edu/bitstream/handle/1721.1/35687/4.1manoff. pdf.

McGilchrist, Iain. 2009. *The Master and His Emissary: The Divided Brain the Making of the Modern World.* New Haven: Yale University Press.

Pearson, David. 2012. *Books as History: The Importance of Books Beyond Their Texts.* London; New Castle, DE: Oak Knoll Press.

Prentiss, George Lewis. 1889. *The Union Theological Seminary in the City of New York: Historical and Biographical Sketches of Its First Fifty Years.* New York: Anson D. F. Randolf and Co.

———. 1899. *The Union Theological Seminary in the City of New York: Its Design and Another Decade of Its History.* Asbury Park, NJ: M., W. & C. Pennypacker.

Slavens, Thomas P. 1986. *A Great Library Through Gifts.* München: K.G. Saur Verlag.

"View from Ginling." n.d. Accessed January 26, 2021. *https://mct.bar-nard.edu/home/overview.*

Notes

1   For most of its history, the Burke Library was simply the Library of Union Theological Seminary. In 1983, it was renamed to honor Walter Burke, a board member and generous benefactor of the Seminary.

2   Another large part of Van Ess's library had been sold several years prior and is now at the Huntington Library.

3   Slavens (1986, 25–6) quotes the University of Michigan's Justin Winsor's 1883 claim that, at that time, Union's library probably held the largest number of incunabula in the country.

4   Ivy Plus, whose best-known service is the Borrow Direct resource sharing network, includes Brown, Chicago, Columbia, Cornell, Dartmouth, Duke, Harvard, Johns Hopkins, MIT, Princeton, University of Pennsylvania, Stanford, and Yale. ReCAP (Research Collections and Preservation) is an offsite shared collection located in Princeton, NJ, and includes Columbia, Princeton, NYPL, and Harvard.

5   The position of "outreach archivist"—a recent addition to the Burke's staffing model—indicates the centrality of teaching with special collections to its present mission.

6   It should be noted that Briggs's daughter, Emilie Grace Briggs—the first female graduate of Union (1897) and an accomplished biblical scholar—is generally acknowledged to have carried to completion his work on the lexicon after her father's death in 1913.

CHAPTER 6

Teaching and Learning with Special Collections and Archives

Introducing Religious and Theological Primary Sources into the Classroom

CHRISTOPHER J. ANDERSON

*A*t the Yale Divinity Library, staff have been actively introducing religious and theological primary sources into the classroom in a variety of ways. These forms of engagement with special and archival collections have been integrated into both the traditional face-to-face classroom context and the non-traditional online environment. By planning and implementing interactive classroom sessions, librarians and archivists are helping faculty and students locate, access, and experience primary sources in both physical and digitized formats. Library resources interwoven into the teaching curriculum, especially digitized archival materials, help demonstrate the value of library collections for stakeholders, such as the Yale Divinity School (YDS) and showcase the educational opportunities theological libraries provide for faculty and students. Special and archival collections intentionally integrated into the curricular design of the classroom shape and enhance the pedagogical practices of the faculty and help make course content more appealing for students and more fully applicable to their coursework, projects, and life experiences.

This chapter provides an introduction to the Yale Divinity Library special collections and archive. The aim of the essay is to spotlight the teaching and learning program of the library by demonstrating how staff introduce and integrate primary sources into the classroom experience for both faculty and students. The chapter will document successful methods of engaging and interacting with students through their experience with special collections materials, including archival documents. Three examples of our program within traditional and non-traditional classroom contexts will be showcased, including our online distance education component using video conferencing technology. Each example spotlights the value and uses of religious and theological special collections and archives in a classroom setting.

Teaching and Learning with Religious and Theological Primary Sources

During the past fourteen years, I have had opportunities as a former college professor to blend my pedagogical experiences of classroom instruction with my more recent work as a special collections librarian. This chapter presents some of the practical opportunities librarians and archivists have while engaging with faculty and students in academic settings. The chapter benefits librarians and archivists working with teaching faculty in theological school and seminary contexts who are considering ways to actively engage students with original, primary source documents in print and digital formats.

Teaching and learning with religious-themed primary sources in a classroom context are essential curricular opportunities for all students. These primary sources are considered "special collections" or "distinctive collections" in academic libraries and, in smaller educational contexts, are often linked directly with the archives of the institution. The materiality and formats of these collections vary in scope and may include such items as rare books, personal papers, manuscripts, and photographs. Silva and McIntosh (2019, 96) note that these items often receive special designation, protection, and care because of an item's condition, year of publication, monetary value, availability, or direct historical connection with the owning institution.

Including special and archival collections in pedagogical situations benefits both faculty and students, and staff of the library and archives should see these moments as opportunities and proactively engage with those who can make these experiences happen. Christoph Irmscher (2016, 134) notes that library or archival staff should attempt to "demystify special collections, to establish them as a place not unlike but in fact very much like the rest of campus, or for that matter, the world." Opportunities to "demystify" primary sources beckon librarians and archivists to consider venues and to actively seek ways to connect these "special" or "distinctive" materials to the school's curriculum.

Library resources, specifically primary source materials, brought into the classroom demonstrate the value of the library by showcasing the educational services libraries and archives provide for faculty and students. Irmscher (2016, 149) notes that most students are prepared and willing to "embrace special collections materials, to handle them, to study them, to make them part of their lives." By linking library resources with the school's curriculum, especially its digitized materials, librarians and archivists demonstrate the inherent value of these collections for the school's administration.

These opportunities also showcase for stakeholders the services libraries provide for faculty and students. Like hosting students in a reading room, these sessions bring together "a synthesis of student learning and experiential learning, while providing opportunities for students to gain hands-on practical skills they can use in their future careers" (Anderson and Brand 2017, 90). Peter Carini (2016, 196) confirms that these opportunities are ways to "create expert users of primary sources," who are better prepared to "find, interpret, and create narratives using primary sources." As a result, primary sources integrated into teaching and learning sessions enhance the classroom and the student's experience with materials in fascinating and enriching ways.

Librarians and archivists are tasked with planning and implementing creative and engaging solutions to help faculty and students find, access, and experience primary resources. Barbara Rockenbach (2011, 298) confirms that methods such as active learning techniques using primary sources in the classroom are some of the "best ways to increase student engagement and teach higher-level critical thinking skills," which help affirm the learning process and the value of the material. This pedagogical approach to active learning is affirmed by Gore and Koelling (2020, 454), who note that students who physically experience archival materials engage their "intellects, bodies, and emotions" in ways that foster critical thinking about the materials under review.

Ultimately, the use of primary sources in the classroom offers opportunities for faculty and students to engage in learning about the past, which then provide real, in-class moments to consider and wrestle with historical questions in the present. Integrating special collections and archives into the classroom and having those materials woven into the framework of the lecture or lesson plan helps students become more aware of past successes and failures from history, while at same time better positioning students to think critically of the present. As I've explored previously (Anderson and Shetler 2019, 158–9), this approach can also encourage classroom participants to critically examine and engage with the materials that present both fascinating and troubling historical narratives. These sessions can inspire and perplex students. They can help make students more aware of the many silences in historical narratives, while spotlighting ways of identifying and interpreting a variety of historical and contemporary complexities that include race, gender, and class in the present. Ultimately, they inform us, while they also help dismantle assumptions and perceptions.

A Brief History of the Yale Divinity Library and Day Missions Library and Collection

The Yale Divinity Library (New Haven, Connecticut) houses in its special and archival collections tens of thousands of items on religious and theological subjects, including a significant amount of material on world Christianity and the history of missions. The Yale Divinity School was founded in 1822 for graduate students with vocational interests in church ministry, education, and missionary service. The Day Missions Library and Collection—the largest of the library's archival collections—originated in part as a gift from Edward S. Salisbury, professor of Arabic and Sanskrit at Yale University. In the 1840s,

Professor Salisbury gave Yale College $5,000 along with his private collection of "Oriental Studies" to generate a research collection, "befitting a true university" (Peterson 1993, 3). The Day Collection was also later sourced by benefactor William E. Dodge, who gave the Divinity School a generous donation of several hundred Bibles that had been published by the American Bible Society and by presses of Protestant missionary organizations throughout the world (5).

The Day Missions Library and Collection received its name from benefactors George Edward Day and Olivia Hotchkiss Day. George Day graduated from YDS in 1838. He worked as Professor of Hebrew Language and Biblical Literature at YDS for several decades, eventually serving from 1888 to 1891 as dean of the Divinity School. During his tenure, dozens of Yale College and Divinity School graduates went on to work as missionaries throughout the world and, by 1900, a total of one hundred and sixty-five Yale alumni had departed New Haven. In 1888, Professor Day toured Europe to explore libraries that included collections on the history of missions and missionary biography. These trips helped confirm his intention of building a library at Yale with a focus on the study and practice of missions.

Throughout the nineteenth century, Day had been actively collecting his own personal library of printed materials on the study of missions. During his final year as dean, Professor Day proposed to the school's "Friends of Christian Missions" group the creation of a new research library that became the Historical Library of Foreign Missions. The proposal was accepted, and Day then donated his personal library to Yale. As a result, by the end of the century, the Historical Library of Foreign Missions comprised "the most full and complete collection of works on foreign missions in the United States and perhaps the world" (Stuehrenberg 1994, 3).

George and Olivia Hotchkiss Day insisted that the library include materials for use by Yale faculty and students. They also envisioned the library as a research collection available for patrons from around the world (Divinity School of Yale University, March 19, 1891, Library of Modern Missions, record group 92, Yale Divinity Library Special Collections). The Days had earmarked funding in their estate for this purpose, alongside an additional endowment of $100,000 raised by YDS mission studies professor Harlan Page Beach (Robert 2020, 113). Following the death of the Days, the Historical Library of Foreign Missions was formally renamed the Day Missions Library.

The original Day Missions Library and Collection comprised six categories of collecting. These resources included the history of missions, missionary biography, the published annual reports of missionary societies, periodicals with mission and missionary statistics and stories, items published by missionaries for missionaries, and material on mission work to Jews. Additional items collected for the library included works on comparative religions, ethnology, geography, and cartography, as well as translations of the Bible, dictionaries and grammars, and printed material prepared and published by missionaries in the original languages of the people where they worked. The original library housed a printing press, photography room, map-making room, and carpentry shop. These spaces were designed to help prepare students going into missionary service with training and vocational skills as printers, photographers, cartographers, and carpenters.

By 1932, YDS and its library had been relocated from its downtown New Haven location to a new space about a mile from central campus along Prospect Street. The property had long ago been the home of the Winchester family, noted for their earlier production of the popular and controversial Winchester rifle. By this time, the Day Missions Library and Collection amounted to over twenty thousand volumes (Tayler 1978, 54). The original vision of the Days—to build a research library with the most complete collection on mission studies—continues in 2021. Current library staff continue to provide researchers with print-based and digitized resources, regardless of whether one visits the special collections reading room in person or the collections found online. During the COVID-19 pandemic, our staff have been especially helpful digitizing primary sources for patrons who cannot spend time on site because of restricted access to our special and archival collections.

The current collection strengths of the Day Missions Library and Collection include print and archival primary sources on the history of Protestant and Catholic missions, items on the religious activities of college and university students (e.g., the Student Volunteer Movement and the World Student Christian Federation), and historical biographies of clergy in the New England area. The Day Missions Library and Collection includes much of the original library alongside a significant collection of manuscripts and ephemera and a wide assortment of print materials, including periodicals, annual reports, and over 325 archival collections, comprised of correspondence, diaries, photographs, and drawings. Our largest archival collection, the China Records Project, spotlights the work of missionaries in China. This collection is a collaboration between the National Council of Churches and Yale Divinity Library and resulted in over three thousand former missionaries and their families being contacted and urged to consider donating their records of missionary work in China (Smalley 1996, 126). The collection documents the work of women as missionaries, how missionaries portray non-Western peoples and cultures, and the institutional histories of missionaries and their roles in the creation of hospitals and centers of higher education around the world.

Day Missions Library books can be discovered by searching the *Yale University Library catalog*, and archival collections can be located through finding aids available at *Archives at Yale*. The Yale Divinity Library also houses a comprehensive assortment of mission-related microforms showcasing archival collections held in other repositories around the world. Finally, grants from the Arcadia Foundation and the National Endowment for the Humanities have supported the digitization of more than fifty-five hundred *print volumes of annual reports and periodicals of missionary agencies, benevolent societies, and religious organizations.*

Introducing Religious and Theological Primary Resources into the Classroom

Academic librarians have an array of opportunities to conjoin religious and theological primary resources within the classroom environment. Special and archival collections built into the design of a course can shape and enhance the student experience and help reinforce classroom content by making faculty lectures more interesting for students as well as more useful for data mining for their course projects. At the Yale Divinity Library, teaching and learning opportunities function as a component of the overall outreach program. As part of our library's mission, we believe that we are charged with connecting faculty and students with primary resources in the classroom. We look for opportunities to help students immerse themselves in our special and archival collections. Once they become aware of the availability and potential uses of our primary sources, they can more critically review and assess the materials. In turn, these experiences help students consider how archival evidence and archival silence apply to or even disrupt their present educational journey or life situation.

Preparing and implementing engaging sessions allows librarians and archivists to assist faculty as their students discover, access, and experience primary sources in physical and online sessions. Introduction and access to these materials create a sense of wonder and promote needed critique and evaluation regarding the past. Hubbard and Lott (2013, 34) note, "The aesthetic qualities of the items, the hands-on experience, and the act of leaving the classroom to visit a new space all seemed to generate excitement and enthusiasm in the students, which encouraged them to engage in the class investigation of the items and the discussion that followed." At the Yale Divinity Library, we have been proactively connecting special and archival collections with Yale University and non-Yale classroom environments in three forms, including: traditional face-to-face teaching, the more recent Zoom online environment, and non-traditional chapel services and group showcase events.

Religious and Theological Primary Resources in a Traditional Classroom Context

The Yale Divinity Library has been actively engaged in connecting religious and theological special and archival collections into the traditional classroom context for many years. By "traditional classroom context," I mean a class session that is held in a brick-and-mortar, physical classroom setting with faculty and students in the room or in the special collections reading room alongside the actual material. For us, the interdisciplinarity of religious and theological studies with other academic disciplines allow for prime opportunities to collaborate with librarians and archivists in classrooms across the Yale University Library system. When Yale faculty request archival sources for their classes, I am often contacted to provide religious and/or theological materials for the teaching session. We also participate with other Yale University Library repositories as part of our teaching and learning program. For example, we have taken our physical primary source materials to the Beinecke Rare Books & Manuscripts Library or to the Yale Manuscripts & Archives classrooms for joint sessions with librarians, archivists, and curators across the Yale Library system.

Germek (2016, 401) confirms that academic libraries can broker teaching opportunities with special and archival collections as primary source information literacy sessions, while also spotlighting the library and archive as an "evolving and holistic learning space." The physical classroom environment allows students to experience primary sources in firsthand, personal ways. Students are encouraged to engage with the material through the use of their senses. Those who are able are allowed to touch the material, actively page through the rare books, and even carefully smell the residual scent put off by the items in order to appreciate the age and materiality of the objects. Irmscher (2016, 136) notes, "Manuscripts allow us a behind-the-scenes look where none seemed possible; they allow us to risk a glance at stories that might and should have been told but weren't." By providing students with a full range of experiential opportunities to view these one-of-a-kind items in a traditional classroom environment, they are given a chance to look back on the past, to physically engage with history firsthand, and to discover stories and narratives that both captivate and inspire.

Three examples of our teaching and learning program in traditional classroom environments include the graduate courses The Bible as Literature, The Bible and the Reformation, and China Mission. For The Bible as Literature and The Bible and the Reformation, I work alongside my colleague Suzanne Estelle-Holmer, who is associate director for research, collections, and access for the Yale Divinity Library. Suzanne and I reach out to the faculty of record for the courses to learn which Bibles and other materials they want made available for their class sessions. We then order, retrieve, and prepare the materials in the library classroom or in our special collections reading room. We have an assortment of foam cradles and book snakes that hold the items for review. Bibles from our collection that we have made available for classes include a 1537 copy of the Matthew's Bible, a 1599 edition of the Geneva Bible, and a 1613 copy of the King James Bible. We also include an assortment of complimentary texts for The Bible and the Reformation, including a 1516 copy of Erasmus's *Novvm Instrumentu[m] omne, diligenter ab Erasmo Roterodamo recognitum & emendatum* and a 1524 copy of Martin Luther's *Eyn Christlicher trostbrieff an die Miltenberger: Wie sie sich an yhren feynden rechen sollen, aus dem 119. Psalm.*

For the China Mission course, I work closely with YDS Professor Chloë Starr. For the first session, I provide an introductory overview to our mission-related collections and bring printed special collections materials (e.g., Chinese-language Bibles and missionary society annual reports) to the session, along with original archival items (e.g., handwritten or typescript correspondence authored by nineteenth- and twentieth-century missionaries and sent to missionary board agencies or the missionary's family and friends). Professor Starr also builds "Library Lab" opportunities into her weekly class sessions. These sessions are held in the special collections reading room, and students are invited to experience the materiality of the items first-hand through active engagement with the collections. Professor Starr attends these sessions and provides content overview, and the students discuss weekly readings, while also working with the original primary source materials. My library staff colleagues Joan Duffy and Sara Azam also assist with ordering materials through our Aeon request tool and then prepare the materials on tables for review.

Religious and Theological Primary Sources in a Virtual Classroom Context (Zoom)

Teaching with digitized religious and theological primary sources is a way to bring special and archival collections from the table to the screen for students who are taking courses online or who are not able to attend classes in person due to COVID-19 restrictions. Librarians and archivists have opportunities to scan, reformat, and ultimately repackage material items through digital imagery and its accompanying online metadata. These formats present faculty and students with multiple modes of viewing and assessing in a virtual environment (Anderson and Shetler 2019, 162). For example, original paper correspondence or glass lantern slide photographs transferred into high-resolution formats can provide a helpful way for students to encounter fragile or unique items in a virtual classroom.

Germek (2016, 401) has effectively argued that, if at all possible, digital surrogates should not replace actual special and archival materials. While it is certainly accurate to claim that providing students with opportunities to interact with archival objects in person presents them with ideal ways to experience special and archival collections, providing digital copies of an original object onscreen can function as an adequate way for students to view the electronic replica of an original item. Depending on equipment availability and pedagogical context, virtual students can even closely examine an object by using the zoom feature provided by most computers and tablets, which allows them an experience similar to using a magnifying glass in a physical reading room. Gore and Koelling concur that, while digital copies of special and archival collections should not replace physical items, they can complement each other, depending on the situation or the educational context (Gore and Koelling 2020, 469).

For several years, I have been using Skype and Zoom video conferencing as an extension of the library's teaching and learning program. In 2018, two years before the COVID-19 pandemic and the proliferation of video classroom technology, I made the decision to begin teaching with digitized primary sources in an online environment, since I had been unaware of other Yale library staff using this approach. These sessions provide us with opportunities to showcase Yale's digitized religious and theological primary sources for non-Yale students. Each interactive session includes a 45-minute virtual in-class experience with faculty and students from colleges and universities throughout the United States. For example, I have met virtually with classes at Albion College, Boston University, Brigham Young University, Prairie View A&M University, and Westmont College. The sessions are broadcast live from my office at the library and from home, depending on the location and time zone of the school.

During the live sessions, I walk students virtually through the Yale Divinity Library website and present examples of digitized primary sources related to the topic of the course. These sessions encourage and enable faculty and students to identify and locate primary sources at the Yale University Library from their classrooms and homes across the country. I explain and assess the similarities and differences between original print-based archival objects and their digitized surrogates. By explaining these differences, students can better appreciate the analog materials and understand that the scanned item on a screen has its source in a static archival object elsewhere (unless the object is born digital). This can be especially enlightening when students are told that the original item has been destroyed or lost to the public and that the only way to currently view the object is through its digitized form.

Each session includes a brief overview of the various Yale University Library special collections and archives repositories and collections. I then narrow the focus of my presentation to the divinity library and spotlight its Day Missions Collection, while showing faculty and students how to access Yale's digitized primary sources, including its thousands of digitized historical images. During the sessions, I also highlight Yale's historical manuscripts, periodicals, and ephemera. Each session concludes with several minutes reserved for student questions and comments, and I invite both faculty and students to contact me following the session so that I can help connect them to Yale's rich and expansive physical and digitized resources. The initiative has been a success, and students from several schools have responded and incorporated Yale's digitized collections into their course projects.

The faculty with whom I have worked have been especially pleased with this virtual presentation discussing our primary sources. I have included several notes sent to me from faculty to show the effectiveness of this approach to online instruction.

Dr. Christopher Jones, assistant professor of history at Brigham Young University, commented,

> Chris has provided an overview of relevant digital and manuscript collections housed at Yale Divinity Library, and several students have used those materials for research papers and projects in my classes, including one student who secured funding to travel to New Haven and take advantage of manuscript sources housed on-site in YDS's archive... Chris has gone above and beyond to assist students in my classes, introducing them to a variety of sources they would otherwise not know about, fielding their questions about those sources, and, in one instance, welcoming a BYU student to New Haven on her first major research trip outside Utah. (email message, May 8, 2019)

Dr. Joseph Ho, assistant professor of history at Albion College, noted,

> Chris's video conference brought Yale Divinity School Library's wealth of visual primary sources directly to my students at Albion College, guiding them through untapped collections of fascinating material as well as fundamental archival practices. Several students explored images and topics recommended by Chris in their final projects, demonstrating the teaching power of such collaborations between a world-class archive and the liberal arts classroom. (email message, May 13, 2019)

More recently, Dr. Marco Robinson, assistant professor of history at Prairie View A&M University, stated,

> Dr. Christopher Anderson's Zoom presentation introduced the students in my Introduction to Historical Methods of Research course to various types of primary sources and ways to utilize these items in their research efforts. Anderson's discussion of the holdings of the archive gave my students a firsthand view of the process of researching in special collections and manuscript collections. Using the zoom platform, Dr. Anderson was able to bridge the distance gap and adjust to the threat of the pandemic because we could not physically be in the facility. By the end of the semester my students were able to apply this knowledge to conducting archival research and composing their research paper. (email message, January 28, 2021)

Ultimately, these sessions have become a useful tool for outreach, both for our library and for the Yale University Library at large. The potential of these teaching sessions is unlimited and, if promoted more widely, the sessions could become an essential component of the library's program to provide access to digitized resources for colleges and universities around the world.

Since the start of the COVID-19 pandemic, I have also been teaching sessions with digitized archival resources on Zoom for Yale University and YDS. One example was the graduate course Chinese Poetic Form, 1490–1990, taught by Professor Kang-i Chang. My former YDS library archivist colleague Elizabeth Peters co-taught the session with me. We showcased several digitized copies of original handwritten and typescript poems authored by American missionaries serving in China during the early twentieth century. We also had the students perform an in-class exercise searching for poetry in some of our digitized mission-themed periodicals. During the Spring 2021 semester, I will be working with additional classes in blended formats. Depending on the situation with the evolving pandemic, the sessions might become a hybrid opportunity of some in-person classroom opportunities working with physical archival items, while also teaching sessions online using digitized archival materials.

Religious and Theological Primary Resources

in a Non-Traditional Classroom Context

The opportunity to showcase and discuss special and archival collections outside the traditional classroom can bring attention to the religious and theological primary sources at one's institution. Staff at the Yale Divinity Library have been actively seeking ways to bring students into contact with special and archival collections in non-traditional, non-intimidating environments. At the divinity library, staff have showcased primary sources in several ways, including the YDS chapel service and through a series of showcases to local religious groups. These opportunities enhance our outreach program to the school's students and to the non-Yale organizations of various local religious communities. These events also allow our staff to see first-hand how people react to and engage with our special and archival collections.

Chapel Service with Special and Archival Collections

In 2018, I met with Yale Divinity School chapel staff to discuss and consider innovative ways to integrate special and archival collections within the daily chapel service. The chaplain agreed to allow library staff to plan, organize, and lead one service per semester. A series of unique chapel services resulted, which included several of our collections. These events provided us with opportunities to showcase original archival materials on the history of the Yale Black Seminarians, the seven oversized and illustrated volumes of the St. John's Bible, and several of our special collections Bibles, written in a variety of languages and published by missionary presses around the world.

For example, for the session with our missionary Bibles, we included a variety of our under-utilized nineteenth- and early twentieth-century volumes from the library's special collections. The chaplain asked the YDS administration to supply us with a listing of the various first languages spoken by students at YDS. We then tracked down and selected several volumes from our collection in those languages. The Bibles were taken to the chapel by library staff and placed on foam cradles with book snakes securing the pages that had been opened to various scriptural passages that were part of the chapel readings for that day.

The staff spotlighted the care that goes into using special and archival collections, including the requirement to wash and dry one's hands prior to handling primary source materials. The chaplain's staff provided and monitored a large basin of water that was placed outside the entrance of the sanctuary. Several dozen towels were made available, and attendees were asked to wash and dry their hands before walking into the service to interact with the Bibles. During the service, I spoke on the "ritual" of handwashing as part of using archival materials and provided a brief reflection on how one's experience with an archive can become a spiritual or sometimes painful reminder of the past.

YDS students read texts from the displayed Bibles in their own languages. Students who read from the volumes actively engaged with special collections materials, and the remainder of the faculty and students who attended the service were able to spend time viewing the various volumes, turning the pages, and engaging with the primary sources. This brought material directly to the students in a comfortable and familiar space and also helped raise awareness of the types of Bibles available for research and use at the library. The service also gave opportunities for students to read and speak in their own languages with peers present. The service drew over seventy-five administrators, staff, and students, and the chaplain and library staff considered the event a successful endeavor.

Special Collections Showcases for Local Religious Groups

Finally, the library also hosts events for local religious organizations in our special collections reading room. These events are similar in style to the "Out of the Vault" program that I helped plan and implement at my former place of employment. Out of the Vault was a series of archival showcases with related talks, sponsored by the Drew University Library. The title of the series originated from staff conversations and an effort to foster and create an image of library staff bringing special and archival collections out of the protected confines of restricted library vaults.

We especially wanted underutilized collections to be viewed, touched, and analyzed in person. Each session lasted forty-five minutes and included brief, informal talks prepared by Drew faculty, library staff, or student staff. Each presenter was limited to fifteen minutes to speak on the provenance, donor information, and research value of the collection on display. Thirty minutes was then reserved for attendee engagement with the collection, which had been mounted and displayed on Wilson Reading Room tables. Each session was designed as a non-intimidating, public venue to explore our collections, and attendees were free to come and go at their leisure and availability (Anderson and Brand 2017, 91–2).

Presently, we offer a similar program for local religious groups. These showcases provide visitors opportunities to interact with our special and archival collections, while also allowing time to touch and closely examine firsthand the materials displayed. To date, we have hosted several New Haven-area groups, and we are planning to broaden the reach of the program to include adherents from a variety of religions and houses of worship. One example of our showcases included hosting a women's group from a regional Episcopal church. The event was organized around our seven-volume set of the St. John's Bible. These lavishly illustrated Bibles were produced in a calligraphic style, and our staff set up and prepared the items in our special collections reading room.

The event began in our library classroom, where the group watched several videos on the history and production of the St. John's Bible. We then gave the group a tour of the library and made our way to the special collections reading room. We discussed the acquisition of the volumes and then allowed participants to examine the materials and to ask questions of staff monitoring the session. The series is currently on hiatus during the COVID-19 pandemic but has been well-received. It provides us with opportunities for teaching and learning outside the four walls of the traditional classroom, and we look forward to expanding the series in the future.

Conclusion

Over the past several years, the staff of the Yale Divinity Library have been intentionally integrating religious and theological primary sources into the classrooms of Yale University and in academic settings across the United States. Our goal has been to bring attention to our collections and to demystify the special and archival collections we manage. As a result, we've learned there are multiple ways to do so. These include traditional face-to-face classroom contexts, online video conferencing environments, and nontraditional classroom outreach, such as chapel services and group showcases. By implementing these interactive classroom sessions in their many modalities, librarians and archivists can increase the visibility of their collections and can help students search, locate, access, and experience primary sources in both physical and digitized formats.

References

Anderson, Christopher J. and Brian Shetler. 2019. "Hands-on Learning: Using Primary Sources as Tools of Information Literacy." In *Information Literacy and Theological Librarianship: History and Praxis*, edited by Bobby Smiley, 157–71. Chicago: Atla Open Press.

——— and Cassie Brand. 2017. "Out of the Vault: Engaging Students in Experiential Learning Through Special Collections and Archives." In *The Experiential Library: Transforming Academic and Research Libraries through the Power of Experiential Learning*, edited by Pete McDonnell, 89–101. Cambridge, MA and Kidlington, UK: Chandos Publishing.

Carini, Peter. 2016. "Information Literacy for Archives and Special Collections: Defining Outcomes." *portal: Libraries and the Academy* 18, no. 1: 191–206.

Germek, George P. 2016. "Starting Almost from Scratch: Developing Special Collections as a Teaching Tool in the Small Academic Library." *College & Undergraduate Libraries* 23, no. 4: 400–13.

Gore, Amy and Glenn Koelling. 2020. "Embodied Learning in a Digital Age: Collaborative Undergraduate Instruction in Material Archives and Special Collections." *Pedagogy* 20, no. 3: 453–72.

Hubbard, Melissa A. and Megan Lotts. 2013. "Special Collections, Primary Resources, and Information Literacy Pedagogy." *Communications in Information Literacy* 7, no. 1: 24–38.

Irmscher, Christoph. 2016. "Teaching with Special Collections." In *Forging the Future of Special Collections*, edited by Melissa

A. Hubbard, Robert H. Jackson, and Arnold Hirshon, 131–56. Chicago: Neal-Schuman.

Overholt, John H. 2013. "Five Theses on the Future of Special Collections." *RBM: A Journal of Rare Books, Manuscripts, and Cultural Heritage* 14, no. 1: 15–20.

Peterson, Stephen L. 1993. "A 'Steady Aim Toward Completeness.'" In *The Day Missions Library Centennial Volume,* occasional publication, no. 2, edited by Stephen L. Peterson, Paul F. Stuehrenberg, and Martha Lund Smalley. New Haven, CT: Yale Divinity School Library.

Robert, Dana L. 2020. "Naming 'World Christianity': Historical and Personal Perspectives on the Yale-Edinburgh Conference in World Christianity and Mission History." *International Bulletin of Mission Research* 44, no. 2: 111–28.

Rockenbach, Barbara. 2011. "Archives, Undergraduates, and Inquiry-Based Learning: Case Studies from Yale University Library." *The American Archivist* 74, no. 1: 297–311.

Silva, Judy L. and Barbara McIntosh. 2019. "An Independent Study Course by an Academic Library Department: Teaching with the Gems of Special Collections." *RBM: A Journal of Rare Books, Manuscripts, and Cultural Heritage* 20, no. 2: 95–118.

Smalley, Martha Lund. 1996. "Archives and Manuscript Collections in Theological Libraries." In *The Theory and Practice of Theological Librarianship: The American Theological Library Association, Essays in Celebration of the First Fifty Years,* edited by M. Patrick Graham, Valerie R. Hotchkiss, and Kenneth E. Rowe, 122–30. Chicago: American Theological Library Association.

Stuehrenberg, Paul F. 1994. *A Library Worthy of the School: A History of the Yale Divinity School Library Collections,* occasional publication, no. 1, Revised Edition. New Haven, CT: Yale Divinity School Library.

Tayler, Merrily E. 1978. *The Yale University Library 1701–1978: Its History, Collections, and Present Organization.* New Haven: The University Library.

CHAPTER 7

"Let Your Eyes Look Forward"

Developing a Digital Repository from the Ground Up

JONATHAN LAWLER AND SHEA VAN SCHUYVER

S pecial collections exist to preserve and make accessible material of enduring historical value. A professional duty to look forward seemingly stands in tension with preserving history. At times, professionals understand preservation primarily as restricting access to material. Looking ahead, however, entails preparing for future threats to preservation, while also taking advantage of opportunities to make collections more accessible.

Developing a digital repository that properly supports both preservation and access is imperative for librarians and archivists considering the future. The issues surrounding digital records cause much excitement and consternation among professionals in special collections and archives. Approaching the challenges of preserving and making accessible digitized and born-digital material requires a consideration of context, cooperation, and commitment.

Contextual consideration allows special collections librarians to carefully study the unique nature of their collections and how best to serve the parent institution and users through a digital repository. Once staff decide on a course of action, cooperation between librarians, archivists, administrators, and information technology professionals is essential to the success of any digital repository project. All stakeholders must commit to the repository's long-term durability.

This chapter examines the development of the digital repository of Southeastern Baptist Theological Seminary's Archives and Special Collections (ASC). As the repository of a smaller theological school, the actions taken by the staff may apply to other repositories and libraries of similar size. An institution does not need to be the size of a leading research university or government entity to pursue digital preservation and access. This case study highlights the essential roles of contextual consideration, cooperation, and commitment in successfully developing a digital repository that preserves digital information and makes it freely accessible to users around the world.

Contextual Considerations

Institutional Context

Southeastern Baptist Theological Seminary (SEBTS) is an entity of the Southern Baptist Convention with the mission "to glorify the Lord Jesus Christ by equipping students to serve the church and fulfill the Great Commission (Matthew 28:18–20)" (Southeastern Baptist Theological Seminary n.d.). Founded in 1950, the Seminary shared the campus of Wake Forest College in Wake Forest, NC, until the college moved to Winston-Salem, NC, in 1956. That year, the seminary took possession of the campus and continued to grow in the number of students and program offerings. By 2020, the seminary offered over 4,700 students "40 different programs with degrees ranging from Associate of Divinity to Doctor of Philosophy, including [its] flagship degree, the Master of Divinity" (Southeastern Baptist Theological Seminary n.d.).

The Library at Southeastern serves the seminary community by offering extensive print and online resources, research assistance, and unique or rare material stored in ASC. Ten full-time and twenty-four part-time staff work to fulfill the mission of the library: "to engage the Southeastern community with services and resources to equip them to serve the church and fulfill the Great Commission" (Library at Southeastern 2020). By 2019, the library offered access to:

> 200,803 books, 461,781 e-books, 38,032 bound journal volumes, and 963 linear feet of archival materials and manuscripts. The Library continues to add thousands of new items every year. Visits to the Library have annually exceeded 99,000. The Interlibrary Loan (ILL) department handled 3,874 requests. More than 575 items have been sent to distance students around the U.S. and the world. (Library at Southeastern 2020)

Since 2015, library leadership increasingly emphasized the need to serve patrons and the institution remotely.

The staff of ASC enthusiastically shared the library leadership's vision to increase online offerings. This vision matched the broad concern of the archives profession to make material accessible to as many users as possible. The Universal Declaration on Archives states as one of its goals, "Archives are made accessible to everyone, while respecting the pertinent laws and the rights of individuals, creators, owners and users" (International Council on Archives 2010). ASC's mission statement manifests a desire to increase access to archival material and special collections in its care. The department exists:

> to procure, preserve, and promote access to rare books, personal papers, institutional records, Baptist materials and church records, and other unique sources of enduring historical value that can be used to better equip Southeastern Baptist Theological Seminary students, faculty, and the broader research community to serve the Church and fulfill the Great Commission. (Library at Southeastern n.d.)

The department's mission statement not only conveys a concern for promoting access but also intentionally mirrors the parent institution's mission.

ASC staff includes two full-time members (the archivist and digital collections manager, and the assistant archivist and digital collections specialist) and five part-time employees (two archives assistants and three digitization assistants). The archives assistants aid in processing collections and assisting researchers. Digitization assistants create digital versions of analog material to make collections available to users across the world.

These staff members preserve and provide access to the repository's approximately one thousand linear feet of material. Notable collections include the Francis A. Schaeffer papers, the John Warwick Montgomery papers, institutional records, and a sizable collection of Primitive Baptist records. ASC also emphasizes material documenting the history of global Christian missions.

In light of the close connection between developing a digital repository and serving the seminary's emphasis on Baptist and Evangelical Christian missions, ASC staff concluded that serving the missional emphasis of the school and its alumni required providing access to archival and special collections material in an online format. As a key component of the department's collecting scope, records documenting global missions would be made accessible via a digital repository for a practical impact on contemporary missions. Through a digital repository, ASC staff trusted that missionaries in the field, perhaps even alumni of the seminary, would learn from their predecessors and be more effective in their work.

To best foster engagement with archival and special collections material, ASC desired to offer global access to the various types of resources in its custodianship. The formats of material housed in ASC include papers, bound volumes, photographic prints, negatives, reel-to-reel tapes, cassette tapes, CDs, Betamax tapes, VHS tapes, DVDs, and various born-digital files. The acquisition of the Francis A. Schaeffer papers in 2010 came with an agreement to digitize the entirety of the collection. Through this project, the staff gained substantial experience in digitizing different types of material—an important factor in developing a digital repository with robust offerings. A significant amount of digitized material (about nine TB) was stored before considering digital repository possibilities. Some of these digitized materials were ready for dissemination and preservation via a proper repository.

A concentrated effort to develop a digital repository began in August 2018. ASC staff considered the resources available for a development project. Resources included finances, hardware (e.g., servers), and the skill sets of staff. This last consideration was perhaps the most important. A successful project required staff members with expertise in a variety of areas, including project management, digital archives, systems development, and website design. For this reason, the archivist hired a digitization assistant with the ability to do complex coding and development work. Fortunately, ASC staff could also call on the seminary's skilled IT staff for support.

The IT department devoted many hours to the project. A systems analyst worked with the digitization assistant to build the repository. The digitization assistant devoted her allotted twenty-nine hours per week to developing the repository. The archivist managed the project, which included setting deadlines and ensuring they were met, fostering efficient communication among staff, and providing feedback on aspects of development impacting archives and special collections best practices and standards.

Key Repository Features

The archivist and digitization assistant considered four primary factors in choosing a digital repository product: (1) the need to preserve and display various file formats, (2) requirements for persistence and fixity of data, (3) the ability to set different access permissions, and (4) an intuitive and functional user interface. In September 2018, a planning group including representatives from the library, ASC, and IT departments evaluated four options to meet the department's digital repository needs: Omeka, DSpace, Islandora CLAW, and Samvera Hyrax. The group focused on Islandora CLAW and Samvera Hyrax as the two most appropriate options. Analysis began with Islandora CLAW, since this was the planned direction of prior ASC leadership, and it was an attractive option for several reasons. It utilized Fedora 4 ("Flexible Extensible Digital Object Repository Architecture" [DuraSpace n.d.b])—the preferred storage and preservation system for ASC. Fedora is "a community-maintained, open-source repository system that supports durable access to digital objects" (DuraSpace n.d.b). The data persistence, fixity, and auditing capabilities of Fedora were critical in this decision. Another factor was Islandora CLAW's user base and sponsors. The community of support from the user base of any repository option was of vital importance. ASC rejected repository options that lacked suitable sponsors and user communities. Sponsors of Islandora CLAW included LYRASIS, McMaster University, York University, and others (Islandora 2020) and so satisfied this requirement.

While these aspects of Islandora CLAW were attractive, other factors led the department to choose Samvera Hyrax. As with Islandora CLAW, Hyrax also utilized Fedora 4 as the storage and preservation system, but the user and sponsor base of Hyrax tipped the scales in its favor. At the time, sponsors and users of Hyrax included Yale University, Columbia University, Digital Public Library of America (DPLA), University of Virginia, and others (Samvera n.d.b). Two other institutions in the local (Raleigh-Durham, NC) area already used or were developing Samvera Hyrax instances. These were Duke University, an established Samvera Partner, and the University of North Carolina at Chapel Hill, which was developing Hyrax and would later become a Samvera Adopter (Samvera n.d.b). Working through development with the aid of staff at these institutions presented the opportunity to strengthen existing ties and cultivate new relationships. The cooperative spirit evident in the strong community of support would be invaluable to ASC and IT staff as development progressed.

In addition, in September 2018, Islandora CLAW was still in development. ASC desired a reliable, production-ready repository to begin developing before December 2018. Related to this was the benefit of reviewing existing Hyrax instances (Samvera n.d.a). These instances revealed excellent speed and quality of audiovisual streaming—an important factor due to the amount of audiovisual material within ASC collections.

Undertaking the web development portion of the project forced ASC staff to consider the structure of the digital repository. Samvera Hyrax used Ruby on Rails as the server-side web application framework, while Islandora CLAW used PHP—a widely adopted programming language for web development and an industry staple. Ruby on Rails is a newer framework for web applications. It is both well-supported and open source, which the digitization assistant and IT staff found compelling. While both Ruby on Rails and PHP are widely used in web development, the team felt there were distinct advantages of the Ruby on Rails platform, including the wide Ruby on Rails community support and the MVC framework.

Both the digitization assistant and IT staff believed the learning curve would be about equal for Islandora CLAW and Samvera Hyrax. Considering staff knowledge as a resource was an important aspect of the early stages of the project. If a staff member possessed substantial knowledge and experience with either repository, the ability to capitalize on that knowledge could well have changed the direction of the project. In the final analysis, ASC staff chose Samvera Hyrax because it was built on Fedora 4 and Ruby on Rails, had significant sponsors and users, offered a responsive development community, and presented an attractive and customizable user interface. Staff recognized that no single repository option was perfect but believed that the project should move ahead with the best available option and collaborate with one another and the broader Samvera Hyrax community for its success.

Cooperation

Repository Design

Once staff selected the platform for the digital repository, development could begin, and the IT department became heavily involved. The first task was to get a server up and running with the necessary components for the Hyrax stack. The IT department completed the initial design and used Nutanix to create a virtual server dedicated to the digital repository. This was a Linux server running Ubuntu 16.04.1. This choice was based on the documentation provided by Samvera on the ideal server environment for the web application. Most of the documentation at the time was geared toward installing Hyrax in a Linux environment (Samvera 2020).

After the server was set up, IT installed the prerequisites for Hyrax: Solr, Fedora, a SQL RDBMS (the IT department chose MySQL), Redis, ImageMagick, FITS, LibreOffice, and FFmpeg (Samvera 2020). Although IT was reasonably familiar with the Linux environment, the remaining prerequisites (including Ruby on Rails) were new to the team. Therefore, the early stages of development were often delayed due to lack of familiarity with the technologies being used. While the IT department worked through the details of installing the prerequisites on the server, the digitization assistant spent time learning the Ruby programming language. Through the utilization of free resources, the assistant became familiar with the Ruby language, which aided the team in the customization of the repository for the institution's needs.

Once the IT department installed the prerequisites, they created a Hyrax app on the server. Following the installation guide, the programmers were able to get the basic Hyrax app running on the server. From there, the task was to make customizations and design choices to fit ASC's specific needs and desires (figure 1). One of the most important choices was the metadata schema and hierarchy of the repository. This decision involved both IT input on the technical specifications as well as the archivist's input on proper archival standards. A video recording from Samvera 2018 entitled, "Architecting

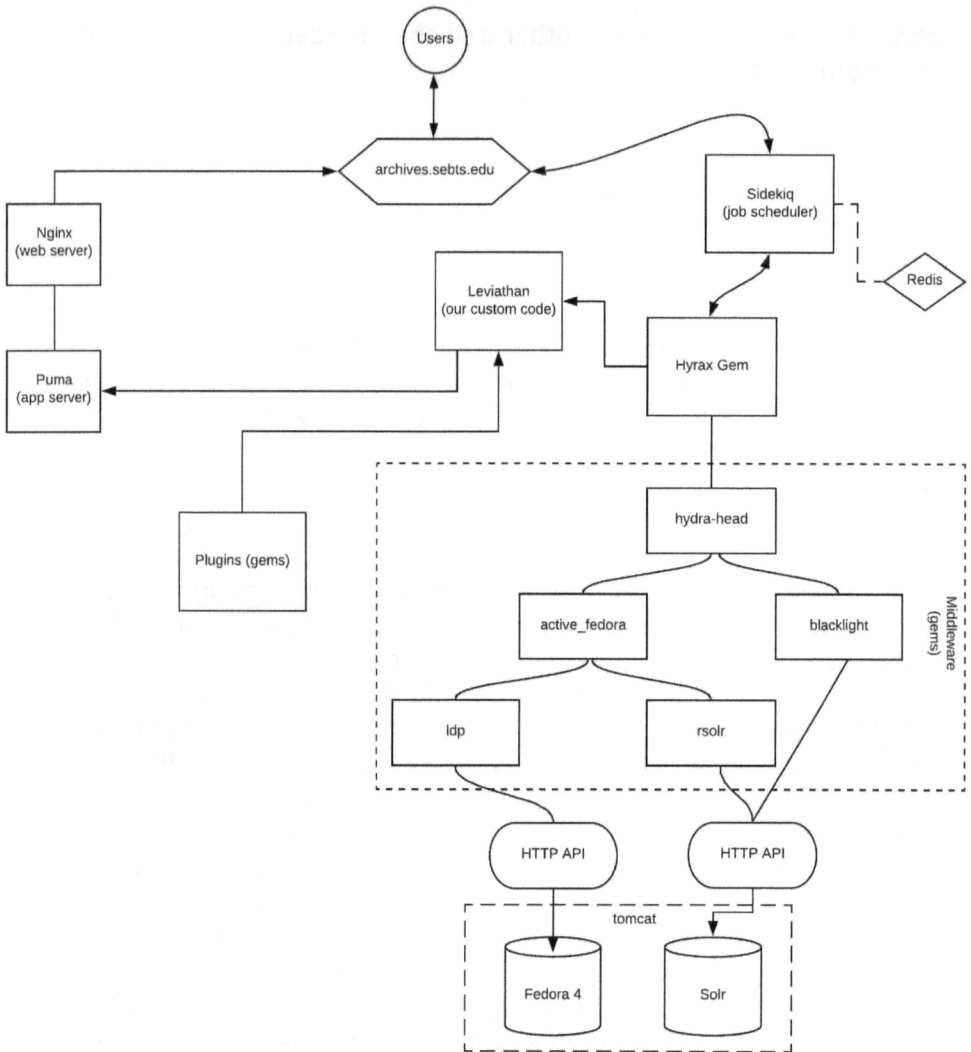

Figure 1: Illustration of Hyrax Stack customized for SEBTS.

Collections," proved to be a helpful resource for the team in thinking through these decisions (Samvera 2018). The team decided to go with a simple structure: one default admin set (which controls general settings), one default collection type (public collection), and a collection hierarchy that matched the archives' physical collection schema.

While matching the existing hierarchical structure was imperative to ASC staff, adhering to other standards and best practices in the fields of archives and special collections was also important. One requirement was well-structured and standards-compliant metadata. The archivist communicated the importance of this aspect of the repository to the digitization assistant, and the assistant worked towards implementing an appropriate method of entering quality metadata.

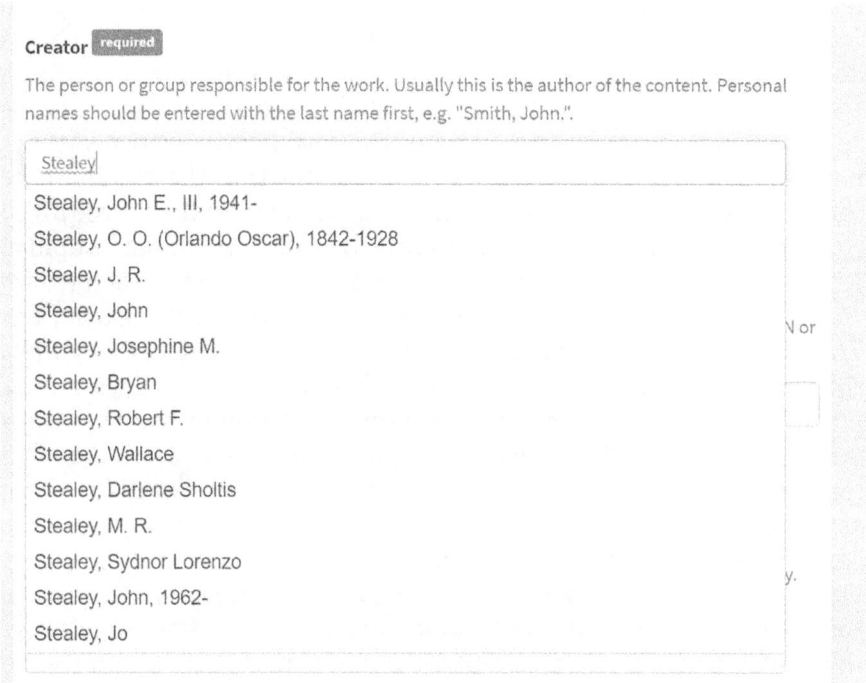

Creator required

The person or group responsible for the work. Usually this is the author of the content. Personal names should be entered with the last name first, e.g. "Smith, John.".

Stealey

Stealey, John E., III, 1941-
Stealey, O. O. (Orlando Oscar), 1842-1928
Stealey, J. R.
Stealey, John
Stealey, Josephine M.
Stealey, Bryan
Stealey, Robert F.
Stealey, Wallace
Stealey, Darlene Sholtis
Stealey, M. R.
Stealey, Sydnor Lorenzo
Stealey, John, 1962-
Stealey, Jo

Figure 2: Screenshot of metadata field with autosuggestions from Library of Congress Controlled Vocabulary.

For the data model foundation of the repository, staff used the model native to Hyrax—the Portland Common Data Model (PCDM), "a flexible, extensible domain model that is intended to underlie a wide array of repository and DAMS applications" (DuraSpace 2018). ASC staff chose to adhere as closely to Dublin Core as possible for descriptive metadata. The assistant was able to link to Library of Congress authorities within most descriptive metadata fields. These fields auto-suggested appropriately formatted authorities when assistants began entering metadata (figure 2). This option helped ensure consistent and accurate descriptive metadata.

Repository Customization

The vast majority of development time was dedicated to customizing the Hyrax application. One of the most important customization features that needed to be developed was the ability to batch upload works to the site via comma-separated value (CSV) files. The archives already had considerable amounts of metadata information in Excel format, but individually uploading each of these assets with its corresponding metadata would take an enormous amount of time. Hyrax natively supports batch uploads but requires that the metadata be the same for each work being uploaded. Therefore, Hyrax required custom development, since ASC required the ability to batch upload works with metadata that reflected the unique nature of each work.

The first step in developing this feature was investigating other institutions' batch upload processes. The team decided to follow the approach of developers at Duke University. Since Duke's code is publicly available online, the digitization assistant was able to track how they developed the feature (Duke Libraries 2020). When the team encountered difficulty integrating Duke's code, the digitization assistant received direct help from one of Duke's developers. Such communication between members of a development community is particularly helpful when customizing a repository, and members of the Samvera community were happy to assist with issues that arose in development. This community was important throughout the development process, especially with the batch upload feature.

Communicating the concerns of archivists and special collections librarians to the development team was also an important aspect of the project. Each profession approaches digital repositories differently, and these differences must be negotiated when an institution conducts a development project. The area of properly citing works within the repository provides a useful example of communicating differences across professions.

The citation field is one of the default metadata fields in Hyrax. This is where the proper citation for a work can be provided. For analog collections, ASC provides citations at the collection level, not the folder or item level. The archivist wanted to be able to set the preferred citation at the collection level and have that applied to each work in order to provide users with a quickly discernable preferred citation format. This is not a feature of Hyrax. Initially, the digitization assistant explored the viability of customizing Hyrax to meet the archivist's requests, but they ran into difficulties executing the idea. This was in large part due to their unfamiliarity with the Hyrax code, as well as difficulty finding an example. Instead, the digitization assistant proposed that they pursue setting automatic citations for each work. The Hyrax code already had examples that gave the assistant an idea of how to achieve this. Together, the team decided to pursue this option because of the decreased time commitment required to make that feature work.

Other existing features of Hyrax also required considerable customization. Natively, the Hyrax homepage has a space to display profiles on "Featured Researchers." Because ASC and IT customized Hyrax to exclude uploads from any users other than library staff members, "Featured Researcher" was an unnecessary offering of the repository. "Featured Collection," however, was important because individual collections are foundational to the arrangement schema of ASC holdings. Since Hyrax already had a "Featured Works" section, the assistant used the general pattern of how that feature was constructed in the code to create the "Featured Collection" segment. However, this took longer than anticipated because of the team's overall unfamiliarity with the Hyrax application and the Ruby on Rails framework. Ultimately, after many failures and dead ends, the team found a solution. Other customization tasks included changing some of the default metadata fields to reflect the schema used by the archives.

As illustrated by the "Featured Researcher" option, Hyrax was initially designed for external users to upload works. However, the nature of the archive's repository is to preserve and display works from its own collections. To that end, Hyrax needed to be customized to prevent non-authorized users from creating accounts or uploading their own content. The archivist also needed to be able to delete internal users. Thus, the next task in customization was to lock down user permissions and improve the existing user management interface. The team used the Devise gem (a packaged Ruby plugin) to implement these changes and created password reset functionality for users. The Devise gem provides a handy authentication module for Rails-based websites. During this phase, the team also added a new role in the system for the archives and the digitization assistants, giving them access to edit and upload works but not to delete works. This choice was made to further protect the assets within the site.

Safeguarding these assets helps fulfill one of the goals of ASC through the digital repository—to preserve the institution's history.

SOUTHEASTERN BAPTIST THEOLOGICAL SEMINARY TIMELINE

Since 1950, Southeastern Baptist Theological Seminary has prepared men and women for ministry in a variety of areas. Use this timeline to explore the history of the GO seminary!

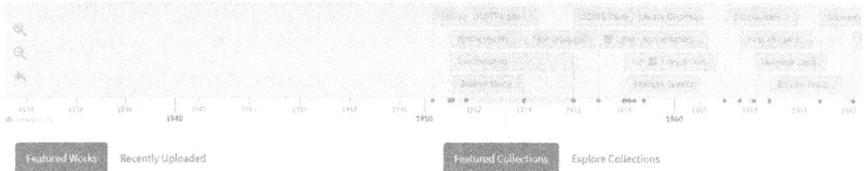

Figure 3: Screenshot of SEBTS History Timeline set as landing page.

Related to this goal is cultivating interest in this history, especially on the part of the students, faculty, and staff of the institution. To that end, the archivist imagined a timeline of SEBTS's institutional history to attract and engage researchers with ASC material. The digitization assistant was initially concerned about the development time needed for such a large feature. However, after some research, the team discovered Timeline JS (Knight Lab n.d.), which served as a simple tool to build an engaging timeline of the institution's history. This timeline was simple to add to the site's homepage (figure 3) and allows the archivist to control the content without additional development time.

Following these major changes, the development team focused on the site's design, branding, and interface and worked toward consensus. The archivist used the opportunity to convey to the seminary's Communications Department the importance of branding for ASC. The Communications Department created a new logo for use on the site, which adhered to the seminary's requirements for institutional branding and purposefully resembled the library's existing logo. The team decided on several small changes, including updating the header, footer, colors, and fonts, as well as improving the contact page. This change would allow for efficient communication between digital repository users and ASC staff.

To better serve these users, a final—and one of the most difficult—customization tasks remained before publishing the repository. The archivist desired a way to filter works on the site by date. Other metadata fields were facet-able and searchable, but the date field was not. This feature proved to be difficult because date and time formats can be inherently complex and require application-language-specific conversion. The first step in improving the date field was to enforce a standardized format. ASC's material often includes a circa date or date range, which presented an additional hurdle. The digitization assistant struggled to work through this particular feature. She located examples from other institutions using Hyrax and sought advice from other users. The Samvera community was indispensable in the implementation and development of the site but, after many failures, the team successfully implemented the blacklight_range_limit gem to facet dates in the repository.

Repository Publication and Promotion

After eight months of development and three months of uploading works to the repository, ASC quietly published the repository in late August 2019. This launch provided additional time to edit the repository before publicizing the site widely. During this phase, the seminary's Communications Department vetted the material on the repository and so ensured that the publicly available material did not violate either legal statutes or internal seminary policy.

By early October 2019, ASC staff actively promoted the repository. The archivist wrote an article for the seminary's magazine, *Southeastern*, about the value of archival material in serving the church and fulfilling the Great Commission (the seminary's mission). He used the article as an opportunity to highlight the newly developed repository. The occasion to do so in this context reached a wide audience, including those most likely to use the repository: students, alumni, faculty, and staff of SEBTS. Communicating the value of the repository to these potential users was an important step in promoting use of ASC material. Promotion of the completed repository was possible due to strong staff partnerships and a collegial spirit between all involved. This collaborative atmosphere prepared staff for continuing development work.

Commitment

Commitment of IT Department

From the beginning of the project, ASC and IT agreed to provide an imperfect, simple site for researchers, rather than delay release until all desired features were implemented. While ASC and the IT department were able to devote significant time to the development of the repository in its early stages, after the site formally launched both departments had to reduce staff time for the project. As a result of the great partnership between ASC and IT during the repository's development, the digitization assistant transitioned into a programming position in the IT department. While ASC hopes to again dedicate staff members to ongoing development, they have been unable to do so since this transition. At the same time, the IT department needed to return to other development projects, and so work on additional features must await the availability of IT staff.

In addition to development leading to the public launch of the site, the IT department needed to commit to the ongoing maintenance of the entire system. This ongoing maintenance is essential to the life and longevity of the digital repository. The IT department considers two general areas when it comes to the ongoing maintenance of the digital repository: hardware and software.

ASC's digital repository necessitates a substantial amount of storage space, which in turn requires significant hardware investment. Initially, the IT department underestimated the amount of storage required and the hardware needed to house all current and future files that would be added to the repository. Most websites present digital media using low-resolution file types and/or screen-quality resolution. However, ASC's digital repository aims to both display and store the highest-available quality for its digitized and born-digital materials. Since meeting the goal of preservation requires that the digital repository securely store these files, the team decided to house the core Fedora object storage database on a Synology NAS (Network Access Storage) device. This NAS consists of eight hard drives, configured in RAID 5 format, providing 27.15 TB of storage. One of the benefits of this configuration is that the NAS has a spare drive that can instantly replace another drive in the NAS if it experiences a failure.

The IT department saw the effectiveness of this NAS system soon after site launch, when the system detected a faulty drive. The NAS system sent a notice that one of the drives had failed, and the "hot spare" automatically replaced it within the array. The IT department swiftly replaced the drive without any further issues. This experience bolstered the confidence in the repository's recovery contingencies for both IT and ASC.

In addition to the main Synology NAS that houses the Fedora database, the team purchased another Synology NAS to serve as a backup device for the system. The Fedora database is backed up every night to this second device. Solr and the MySQL database are also backed up each night. These backups allow the site and its digital works to be restored in case of catastrophic failure. These two devices are housed in separate buildings at the institution in the hopes that, in a major disaster, one of the two devices will survive. The IT department performs daily checks to ensure that these NAS devices are functioning properly and backing up the system. The IT department also employs a program that automatically checks the devices' network availability every five minutes. If either device has problems, the IT department is ready to respond and investigate potential issues.

While maintaining the digital repository's storage, the IT department also makes sure that the virtual server on which the site is running is backed up. This is accomplished by taking daily server snapshots. The IT department can restore the server to its previous state from one of these snapshots in the event of catastrophic system error.

The IT department also has ongoing responsibilities to maintain the software of the digital repository. The Samvera community is continuously developing and improving the Hyrax platform. When new versions or patches of Hyrax are released, the IT department takes time to test and upgrade the current version of Hyrax on the site. This process is facilitated by a secondary virtual server, which serves as a "sandbox" for development and testing. Since the repository launched in October 2019, the IT staff upgraded the site from Hyrax version 2.5.1 to 2.9.0. The staff are looking forward to upgrading the site to Hyrax 3.x, which is currently under development. This upgrade has the potential to bring even more improvements and features to the digital repository. Ongoing maintenance, along with further development needs, requires commitment from the IT department and ASC to the maintenance of the site and its resources.

Commitment of ASC

ASC is committed to promoting existing material and adding new offerings to the digital repository. This commitment entails exploring how the department may successfully meet future needs of researchers. Such proactivity can be daunting and easily swept aside when faced with the myriad day-to-day responsibilities of managing an archives and special collections department. However, this is necessary to continue ASC's record of serving its patrons.

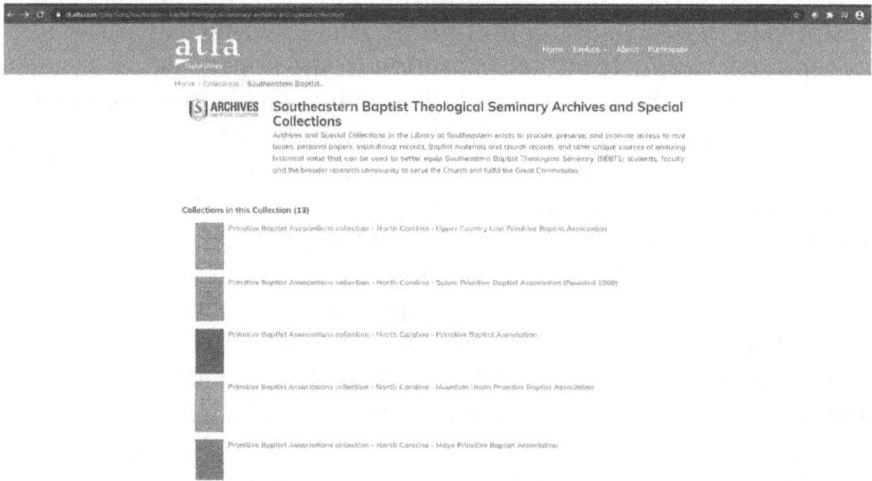

Figure 4: Screenshot of results of OAI-PMH partnership between ASC and Atla.

Beginning in January 2020, ASC and IT staff began the process of implementing the Open Archives Initiative Protocol for Metadata Harvesting (OAI-PMH), which is supported by Hyrax. An existing relationship with Atla led to a partnership using OAI-PMH for harvesting metadata from the SEBTS Digital Repository for the Atla Digital Library. Staff limited the harvest to material relating to Primitive Baptists, which fit the collecting scope of the Atla Digital Library. Completed in October 2020, this project offered ASC staff the opportunity to reach a wider audience interested in the history of religion and theology and better connect users with ASC material (figure 4).

The advocacy and awareness benefits of such partnerships are clear. Roe writes that successful advocacy and awareness efforts include "[c]ollaboration with allied institutions in the library, historical and genealogical communities, and developing coalitions that cross disciplinary boundaries" (Roe 2019, 33). The utilization of OAI-

PMH to allow other organizations to harvest and make accessible ASC metadata is an example of collaborating in order to connect with other user communities.

A commitment to collaboration is an important aspect of promoting the digital repository's longevity. In the summer of 2020, ASC staff began work with OCLC on harvesting metadata for inclusion in their Digital Collections Gateway. This collaboration brings many of the same benefits as those arising from the Atla partnership, has significant reach, and includes all ASC collections.

Collaborating with outside institutions like Atla and OCLC also helps promote ASC's value to various stakeholders and resource allocators. Recognizing that the seminary, as the parent institution, is the primary stakeholder in the digital repository led ASC leadership to consider how to best serve its needs. One planned addition to the digital repository is adding access to electronic theses and dissertations produced by seminary students. As theses and dissertations are primarily, or exclusively, produced in electronic format, a convenient portal on the digital repository would allow for efficient use of these resources. Offering such material would provide the broader scholarly community access to the wealth of academic work produced by the seminary. Students, faculty, and staff would also clearly benefit from such an addition to the repository.

Serving the students, faculty, and staff of SEBTS also includes the planned creation of online displays that highlight the history of the school. For many years, ASC created static displays for the common area of the library. The prominent location of the two display cases meant that the displays received a fair amount of engagement. Static exhibits, however, are only on display for six months. An online exhibit could reach far more users and remain "live" for a much longer period. Thus, creating an online exhibit in conjunction with a static exhibit should increase interaction with archival and special collections material.

Online exhibits can also engage users with ASC material in new ways. Although using the search box may well be the easiest way to locate ASC material on the digital repository, online exhibits may expose users to material they would never have considered. Ranade (2018, 90) writes on digital reference services, "Alternatives to search and browse have emerged in the form of exhibition-style content, designed to help users understand what the archives might contain." Such exhibition-style content "can be highly engaging." ASC and IT personnel are looking for the most effective method to create engaging online exhibits, and staff are considering both using the internal capabilities of Hyrax and linking to exhibits created with other software, such as Omeka.

One capability of Hyrax, which ASC staff prioritized for development, is its ability to incorporate Encoded Archival Description (EAD) finding aids, which should better serve users and maintain professional standards and best practices. ASC staff create EAD finding aids that adhere to the standard *Describing Archives: A Content Standard* (DACS). Rather than provide access only to individual items within the collection, these encoding and description standards give users more streamlined access to the larger context of ASC holdings. Hyperlinks to individual assets included within finding aids will serve all users, especially those who choose to research through browsing. While ASC and IT staff provided researchers a digital repository capable of enabling long-term access to digital material, the continued success of the repository will require ongoing improvements that reflect changes in standards and best practices.

Conclusion

Developing a digital repository was a daunting task for the Archives and Special Collections at Southeastern. Despite the many challenges encountered, ASC and IT staff successfully developed a robust repository through their devotion to contextual consideration, cooperation, and commitment. This experience should encourage the staff of other archival repositories and special collections libraries.

Any digital repository development project requires careful consideration of the options that will best fit institutional needs. No one-size-fits-all solution exists for digital repository development. However, once the most appropriate solution is selected, cooperation between various professionals and stakeholders is essential. As with all preservation and reference service relating to digital assets, work does not cease with the initial completion of a repository project.

Initial completion must be followed by attentive stewardship of the repository. ASC's commitment to its users requires continued development including adding content, continuing adherence to evolving best practices, and vigilance regarding hardware and software integrity. Archivists and special collections librarians have a duty to both preserve the material in their care and serve users by alertness to future opportunities and threats and so realize the wisdom of Proverbs 4:25: "Let your eyes look forward" (CSB).

References

Duke Libraries. 2020. "rdr." Last modified September 1, 2020. *https://gitlab.oit.duke.edu/ddr/rdr.* Captured at *https://perma.cc/QBV6-9RC5.*

DuraSpace. n.d.a "About Fedora." Accessed August 27, 2020. *https://duraspace.org/fedora/about/.* Captured at *https://perma.cc/77EH-RMLY.*

———. n.d.b "Fedora and Digital Preservation." Accessed August 27, 2020. *https://duraspace.org/fedora/resources/publications/fedora-digital-preservation.* Captured at *https://perma.cc/X299-TDEZ.*

———. 2018. "Portland Common Data Model." Accessed October 8, 2020. *https://github.com/duraspace/pcdm/wiki.* Captured at *https://perma.cc/J9V4-EUDY.*

International Council on Archives. 2010. "Universal Declaration on Archives." Accessed August 31, 2020. *https://www.ica.org/sites/default/files/20190510_ica_declarationuniverselle_en_0.pdf.* Captured at *https://perma.cc/332Q-36UY.*

Islandora. 2020. "Islandora 8 Documentation." Accessed August 31, 2020. *https://github.com/Islandora/documentation.* Captured at *https://perma.cc/NG8H-EZGG.*

Knight Lab. Northwestern University. n.d. "Timeline." Accessed August 29, 2020. *https://timeline.knightlab.com.* Captured at *https://perma.cc/WS45-HALZ.*

Library at Southeastern. 2020. "About." Accessed October 8, 2020. *https://library.sebts.edu/About.* Captured at *https://perma.cc/F5KW-WMN8.*

———. n.d. "Archives and Special Collections at Southeastern." Accessed August 27, 2020. *https://library.sebts.edu/Archives.* Captured at *perma.cc/H3UD-QFCK.*

Ranade, Sonia. 2018. "Access Technologies for the Disruptive Digital Archive." In *Archival Futures,* edited by Caroline Brown, 79–97. London: Facet Publishing.

Roe, Kathleen D. 2019. *Advocacy and Awareness for Archivists.* Archival Fundamentals Series III 3. Chicago, IL: Society of American Archivists.

Samvera. n.d.a "Applications & Demos." Accessed August 31, 2020. *https://samvera.org/samvera-open-source-repository-framework/ applications-demos.* Captured at *https://perma.cc/N3WD-553K.*

———. 2018. "Architecting Repository Infrastructure with Collection Types, Admin Sets, and Collections." YouTube. Video, 1:48:02. *https://www.youtube.com/watch?v=7pHN1om6n6w.* Captured at *https://perma.cc/BH3M-43BJ.*

———. 2020. "ReadMe." Last modified August 26, 2020. *https://github. com/samvera/hyrax#getting-started.* Captured at *https://perma.cc/ N5DD-XD8N.*

———. n.d.b "Samvera Partners." Accessed August 31, 2020. *https:// samvera.org/samvera-partners.* Captured at *https://perma. cc/96E5-6XJQ.*

Southeastern Baptist Theological Seminary. n.d. "Main Webpage." Accessed October 8, 2020. *https://www.sebts.edu/about/default. aspx.* Captured at *https://perma.cc/GQ88-FMVW.*

Collection Development & the Future of Special Collections

CHAPTER 8

Shipping Container Librarianship

Creating Comprehensive Research Collections in Theological Libraries

STEPHEN D. CROCCO

This chapter tells the story of two comprehensive research collections created several decades ago by library staff at Princeton Theological Seminary: one devoted to the Swiss theologian Karl Barth (1886–1968) and one to the Dutch pastor, theologian, journalist, educator, and politician Abraham Kuyper (1837–1920). At this writing, the Center for Barth Studies, which houses the Barth collection, is thriving. The Abraham Kuyper Institute of Public Theology closed as an institute several years ago, but the massive collection acquired to support research in Kuyper studies and Neo-Calvinism remains in the Princeton Seminary library. Accounts of the origins of these two collections illustrate that comprehensive collecting inevitably has backstories. The narratives presented here provide opportunities to consider "lessons learned" and function as an "after-action report" of what worked and what did not and may be useful for libraries considering comprehensive collecting. As such, the stories reveal some of the goals, methods, and pitfalls awaiting those who take this path.

There are three questions that beg to be answered at the outset. What are comprehensive research collections? Why is there a chapter about them in a volume devoted to special collections? Why would any library want to create a comprehensive research collection in the first place? To answer the first and third questions, I turn to "collecting levels" as described by the Library of Congress ("Collecting Levels" n.d.). These levels are offered to libraries as tools to describe existing collections as well as goals to guide ambitions in collecting. Inevitably, these collecting levels are aspirational and subjective. The levels go from zero to five, from 0—"Out-of-Scope," meaning the library does not collect in an area, to level 5—"Comprehensive Level," meaning that the library collects everything in an area. In between, are levels 1—"Minimal Level," 2—"Basic Information Level," 3—"Instructional Support Level," and 4—"Research Level." University libraries typically acquire materials at level 4 in areas for which they have some responsibility. Most theological libraries collect materials at levels 3 and 4, which (in comparison to university libraries collecting at levels 3 and 4) suggests the aspirational or relative character of the levels. When librarians talk about their collections being at a "research level" and needing an appropriate level of funding, they often have these levels in mind. Almost by definition, level-5 collections are few and far between, even at major university libraries. They imply commitments to long-term—even perpetual—spending for materials and curatorial support, which few libraries are willing or able to make. Early in my time at Yale, I recall a conversation with a collection development librarian about the Barth and Kuyper collections. He could not grasp that those collecting areas were set up without substantial and permanent endowments to fund acquisitions and staff. He had a good point.

Why is a chapter on comprehensive collecting included in a book on special collections, when "special collections" materials normally include manuscripts, rare and antiquarian books and pamphlets, photographs, and realia, all used by patrons under the supervision of library staff? The Library of Congress's ("Collecting Levels" n.d.) full description provides the rationale. A comprehensive collection is one

Preserving the Past & Engaging the Future

which, so far as is reasonably possible, includes all significant works of recorded knowledge (publications, manuscripts, and other forms), in all applicable languages, for a necessarily defined and limited field. This level of collecting intensity is one that maintains a 'special collection.' The aim, if not achievement, is exhaustiveness. Older material is retained for historical research. In law collections, this includes manuscripts, dissertations, and material on non-legal aspects.

The explicit reference to manuscript material and the inference that curators would need to acquire it and patrons would need to be supervised in its use, hints at the "special" character of comprehensive collecting. After word got out that Princeton was collecting Barth and Kuyper, opportunities quickly surfaced to acquire manuscripts, photographs, annotated books, and ephemera, which immediately thrust its curator into issues normally associated with special collections.

What sorts of materials lend themselves to comprehensive collecting? Consider the following categories, from the bottom to the top, most general to most particular.

Karl Barth	Abraham Kuyper
Confessing Church	Anti-Revolutionary Party
Swiss Neo-Orthodoxy	Dutch Neo-Calvinism
Modern Swiss Protestantism	Modern Dutch Protestantism
Swiss Protestantism	Dutch Protestantism
Swiss Christianity	Dutch Christianity

For all intents and purposes, it may be impossible for a library to collect any of these categories at the comprehensive level, except the top one in each column. Even collecting an individual at a comprehensive level has its challenges, but it is at least within the grasp of a library. Aspiring to collect anything more general than an individual, an organization, or an institution is possible, but doing so runs the risk of missing the weightiness and demands of comprehensive collecting. In other words, the more general the subject, the more aspirational comprehensive collecting becomes. With Barth and Kuyper collecting up and running, Princeton also considered creating comprehensive collections to support two other interests: Korean Presbyterianism and American Presbyterianism. While the library had strong holdings in both areas and patron groups interested in them, there was no way to put borders around these areas that would allow for even aspirational comprehensive collecting. They both failed the test of being a "necessarily defined and limited field."

More basic than a budget for materials and a curator, comprehensive collecting requires a worthy subject, a desire to promote it, and an iron determination to will it into existence. Why collect anything comprehensively? Someone needs to have decided that the subject is important and therefore worth the cost and the effort. The Hong Kierkegaard Library at St. Olaf College, the H. Henry Meeter Center for Calvin Studies at Calvin University, the Jonathan Edwards Center at Yale University, and the Marion E. Wade Center at Wheaton College, which collects C. S. Lewis and six other authors from the United Kingdom often called the Inklings, all started with an idea and found the funding and support for it.[1] Today, the collections at St. Olaf, Calvin, Yale, and Wheaton all aspire to some level of comprehensive collecting.[2] As these ideas settled into their institutions and comprehensive collecting began to take shape (often around a gift of money and/or materials), someone had to will these collections into existence. Doing so is no small feat. The status or significance of the subject contributes to the complexity and the perceived value of the task. Both Barth and Kuyper were prolific authors, generated a massive secondary literature, and have deep and wide legacies to the present day, all of which contribute to the complexity of the task and the value of their collections. Conversely, a smaller output and less influence make comprehensive collecting easier, but perhaps less significant too in terms of the breadth of interest. For example, comprehensively collecting works by and about Eduard Thurneysen (1888–1974) or Herman Dooyeweerd (1894–1977)—two important figures in Swiss Neo-Orthodoxy and Dutch Neo-Calvinism, respectively—would be much more manageable than collecting Barth or Kuyper, simply because they did not generate the same amount of literature, and their legacies are not as extensive. However, they do have legacies. Thurneysen remains important for those seeking to think theologically about pastoral care, and Dooyeweerd is significant for those seeking to articulate a distinctly Christian philosophy. There are plenty of figures who lack the status of Barth and Kuyper yet are deemed worthy of attention by scholars. For any comprehensive collecting, someone must be passionate about the subject and have a vision for its usefulness in the modern world. It is difficult to imagine any institution aspiring to collect comprehensively without thinking the individual collected is worth the attention. Ideally a comprehensive collection should be a gift to scholars and students and should be a jewel in the crown of the institution that hosts it. The link between collecting and promoting raises the question of the amount of purchase the subject has or should have on the school and those who teach and study there. That question, in turn, raises questions about the authority or freedom of a library to create such collections.

Not surprisingly, there are institutions in Europe that have collections of Barth and Kuyper materials, often built around original archival collections. What comprehensive collecting at Princeton brought to archival collections in Basel and Amsterdam was a renewed conviction that the world would be a better place if materials by and about Barth and Kuyper were curated and promoted. It also brought an energy to create partnerships and, to varying degrees, to provide the funding to make materials available to wider audiences. In addition to collecting primary and secondary materials, Princeton held conferences, acquired background materials, preserved at-risk items, digitized materials, and translated texts. The result was to change the nature of Barth and Kuyper scholarship. To illustrate, this chapter now turns to brief accounts of the two Princeton collections to show how they were conceived and then willed into existence. By telling these stories—of Barth more than Kuyper—the chapter illustrates the kinds of histories and settings out of which comprehensive collecting can rise and fall. Good fortune and the human capacity for relationships across cultures and languages figure heavily into the accounts, as do human foibles and prejudices.

The Center for Barth Studies

By the time of Karl Barth's death in 1968, a plan was in place to edit and publish his extensive literary remains. That plan would move forward by the work of a *Nachlasskommission* (legacy commission) consisting of Barth's living children and his son-in-law Max Zellweger. Its goals were to make the works of Barth known and to encourage the study of his thought, to collect and preserve all writings by and about him, to publish a critical edition of his works, and to promote serious biblical and theological work through conferences and publications. Another provision of the plan was to create a *Karl Barth-Stiftung* (foundation) to raise funds to help with the publication of his posthumous works, support research, and arrange conferences. In 1971, that plan led to the transformation of Barth's house at Bruderholzallee 26 into the Karl Barth-Archiv, keeping Barth's and Charlotte van Kirschbaum's studies basically intact. The house also contained over one hundred thousand documents and Barth's personal library of approximately ten thousand volumes. His home would also serve as the residence for an archivist, whose work was essentially that of the editor of the editors of the Karl Barth *Gesamtausgabe*. Without question, the driving force behind these activities was Barth's oldest son, Markus (1915–94). From 1940 to 1953, he was a pastor of a Reformed church in Bubendorf, a town southeast of Basel, during which time he received a doctorate in New Testament from the University of Göttingen. Markus left Switzerland in 1953 to accept a teaching position at Dubuque Theological Seminary in Iowa. Two years later, he moved to the University of Chicago, and, in 1963, he took a position at Pittsburgh Theological Seminary, where he remained until 1972. Karl Barth died in late 1968, putting his son's plans into effect. Markus was aware of the steady stream of Americans who studied with his father and hoped their interest would lead to financial support for the *Karl Barth Gesamtausgabe*. He also believed his father's theology could make important contributions to the American theological and social situation. To help institutionalize these goals, Markus envisioned a Karl Barth society in North America, a substantial collection of publications by and about his father, and an ecumenical center for theological study located at Pittsburgh Seminary. His plans quickly hit roadblocks; chief among them was Pittsburgh's lack of interest in supporting these projects financially. Markus was a man on a mission and wasted little time taking the plans to his friend and colleague David Demson at the University of Toronto. The result was the same. At Toronto, like Pittsburgh, there were no hearty welcomes or blank checks. While the idea of an ecumenical theological center had some appeal, there was little interest in tying it closely to Karl Barth, whose influence in North America had supposedly peaked and was on the wane. Discouraged, Markus gladly accepted an offer from the University of Basel and returned to Switzerland in May of 1972, taking the extensive correspondence related to these matters with him. The main thing to come of his American efforts was the creation of the Karl Barth Society of North America, which flourished primarily in its Midwest chapter (KBSNA).

In 1983, I joined the faculty at Elmhurst College in the western suburbs of Chicago. Ronald Goetz, a theologian at Elmhurst, was an active member of the KBSNA and friend of David Demson.[3] Given its central location in the Midwest, Elmhurst College was the scene of many KBSNA Midwest chapter meetings. After four enjoyable years at Elmhurst, I followed a deep urge to give up full-time teaching and pursue a career in theological librarianship, replacing Dikran Y. Hadidian as the library director at Pittsburgh Theological Seminary. While getting the tour of the library from Hadidian, we stopped and admired the desk of Karl Barth, which Markus arranged to give to the school in 1962 for its new library building (Busch 1975, 475).[4] A New Testament scholar and close friend of Markus Barth, Hadidian told me the story of Markus's efforts to start a Karl Barth center at Pittsburgh Seminary fifteen years earlier and that, like Markus, he too had been dismayed by the school's lack of interest. There was no collection of Markus Barth's papers in the Pittsburgh archives, so my knowledge of the plan came almost entirely from Hadidian. That was the end of story, except that I started a small collection of Barth's writings at his desk and set out a few artifacts that belonged to Barth—a pen, a pair of glasses, and a pipe—also gifts of Markus— in a nearby display case. A few years later, I encountered Thomas F. Torrance, who was on campus for a lecture, staring at Barth's desk. I remember him shaking his head with a sense of awe at Barth's achievement. Maybe it was time to revisit Markus Barth's idea for a collection of materials by and about his father.

There was not much interest in Barth at Pittsburgh Seminary in those days, and so the idea of a Barth research collection there made little sense... but perhaps somewhere. To that end, I suggested to the Executive Committee of the KBSNA that it put out an RFP to see if a theological institution would step up to host a center for Barth studies. Instead, they named me to the executive committee and tasked me to issue an RFP. News of this process was published in the Fall 1995 *Karl Barth Study Newsletter* under the heading "A Center for Barth Studies?" A year later, two schools had submitted RFPs: Yale Divinity School and Princeton Theological Seminary. Both schools could make a claim for the importance of Barth to the theological ethos of their schools, but Princeton was chosen by the KBSNA because it committed two spacious rooms in the new Henry Luce III Library and a salary for a director.[5] Midway through the executive committee's work, Princeton Seminary approached me about becoming its library director, and I recused myself from the KBSNA's final deliberations. On September 8, 1997, about three months after I began at Princeton, President Thomas Gillespie announced the formation of the Center for Barth Studies (CBS) with well-known Barth scholar George Hunsinger as its first director.[6] Bruce L. McCormack, a systematic theologian at Princeton, also brought much to the fledgling center. His 1995 book, *Karl Barth's Critically Realistic Dialectical Theology: Its Genesis and Development, 1909–1936,* established him as a first-rate Barth scholar. McCormack completed the research for his book at the Karl Barth-Archiv, under the supervision of archivist Hinrich Stoevestandt. In Basel, McCormack became friends with Markus Barth and familiar with the Karl Barth *Nachlasskommission* and *Stiftung.* More than anyone, McCormack had his eye on ways the CBS at Princeton might support the publication of the *Karl Barth Gesamtausgabe.* It was also a boon to the CBS that McCormack had remained friends with Niklaus Peter, a ThM student at Princeton Theological Seminary a decade earlier, who was the husband of Verena (Vreni) Barth, the daughter of Hans Jacob Barth and Renate Ninck, and a granddaughter of Karl Barth. From 2000–04, Peter was head of Theologischer Verlag Zürich (TVZ), publisher of *Die Kirchliche Dogmatik* and the *Karl Barth Gesamtausgabe.* These relationships opened doors, made connections, and provided energy to the developing partnership between Basel and Princeton.7

During the CBS's early months, another Princeton faculty member—a Barth scholar, at that—questioned what right I had, as the school's librarian, to set up an academic center—a decision he thought should be left to the faculty. Telling him that I had the rank of professor did not satisfy him, though, when he started seeing the results, he became an active participant and supporter of the CBS. A few Princeton faculty members complained because Barth was too conservative for their liking, though there was a general sense that a CBS made sense at Princeton Seminary, given the school's role as a major broker of Barth's thought to the English-speaking world. More than once, I heard from faculty members that, had they known there was money and space in the library for a research center, they would have proposed one of their own. I invited them all to conversations about their ideas, but no one made a proposal. The relationship between the subject of a comprehensive collection and faculty opinion is an important issue that will be considered again in the discussion of the Kuyper Institute.

The CBS opened its doors with two spacious but empty bookshelf-lined rooms: several desks with computers and file cabinets in one room and a seminar room set up in the other. Hunsinger offered Barth reading groups for Princeton students and pastors in the area. He also took the lead in establishing annual conferences, beginning in June 1999 with "For the Sake of the World: Karl Barth and the Future of Ecclesial Theology"—a conference that attracted over three hundred people. Both activities suggested that Barth's thought was useful and important in the United States. The CBS was eager to start acquiring publications by and about Barth and did so in close cooperation with the collection development librarian because Princeton was already acquiring Barth at a level 4—research level. Working out this division was one of the early issues facing the CBS, since there was only so much duplication the library could afford. A Barth bibliography by Hans Markus Wildi gave Princeton a good start collecting literature, especially since Wildi managed to track down many obscure sources (Wildi 1984).[8]

Before long, it was time for a trip to Switzerland. First stop was the headquarters of Theologischer Verlag Zürich. At TVZ, we were politely received, as we shared a vision for digitizing Barth's *Kirchliche Dogmatik* and *Church Dogmatics*. However, without funds in hand, there were no next steps. From Zurich, we went to Basel, where we met the new archivist, Hans-Anton Drewes—a DTheol from Tübingen and a student of Eberhard Jüngel. Drewes was far less formal than his esteemed predecessor was rumored to be. Sitting in Barth's study, drinking tea, we encountered someone who grasped our vision and went out of his way to support us, including introducing us to Barth's relatives in the Basel area. These encounters set up the CBS's first big break. With Drewes's encouragement, we were contacted by the children of Markus Barth. With the passing of their parents, they were interested in finding a home for their father's extensive library and papers. Surprisingly, and to the great benefit of the CBS, Drewes directed the family to Princeton, even though he knew the papers contained much material directly relevant to the work of the Karl Barth-Archiv, e.g., many letters between father and son. Perhaps even then Drewes realized that Princeton and Basel would form a partnership that made the ownership of such materials ultimately irrelevant for purposes of research and publication. I suspect he could afford to be prescient on this issue, because he was the single greatest force in Switzerland making it happen.[9] Before long, a large shipping container arrived in Princeton with thousands of books, including Markus's *Weimar Luther*.[10] Of greater interest were many boxes of Markus's correspondence, going back to his youth—including records of his efforts to establish a Barth center in North America. Correspondents included prominent scholars, church leaders, and family members (including his father).[11] Of special interest were primary source materials related to the Confessing Church movement and student notes of his father's classes, including provisional publications of *Die Kirchliche Dogmatik*. If there was one treasure in the collection—and there were many!—it was a copy of a first edition of Barth's *Römerbrief* with an inscription to his wife Nelly, translated: "My love, wife, and helper, Nelly. Christmas 1918." The Markus Barth family was not interested in payment for these materials; instead, they asked Princeton to make a gift for Roma relief. By acquiring this collection, with its correspondence, manuscripts, photographs, rare materials, and ephemera, the "special" character of the CBS collection was undeniable.

The CBS's second big break came in November 2000 with a grant from the Lilly Endowment. Princeton's appeal to Barth's great influence in the United States persuaded Lilly to look favorably at a proposal to preserve Barth's legacy and to present it in new formats. The $1.1 million grant was designed to support the digitization of Barth's published works, including the *Church Dogmatics* and *Die Kirchliche Dogmatik*. It also provided for the manuscript materials in the Archiv to be organized, microfilmed, and digitized. Until that time, there were no copies of those one hundred thousand pages in other locations.[12] The Lilly grant supplied the funds for filming interviews of a dwindling number of Barth's personal acquaintances, including his daughter-in-law Renate Ninck Barth and Herta Baier, Barth's housekeeper from 1934–37. Also included in the filming project were interviews with Barth scholars and historians in the United States and Europe. The partnership between Basel and Princeton was celebrated in April 2002 with the signing of a formal agreement in the Bischofshof in Basel, speeches by dignitaries, and a banquet. By intention, the agreement allowed a great deal of Barth research to shift from Basel to Princeton, although the Archiv retained the right to grant permission for access to certain manuscripts, a number that dwindled with time. While there were still reasons for Barth students and scholars to visit the Archiv—to consult with the archivist, to do studies that required the investigation of actual manuscripts, examine Barth's personal library, or have a tour, for example—the archivist was able to direct researchers with routine requests to Princeton, which allowed him to focus on editing volumes of the *Karl Barth Gesamtausgabe*. This was Princeton's indirect contribution to financially supporting the publication of Barth's works. Along the way, it became the CBS's informal mission to be a "one stop" location for Barth scholars anywhere in the world. A project that Princeton was not able to fund was to deacidify and digitize Karl Barth's personal library. That work still needs to be done. A catalog of Barth's library is available through the University of Basel Library.[13] Another unfinished project was to provide a conceptual framework around the Markus Barth collection and a collection received a few years later—the papers and library of Thomas F. Torrance. Both men were heavily influenced by Karl Barth, and some thought was given to a secondary layer of comprehensive collecting that acquired the writings of prominent scholars deeply influenced by Karl Barth. The next thinker on my radar screen was the French Christian thinker Jacques Ellul, who readily acknowledged his significant debts to Karl Barth.

The story of the CBS frequently turns to McCormack, who had become acquainted with Gerritt Neven of the Theological Universiteit Kampen in the Netherlands, through their collaboration on the *Zeitschrift für dialektische Theologie*. McCormack and Neven proposed holding biennial meetings between Princeton and Kampen, which began in 1999.[14] Neven and his research assistant Hans van Loon sketched out plans for a freely accessible online bibliography of the works of Barth and invited Princeton to join. For its part, Princeton secured the rights to publish the Wildi bibliography in digital form. In 2004, a call went out to Barth scholars in designated countries and languages to funnel bibliographic references for inclusion in the online bibliography. This is a good place to mention that, in developing various programs, we soon discovered other centers related to Barth (and Kuyper) around the world. All of them were eager to cooperate. The *CBS website* provides an overview of its history and current activities.

During these years, Clifford B. Anderson moved from student worker and doctoral student to curator of Reformed research collections to head of special collections.[15] With a dissertation on Barth's view of science, facility with the German and Dutch languages, and computer programming skills, Anderson was exactly the kind of person Princeton needed to take its efforts to the next level. With news of the Lilly grant, Barth's publishers—TVZ and T & T Clark—suddenly had reason to pay attention, and they did. Princeton soon had a digitized text of *Die Kirchliche Dogmatik* and the *Church Dogmatics* as well as translations of the hundreds of Greek and Latin phrases in those volumes. Plans were also in place to identify and re-translate troublesome English passages and to identify individuals, cultural references, and literary allusions for English readers. Publisher William B. Eerdmans allowed Princeton to digitize some of its Barth titles to add to the mix.[16]

Princeton had high hopes for a long-term partnership with T & T Clark and Continuum, its parent company at the time (now Bloomsbury Publishing). We envisioned that Princeton's substantial investment in digital editions of Barth's works would encourage Continuum to reciprocate by incorporating these improvements in a new edition of the *Church Dogmatics*. A team of Princeton scholars managed to include Greek and Latin translations and make other improvements in the first three volumes of Continuum's forty-volume student edition of the *Church Dogmatics*—the equivalent of volume 1/1 in the regular edition. What happened? Sensing a market, it appears that Continuum was eager to publish a student edition, even though the rest of the volumes used the same text as the original T & T Clark edition. Without adequate funding, Princeton's efforts to improve the remainder of the texts ran out of steam. Princeton retained copyright to the electronic edition of the *Church Dogmatics* and was free to make improvements but was greatly restricted in providing access to it. On a brighter side, an annual seminar for young translators led to three volumes of the *Karl Barth Gesamtausgabe, Gespräche* published as *Barth in Conversation* (Busch 2017; 2018; 2019). A lesson to be learned here is the complexity and difficulty of using funds raised by a center to promote publication of materials with strict copyright restrictions and publishers eager to monetize them.

The Kuyper Institute and Collection

The story of the Kuyper Collection at Princeton is more quickly told, because it lacks a pre-history. Also, Princeton collected and promoted Kuyper in many of the same ways it collected and promoted Barth, and so there is no need to repeat them here. The few differences are worth mentioning and will be the focus of this section. What was the origin of this interest in collecting Kuyper? In the nineteenth and early twentieth centuries, Princeton Seminary had strong connections to Dutch theological thought, which was noted for its robustness and orthodoxy. Kuyper delivered his famous *Lectures on Calvinism* at Princeton Seminary in 1898. Geerhardus Vos and Cornelius van Til were Princeton faculty members in the late nineteenth and early twentieth centuries, respectively. However, by the 1990s, there were few traces of Kuyperian theological thought to be found at Princeton Seminary.[17] Around 1995, Rimmer de Vries, an immigrant from the Netherlands who served as chief economist at J. P. Morgan, approached Princeton Seminary about a gift to endow a lecture series that came to be known as the Abraham Kuyper Prize for Excellence in Reformed Theology and Public Life. De Vries had a passion for the Reformed faith in its Dutch expressions and, like Kuyper, an interest in that faith as it expressed itself in all areas of life, not just theology and ministry. He sought a venue that would promote Kuyper in mainstream American intellectual life, and so he approached Princeton Seminary rather than one of the historically Dutch institutions about setting up an annual lecture and a generous prize. The prize was first awarded to Dutch historian George Puchinger in 1996.[18]

George Harinck, an historian at the Documentation Center at the Vrije Universiteit (Free University) Amsterdam, was a frequent visitor to Princeton in those years.[19] As a one-time student of Puchinger, Harinck was aware of the Center for Barth Studies. He started wondering out loud—with Princeton professor of ethics Max Stackhouse—whether there was room at Princeton for a similar center devoted to the thought of Kuyper. Clifford Anderson and I were soon included in the conversation. Anderson had traveled in the Netherlands and had a good grasp of the Dutch language and Neo-Calvinist thought. In my graduate school days, I had exposure to Neo-Calvinism through the Institute of Christian Studies in Toronto and the writings of the contemporary Dutch theologian G. C. Berkouwer (1903–96). I was also aware that Berkouwer's book, *The Triumph of Grace in the Theology of Karl Barth*, was deeply admired by Barth (Barth 1958, xii).[20] We began to imagine some interesting connections between the CBS and a possible center for Kuyper studies. Although no one on the faculty was particularly interested in Kuyper or Neo-Calvinism, we envisioned a center with a collection and similar activities and programs as the CBS, but we had to do so without the help of a $1.1 million Lilly Endowment grant.

At Harinck's suggestion, I traveled to the Netherlands to talk to Puchinger about his personal library. Puchinger, who had just moved to a retirement home, said to me, "I hear you want to start a Kuyper Center. Then you need a library. I have a library." I soon discovered that he was a bachelor married to his books, which filled nearly every room in his spacious house in The Hague. Princeton Trustee Henry Luce III, a member of the library committee of the board, funded the purchase. He was glad to see that the Princeton librarian was traveling to Europe to buy books. Puchinger had no family, and his house was being emptied, and so whatever Princeton did not want was going to be sold. Since there was still room in the large shipping container after it was packed with books, we added a massive two-sided antique desk and chair, decorative items, and a portrait of Puchinger to give an historical look to the Kuyper Institute reading room we envisioned. One thing led to another and soon approximately thirty thousand volumes of European—but mostly Dutch—history, theology, philosophy, and literature were on their way to Princeton. Puchinger's library was not a comprehensive collection of Kuyper. What it did was to get Princeton a significant collection of Kuyper in a single action and a substantial collection of background materials related to the study of Kuyper and European theology, too. Puchinger was perhaps best known for a series of interviews he conducted, including one with Barth that was done on April 15, 1965 and eventually published in English in *Barth in Conversation: Volume 3, 1964–1968*.

There are two points to make here. The first is that it is much easier to build on a collector's work than to start from scratch. Comprehensive collecting can get a huge boost by discovering individuals willing to part with their collections.[21] The second point is that, when the word gets out that an institution is in the market for materials, people step up. Many collectors reach a point in their lives when finding a home for their collections becomes a nagging concern, eventually as important as their collections themselves. Two other Kuyper collectors approached us during this period, and Princeton acquired both sets. Puchinger's library contained many Kuyper materials, but nothing compared to the collection gradually and obsessively acquired by Tjitse Kuipers, a pastor in the Dutch Reformed Church. At the front of Kuipers's sixteenth-century house, overlooking a canal in the city of Kampen, was the Kuyper Room—a small museum and antiquarian book library. The second floor library was dwarfed by the massive attic that was full of materials related to Kuyper's ecclesiastical and political contemporaries—friends and foes. Kuipers also collected different editions and even different printings of books and pamphlets, as well as duplicates. The best copies were kept in the Kuyper Room and the rest were in the attic. The Kuipers collection came with many things commonly associated with special collections: manuscripts, photographs, presentation copies, and ephemera such as busts, coin banks used for fundraising, celebratory cigar bands, and commemorative stamps. Kuipers's materials filled the third shipping container sent to Princeton Seminary during these years.[22]

Princeton's collection of Kuyper materials soon became the foundation for Brill's *Abraham Kuyper: An Annotated Bibliography 1857–2010* (Kuipers 2011). Nearly three hundred digital editions of Kuyper's books and pamphlets can still be found in Princeton Theological Seminary's *Theological Commons*. Princeton entered a partnership with the Vrije Universiteit Amsterdam to digitize Kuyper's extensive correspondence and secondary Kuyper literature. Unlike the situation with Barth, there were few copyright issues with Kuyper's materials. Princeton had plans to sponsor translations of Kuyper's works, but that work was picked up by the Acton Institute and published by the Lexham Press. Bravo!

What happened to the Abraham Kuyper Institute for Public Theology at Princeton Theological Seminary? It is a tale of woe that points to some of the pitfalls associated with comprehensive collections and the efforts to promote them. It was soon obvious that, while the idea of a Kuyper Institute had some support in the faculty, that support was directed more to public theology generally than anything to do with Kuyper or Neo-Calvinism. A center in the spirit of Kuyper's broad interests and accomplishments was one thing. A center devoted to promoting Kuyper's thought and Neo-Calvinism generally was another. Recall that Barth had strong support among some of the Princeton faculty. Kuyper had little or no support among faculty members; in fact, few people had heard of him. One vocal faculty member could not get past the fact that, long ago, some Afrikaner theologians in South Africa appealed to Kuyper's notion of *verzuiling* (pillarization) to justify apartheid.[23] While De Vries was pleased by the status of Kuyper Prize winners, the research collection, and the conferences sponsored by the Kuyper Institute, he regretted that Kuyperian thought played no role in the curriculum of the school. To address that situation, De Vries endowed a chair in Reformed theology and public life as a new faculty position. Realizing that he could not dictate a faculty appointment, he expected Princeton to hire a faculty member who could or would occasionally teach Kuyper and Neo-Calvinism, whether that person was a Neo-Calvinist or not. It is not difficult to see where this led. Some faculty members protested, complaining that donors were dictating the curriculum, encroaching on faculty turf. The school struggled to make an acceptable appointment until Dirk Smit was hired in 2017. Smit, a South African from Stellenbosch University, was trained in the Netherlands and worked comfortably in Neo-Calvinist and Barthian traditions. That same year, protests about an announced Kuyper Prize winner plunged the

Kuyper Institute into controversy from which it never recovered. To make a long story short, the Kuyper Institute closed.[24] Although the large collection gathered to support it remains in the library's special collections, there are few traces of Kuyper at Princeton Seminary today.

The closure of the Kuyper Institute points to what seems to be the inevitable political dimension of comprehensive collecting. Do the long-term commitments to materials and staff make comprehensive collecting feasible? It seems an open question, until we try to imagine the worlds of Calvin, Edwards, Kierkegaard, Inklings, and Barth scholarship without the centers and collections devoted to them. If these collections were all adequately endowed to exist in perpetuity, the winds of change could be mostly ignored. Short of that, perhaps there is a need for an informal association of comprehensive research collections that would monitor the political and financial climates at such centers and, if necessary, attempt to move centers from institutions no longer wanting them to those that do. This might seem far-fetched, but it would be far better than watching a research collection become stagnant due to shutting off funds, or worse, watching it be broken up and sold. When contemplating comprehensive collecting, administrative buy-in seems to be essential, particularly given the inevitable fact of leadership turnover. Faculty support is desirable too, though the required extent is not clear, and it is also the case that faculty turnover is an issue. Do faculty members hold veto power over the origins and growth of comprehensive collections? How many faculty members does it take for a comprehensive collection/center to be born and live—or die? For example, it may be that no one at Yale Divinity School complains about the Jonathan Edwards Center because it is accepted that this is something Yale simply "must" do, since Edwards is one of their own and his papers are there. Plus, for now, the Edwards Center has its own funding. Moreover, it is doubtful that any faculty members see Edwards as a threat to their politics.[25] Recall the Princeton faculty member who questioned my "right" to set up a Center for Barth Studies without faculty buy-in. Of course, he had a point, but deciding how to gauge faculty buy-in and then taking it into account could have led to there being no CBS at Princeton.

In closing, I want to suggest that librarians should have some say about these matters, regardless of faculty opinions. Otherwise, librarians are only servants of the faculty and the curriculum and not also educators, caretakers, and curators of important ideas and figures. In the cases of Calvin, Edwards, Kierkegaard, Barth, the Inklings, and even Kuyper, librarians and archivists stepped up as caretakers of those who shaped significant parts of the Western theological tradition in ways and to degrees that no one else did. Pitfalls notwithstanding, comprehensive collections make genuine and substantial contributions that will cause generations of scholars and students to rise up and call the libraries and schools that sponsor them blessed.

References

Barth, Karl. 1958. *Church Dogmatics,* IV/2. Edinburgh: T & T Clark.

―――, ed. 2017. *Barth in Conversation: Volume 1, 1969–1962,* dited by Eberhard Busch. Westminster/John Knox Press.

―――, ed. 2018. *Barth in Conversation: Volume 2, 1963,* dited by Eberhard Busch. Westminster/John Knox Press.

―――, ed. 2019. *Barth in Conversation: Volume 3, 1964–1968,* dited by Eberhard Busch. Westminster/John Knox Press.

Busch, Eberhard. 1975. *Karl Barth: His Life from Letters and Autobiographical Texts.* Philadelphia: Fortress Press.

"A Center for Barth Studies?" 1995. *Karl Barth Society Newsletter,* no. 13 (Fall): 1–2.

Kuipers, Tjitse, ed. 2011. *Abraham Kuyper: An Annotated Bibliography 1857–2010.* Translated by Clifford B. Anderson. Leiden: Brill.

Library of Congress. n.d. "Collecting Levels." *https://www.loc.gov/ acq/devpol/cpc.html.* Accessed February 10, 2021.

Wildi, Hans Markus. 1984. *Bibliographie Karl Barth.* Zurich: Theologischer Verlag Zürich.

Notes

1   I am not suggesting that these collections aspire to be comprehensive as per Library of Congress guidelines or, if they are, that they are comprehensive in the same ways. There is no checklist of what it means. For that reason, most comprehensive collecting is subjective and aspirational. After some deliberation, I decided to include the Jonathan Edwards Center at Yale. Like other centers, it sponsors conferences and publications as well as maintains associations with Edwards centers around the world. However, most of its work transcribing and publishing Edwards is with images of his manuscripts on deposit in the Beinecke Rare Book and Manuscript Library. Moreover, it does not actively collect published literature by and about Edwards.

2   Consider the following mission statements:

> The H. Henry Meeter Center for Calvin Studies is a research center specializing in John Calvin, Calvinism, the Reformation, and Early Modern Studies. Since opening in 1982, our extensive book, rare book, article, and microform collections has attracted scholars from all over the world. The Meeter Center sponsors lectures, hosts seminars sponsored by the National Endowment for the Humanities, awards scholarships to faculty, pastors, graduate students and high school seniors, offers occasional courses on Early Modern French paleography and hosts events for the Friends of the Meeter Center and the local community throughout the year (*https://calvin.edu/centers-institutes/meeter-center/about*, accessed December 21, 2020).

> The Hong Kierkegaard Library (HKL) serves as the world's official repository for books by Søren Kierkegaard as well as those influencing and influenced by his authorship. The HKL offers programs and courses aimed at stimulating and nurturing the study of Kierkegaard among St. Olaf students and faculty, as well as domestic and international scholars. The HKL is both a Special Collection and a Center for Research and Publication and as such, it fosters an intellectual community highly conducive to reflection on faith and values. (*https://wp.stolaf.edu/kierkegaard*, accessed December 21, 2020).

> The Marion E. Wade Center promotes cultural engagement and spiritual formation by offering a collection of resources available nowhere

else in the world. We emphasize the ongoing relevance of seven British Christian authors who provide a distinctive blend of intellect, imagination, and faith: C. S. Lewis, J. R. R. Tolkien, Dorothy L. Sayers, George MacDonald, G. K. Chesterton, Owen Barfield, and Charles Williams. (*https://www.wheaton.edu/academics/academic-centers/wa-decenter*, accessed December 21, 2020)

The mission of the Jonathan Edwards Center is to support inquiry into the life, writings, and legacy of Jonathan Edwards by providing resources that encourage critical appraisal of the historical importance and contemporary relevance of America's premier theologian. The primary way that we do this is with the *Works of Jonathan Edwards Online*, a digital learning environment for research, education and publication, that presents all of Edwards's writings, along with helpful editorial materials that allow the reader to examine Edwards' thought in incredibly powerful, useful ways. (*http://edwards.yale.edu/about-us*, accessed December 21, 2020)

3   At KBSNA meetings at Elmhurst, Demson spoke occasionally of a small Barth research collection he had assembled in Toronto.

4   The desk given to Pittsburgh Seminary was Barth's father's desk and the desk at which he wrote the *Church Dogmatics*. In exchange, Barth received a "splendid new desk."

5   Yale Divinity School expressed serious interest in hosting the CBS. However, at that time, the Yale Divinity Quadrangle was in a state of disrepair to the degree that serious thought was given to razing it in favor of a compact Divinity School building—minus housing and a separate library—in downtown New Haven. In any case, Yale easily envisioned space in its renovated Divinity Quad but could not make the concrete commitment Princeton did.

6   Hunsinger, a well-known Barth scholar, was married to Deborah van Deusen Hunsinger, a member of the faculty at Princeton. His availability for the position secured instant credibility for the CBS. A few years later, Hunsinger left the CBS to join the faculty.

7   A great deal of the early business between the CBS and interested parties in Switzerland was conducted at a fine Italian restaurant in Basel on several memorable occasions.

8   Wildi's three volumes—works by Barth, about Barth, and an index—were prepared in cooperation with the Karl Barth-

Stiftung, the Aargau Canton library, and the Karl Barth-Archiv.

9   On more than one occasion, Drewes indicated he believed that, with the establishment and success of the CBS, the locus of Barth studies shifted from the German-speaking to the English-speaking world.

10   Princeton accepted these books with no conditions that they would be kept or kept together. Making such arrangements unnecessarily ties the hands of the library in terms of providing space and bibliographic control for items that are already in the collection. Heavily annotated books were a different matter, as were books that belonged to Markus's father. Karl Barth's books were returned to Basel.

11   At one point, the *Karl Barth Gesamtausgabe* planned for a volume of letters between Karl and Markus.

12   After the Barth manuscripts were digitized and microform copies were scattered for safekeeping, Hans-Anton Drewes expressed great relief that he could leave the Archiv for the weekend without fearing he left the oven on.

13   The path to accessing Barth's personal library in the OPAC at the University of Basel Library is a complicated one. Researchers interested in getting access are advised to contact the library directly at *https://ub-easyweb.ub.unibas.ch/en/contact*.

14   Barth scholars with Neo-Calvinistic roots and interests provided an unanticipated dimension to the CBS that readily spilled over into the Kuyper Center.

15   Anderson was the curator of Reformed research collections from 2002–06 and head of special collections from 2006–12.

16   The Digital Karl Barth Library was published by Alexander Street Press. See *https://dkbl.alexanderstreet.com*.

17   J. Wentzel van Huyssteen was an exception in that he knew of the Neo-Calvinist tradition. Van Huyssteen was a professor of theology and science at Princeton Seminary from 1992–2014. Born in South Africa, he was ordained in the Dutch Reformed Church in South Africa and received his PhD from the Vrije Universiteit Amsterdam.

18   Other Kuyper Prize winners included novelist Marilyn Robinson, philosopher Alvin Plantinga, former Atlanta Mayor Andrew Young, and Prime Minister of the Netherlands Jan Peter Balkenende.

19   Harinck was, until his recent retirement, the director of the

Archives and Documentation Center of the Reformed Churches, Kampen, and a staff member of the Historical Documentation Center for Dutch Protestantism at the Vrije Universiteit Amsterdam.

20 Here Barth praised G. C. Berkouwer's *De Triomf de Genade in de Theologie van Karl Barth* (Kampen: J. H. Kok, 1954).

21 The Kierkegaard Library at St. Olaf College was built on a major gift by Howard and Edna Hong, fixtures in the philosophy department at St. Olaf for four decades. "In the course of their translation efforts, the Hongs collected an enormous body of literature which includes writings from Kierkegaard's contemporaries and the thinkers who influenced him as well as interpretive studies about Kierkegaard. Their private collection was donated to St. Olaf College in 1976 as the foundation of the present Howard V. and Edna H. Kierkegaard Library" (*https://wp.stolaf.edu/kierkegaard/history*, accessed December 21, 2020).

22 At least one tractor-trailer's worth of materials came from within the United States. In 2000, Princeton acquired fifty file cabinets and hundreds of boxes associated with Presbyterian firebrand minister Carl McIntire.

23 "Pillarization" was Kuyper's proposal for how different worldviews might relate in the public sphere. He envisioned a society where Protestants, Catholics, socialists, etc. would be free to develop their own institutions—labor unions, political parties, schools, newspapers, etc.—without interference. As Kuyper envisioned them, these pillars were voluntary associations. However, in South Africa, some appealed to Kuyper's concept to justify apartheid—a bastardized version which resembled a separate but equal status that was not equal. See George Harinck, "Abraham Kuyper, South Africa, and Apartheid," remarks delivered at the opening ceremony of the Abraham Kuyper Institute for Public Theology at Princeton Theological Seminary, Nassau Inn, February 1, 2002. Published under the same title in the *Princeton Seminary Bulletin* 23, no. 2 (2002): 184–7, *https://commons.ptsem.edu/id/princetonseminar2322prin-dmd007*.

24 The Kuyper Prize and the conferences developed around it went to Calvin University. As for some of the digital projects Princeton helped to develop, they were picked up by institutions in the Netherlands. "The Archive of Abraham Kuyper (1837–1920)" belongs to the collection HDC [Historical Documentation Center]/Protestant heritage of the University

Library of the Vrije Universiteit Amsterdam (UBVU). This archive occupies a central position amid the source material concerning the history of Neo-Calvinism. It contains many works on the Anti-Revolutionary Party, the Free University, the *Doleantie*, the school struggle, Kuyper's ministry, his network, and his personal life; the archive includes nearly nine thousand letters. A decade ago, Princeton Theological Seminary (USA), together with the HDC, started digitizing the archive. Eventually, the NRI took over and completed the work that Princeton began. See *https://en.tukampen.nl/news/kuyper-and-bavinck-online* (accessed December 21, 2020).

25   Edwards owned a series of house slaves, so "cancelation" is a possibility.

CHAPTER 9

Engaging the Alumnus/a Donor

*A Case Study Based on Drew University's
R. S. Thomas Collection*

BRIAN SHETLER AND JESSE D. MANN

Donors are, in many ways, the life-blood of special collections. They provide financial support that pays for supplies and salaries; donate materials that fill our shelves; promote our institutions to potential patrons, researchers, and other donors; and become part of the active community that surrounds and supports our work. As E. Haven Hawley (2016, 9–10) has put it, "[t]he donors and communities with whom we engage embed themselves within how we do our work, generate new possible trajectories, and with us cocreate a system of authority, authenticity, and cultural persistence." There are, perhaps, no more "embedded" donors in our midst than alumni/ae. This population of supporters of academic institutions in general, and of academic libraries in particular, is among the most invested and informed of potential donor groups.

It is with this population that this chapter is concerned—a population that is sometimes overlooked, taken for granted, or both. While countless articles, books, and book chapters have been written about library donors in general, far too few focus on (or even mention) alumni/ae donors specifically. Within recent important publications in the field, such as Sidney Berger's *Rare Book and Special Collections* (2014) and the edited volume *Forging the Future of Special Collections* (2016, from which the Hawley quote above is taken), no significant mention is made of alumni/ae donors. A recent search of articles published in *RBM* (ACRL's journal dedicated to issues related to special collections) resulted in only three articles within the last decade that even mention alumni/ae in the context of donor relationships (search conducted by authors in December 2020 via *https://rbm. acrl.org/index.php/rbm/search/search*). This is not to say that alumni/ae donors are completely ignored by the profession or forgotten by special collections librarians. Rather, they are relatively absent from the literature and, therefore, worthy of discussion. With this in mind, the authors present the following case study as representative of our larger collaborations and partnerships with alumni/ae donors in the world of special collections.

Drew University's Special Collections and University Archives Department consists of more than 100,000 items, including manuscripts dating from the eleventh century and printed books dating from the fifteenth century. It also houses significant archival collections related to the history of the university and its founding as a Methodist seminary in 1867. While the majority of Drew's rare book and archival holdings have come through 150 years of institutional purchases, faculty contributions, and outside donations, recent years have brought a number of important collections donated by alumni of the undergraduate college, graduate school, and theological seminary. These include a collection of illustrated botanical books, an archival collection detailing the adventures of American college students on a goodwill tour of South America in the 1960s, and numerous donations to Drew's large collection of Methodist books and realia. This chapter, however, focuses on the donations of Rev. John Galen McEllhenney, who graduated from Drew's Theological Seminary with a BD in 1959.

During his more than sixty-year association with Drew, Rev. McEllhenney has been an active student, educator, patron, researcher, and donor. Most of his scholarly work centers around Methodist history in America, and his publications have become important reference works for students and scholars studying Methodism (see McEllhenney 1982, 1992, 1996; McEllhenney and Yrigoyen 1984; and McEllhenney, Yrigoyen and Rowe 2008). In addition to his contributions to and expertise in Methodist history, Rev. McEllhenney is also an avid collector of poetry. One of his major gifts to Drew's rare book collection was his significant holdings of material published by and about Robert Frost. The Frost Collection (see Drew University n.d., "Frost Collection") is a treasured part of the rare book holdings at Drew and has attracted scholarly interest both from within the university and worldwide. Along with his contributions to the Methodist collection, the Frost donation of more than sixty volumes would be enough to establish John McEllhenney as one of Drew's most important alumni donors. But the material that is at the heart of his connection to Drew is even more significant: the R. S. Thomas Collection of printed books, manuscripts, and archival documents.

Ronald Stuart Thomas (1913–2000) was a Welsh poet and clergyman whose literary work touched on a wide range of topics, including the Welsh countryside, questions of faith and religious uncertainty, and the struggles of everyday life (see Keith 1978; Morgan 2009; Perry 2019; and Poetry Foundation n.d.). Thomas was highly regarded by contemporaries and proved popular among readers in Wales and beyond, and he was nominated for the Nobel Prize in Literature in 1996. His poetry was wrapped up in—even warped by—an irascible personality that permeated his personal life as well as his poetry. This personality is fully on display within the material that Rev. McEllhenney has collected and donated over the years, beginning in 2006. In addition to more than 200 printed editions of Thomas's works, the collection also includes an important archive of hundreds of periodicals, essays, pamphlets, reviews, etc. that explore Thomas and his work. In addition, McEllhenney's own research into Thomas, his poetry, and his life represents a significant insider's perspective on the poet. This includes an important and illuminating personal correspondence between Thomas and McEllhenney that spanned the last dozen years of Thomas's life. This personal research served as the basis for McEllhenney's own published study of the poet, *A Masterwork of Doubting-Belief: R. S. Thomas and His Poetry* (2013). The collection, taken as a whole, is the largest dedicated solely to R. S. Thomas in the United States and is regularly expanded through purchases and donations by Rev. McEllhenney that continue to this day—more than 45 years since he first picked up a book of Thomas's poetry and started collecting his work (McEllhenney, email to authors, September 17, 2020).

This essay uses Rev. McEllhenney's Thomas Collection donation as a way to illuminate the importance of the alumnus/a donor, particularly the donor of gifts-in-kind (see Kuhn 2016, 11–12; Berger 2014, 176ff.; Leonhardt 2011, 207; and, more generally, Clotfelter 2001; Purcell 2015, 121–40). At the same time (and as the McEllhenney example illustrates), the alumnus/a donor is often also a collector. Therefore, we will reflect on alumni/ae as collectors as well as donors. We have chosen McEllhenney's donation of the Thomas Collection as our case study not only because this collection has obvious connections with the concerns of theological libraries but also because this collection has a uniqueness that makes it especially appealing to librarians and scholars. We will explore that uniqueness and its relevance to our decision to accept the donation. Also appealing, as we will discuss below, is the interdisciplinary nature of this collection. As a poet and clergyman, Thomas's work has potential appeal to students of literature and theology, but, as noted, his themes included Wales and Welsh history as well as the fate of country life in the face of growing mechanization (Keith 1978, 347). Consequently, the Thomas Collection presents opportunities for outreach to students and faculty in a variety of disciplines, some of which we will explore below. Finally, we will discuss how McEllhenney's donation has proven to be a gift that has kept on giving. Not only did that donation lead to significant subsequent donations by the same donor, it also resulted in additional donations by other donors who knew of our relationship with Rev. McEllhenney and his books. Rev. McEllhenney himself has remained involved with Drew's special collections around the Thomas Collection and, as described below, has engaged students using his donations as a departure point. Of course, such outreach to students (and faculty) serves to promote special collections more generally and to encourage students at all levels to become collectors themselves and perhaps even alumni/ae donors.

Alumni/ae Donors

The phenomenon of the alumnus/a donor is certainly not new. To cite but one rather early example: the Spanish theologian Juan de Segovia (d. 1458)—a former student and professor at the University of Salamanca—donated his substantial personal library to his alma mater in 1457 (Hernández Montes 1984). He did so for many of the same reasons that still motivate donors today: to express gratitude to his institution, to benefit less fortunate students, and to preserve his collection (Hernández Montes 1984, 78–9, 84; Allen 2012, 235–6). Casey and Lorenzen (2010, 517–20) provide other renowned examples of academic libraries, including Harvard's Widener Library, built or enhanced by donations of personal libraries, although not all their examples involve donations made by alumni/ae.

Nonetheless, some fund-raising literature suggests that academic libraries, unlike the colleges and universities they serve, "offer no degrees and thus have difficulty building a loyal base of support" (Clark 1986, 20; see also Wedgeworth 2000, 531; Casey and Lorenzen 2010, 521–2). According to this argument, libraries do not have alumni/ae in the same way that the schools themselves or other associated institutions, such as academic departments, sports teams, or Greek societies do. Not surprisingly, this literature focuses on financial gifts rather than on gifts-in-kind such as book donations to special collections. Even so, this literature does not tell the full story. Many alumni/ae do recognize the significant role played by libraries and librarians in their education, and they see the library as a worthy recipient of support both financial and material (Brittingham and Pezzullo 1990; Konzak and Teague 2009). Library usage statistics at Drew University indicate that Theological School students are the most active library users among all student populations, and some no doubt feel a special denominational fondness for Drew's special collections department, housed currently in the Methodist Archive. We know from his very first letter to R. S. Thomas that Rev. McEllhenney felt a keen allegiance to the institution where he had received his BD degree and that he intended to donate his Thomas collection to Drew, "his theological school," many years before he actually did so (McEllhenney – Thomas Correspondence, 16 July 1988). The presence of an inviting, appropriate, and well-maintained space only facilitated the decision.

One of the ways that special collections can demonstrate the appropriateness of their space to take on such donations is through the development and curation of exhibitions. Exhibit facilities offer the institution a place to highlight parts of their collections, often in a manner that will equally highlight the donor(s) who contributed the items. At Drew, the special collections department is fortunate to have a dedicated exhibit space alongside the front lobby of the archives building. This space allows for departmental staff to feature a large selection of material in more than ten large display vitrines. The very public placement of these exhibit cases not only invites visitors to peruse selected portions of Drew's collections but also provides potential donors with a model for how their own donations could be highlighted. This was an important aspect of another alumni-related donation that came to the department early in this century and that deserves mention here.

The Richard L. Walker Papers represent the political, professional, and personal life of Richard "Dixie" Walker, a Drew alum and former United States ambassador to South Korea in the 1980s (Drew University n.d., Walker Papers). The collection came to Drew through Amb. Walker's family, starting in 2003, partially supported by funds raised and donated by Walker's family and friends. One of the conditions of the donation, and something that is not uncommon with large donations to special collections, was the requirement for an exhibition of a selection of the materials after they had been processed. Such an exhibition was mounted, using the large exhibit space in the archives building, and a series of events were held in the building to celebrate the collection and honor Amb. Walker's legacy. The exhibit itself was curated by special collections staff, who worked alongside the university's advancement office to ensure that the donors were supported and included during the process. It was a great success and demonstrated how valuable exhibitions can be in both the highlighting of alumni/ae collections and the potential they have to recruit new alumni/ae donors. The Walker exhibition prompted additional donations from Drew alumni/ae who had seen the exhibit and generated additional interest among current students who wanted to learn more about Drew's connection to the ambassador and his time in South Korea. While McEllhenney's Thomas collection has not yet been featured in a dedicated library exhibit, his Frost collection has been the subject of a smaller, "Out of the Vault" event that allowed for the collection to be displayed to the public in a one-time, pop-up presentation.

Of course, for many libraries and special collections departments, the problem often is not a shortage of alumni/ae book donors, but rather a surplus (Little 1987; Nelson 1988; Wedgewood 2000, 537; Berger 2014, 175). Offers of unwanted or unneeded collections can be problematic. And gifts-in-kind only underscore other related concerns, such as space limitations and processing costs (Lindseth 2016, 31; Berger 2014, 179; Cox 2004, 34). Nelson (1988, 54) has emphasized the importance and value of a "sensibly worded," written gift policy as one way to address these concerns. Clearly, not all willing alumni/ae donors will have material suitable for a circulating collection, let alone for special collections. But alumni/ae collectors, especially those with distinctive collections, present us with a different situation. It is often these more specialized and unique collections, such as the Thomas or Walker materials, that special collections departments want to pursue and promote. This is particularly the case when the alumnus/a in question is a collector of material that fits well within the collecting policies of the institution.

Alumni/ae Collectors

If, as Lindseth (2016, 31) has noted, "library special collections material often comes from collectors," and if, as Casey and Lorenzen (2010, 522) rightly observe, "alumni are the most obvious potential donors to an academic library," then alumni/ae collectors should constitute the most likely and attractive pool of alumni/ae donors to academic special collections. There is ample evidence to confirm that many alumni/ae collectors, including many distinguished collectors, have indeed donated collections to "their" schools (see, among many examples, Washington University, n.d.; Dartmouth College n.d.). Perhaps the most famous, and certainly the most valuable financially, alumni donation was that of William Scheide to Princeton University (Princeton 2015). Though housed at Princeton since 1959, the Scheide Library officially became a donation to the university upon William's death in November 2014. The collection of 2,500 volumes was valued at the time at around $300 million and represents one of the finest private rare book and manuscript collections ever assembled. While most alumni donations are not going to reach the heights of the Scheide Library, many donor-collectors have much to offer their degree-granting institutions, and, in return, these institutions have much to offer donor-collectors.

As suggested above, a critical part of accepting such donations involves publicizing them as widely as possible, or at least as widely as donors find agreeable (see Berger 2014, 178). Such publicity is a boon for the institution and its special collections holdings, but it is also often an honor for the donor as well. By highlighting alumni donations through publications, press releases, exhibitions (physical or virtual), social media posts, etc., special collections can demonstrate the importance of the material and, by inference, the importance of the donor. This need not necessarily be an effort to fluff the ego of a donor or to solicit an additional donation. Rather, it is a way to demonstrate the legacy of the donor and his/her donation and its long-term impact on the institution and its faculty and students. For alumni donors who are serious about their collections, whether they be 200 R. S. Thomas items or 2,500 of the rarest books in the world, there is an element of pride and honor associated with donating their materials. These are items that have been collected with care and passion and often at no small expense. Promoting their donation to one's institution is a way of honoring the work of collecting that has been done by the alumnus/a and their family.

For this reason, special collections departments should be as attentive as possible to the collecting habits of alumni/ae. This is especially important for smaller institutions with more limited resources. Knowing who is collecting, and in what areas, is important. While one does not need to check in constantly on potential alumni/ae donors, it is important to have a finger on the pulse of their collecting habits and areas of interest. For small institutions, this can often serve to expand or build upon existing collecting areas. At Drew, that often means expanding the large Methodist Library collection—something that not only serves the immediate university community but also supports Drew's existing partnership with the General Commission on Archives and History of the United Methodist Church. Many of Drew's most active alumni/ae donors, like Rev. McEllhenney, contribute books to the Methodist studies portions of our special collections.

Tapping into alumni donors can also create new areas of collecting when they are needed. This has also happened in Drew's special collections, particularly in recent years, as we have expanded our holdings in areas related to popular culture and graphic narratives. Specifically, we looked to expand upon an existing collection of cartoon art and graphic satire (the Chesler Collection; see Drew University n.d., Chesler Collection) that has had significant growth in terms of usage and student interest over the past few years. The Chesler Collection includes a number of comic books, graphic novels, and secondary sources related to the history of comics. Because of the increasing interest in these materials, we began to seek out additional comic books to supplement the collection and to support new and existing course offerings. Rather than spend our somewhat limited budget to purchase comics for the collection, we reached out to existing donors and alumni friends who were themselves comic book collectors. These efforts were notably rewarded and resulted in a series of comic collections, all donated by alumni collectors, amounting to nearly 12,000 comic books (see Drew University n.d., Comic Collection). These donations represent a vast resource for current students—one that the special collections department could not have purchased or otherwise acquired without the generosity of our alumni collectors.

Rev. McEllhenney's donation of his R. S. Thomas Collection was a similar case. Although Drew did not have a specific collection related to modern poetry, much less to Welsh poetry, the need for such a collection was increasingly evident on campus at the time of McEllhenney's donation. At that time, Drew had a strong MFA in poetry program and was looking to add collections to support that program. This resulted not only in the Frost and Thomas donations, but also the addition of world-renowned collections such as the Byron Society of America Collection and the Maxine Kumin Collection. The Thomas Collection, however, was the most significant one donated by an alumnus of the university. The donation began when Drew's dean of the library at the time responded positively to Rev. McEllhenney's initial overture. He visited McEllhenney's home several times, reviewed the Thomas Collection with the donor, and clearly communicated his desire to obtain it for Drew's special collections. This desire was equalled, if not exceeded, by the donor's own aspiration:

> Meanwhile, I collected everything I could find by or about [R. S. Thomas]: first editions, limited editions, anthologies, critical studies, biographical materials, his letters to me, recordings of him reading his poems, even a coffee mug. Where was this collection to live when I no longer lived? At Drew was the obvious answer. I was a Drew graduate. In the late 1990s, I wrote and taught an online course in [United Methodist] history, doctrine, and polity for Drew, followed by a short course for women preparing to be commissioned as deaconesses. I knew the archives building at Drew from the time it was a hole in the ground, was present for its opening ceremonies, and wrote the brief history of Methodism included in the Drew-published volume celebrating the building. Dean Andrew Scrimgeour told me about each step in his plan for expanding the space for collections. His visits to my home, to see the collection, to develop a relationship that became a deep friendship, were crucial. Because of the nature of my collec-

tion, the works of a poet who was nominated for the Nobel Prize in Literature and who was an Anglican parish priest, it needed to be placed where researchers had the support of scholars of English literature and theology. (McEllhenney email to authors, September 17, 2020)

That place, it was clear, was Drew University's special collections.

As Dow, Meringolo, and St. Clair (1995, 119) note, and as the McEllhenney case demonstrates, "if handled properly, the acceptance of gifts-in-kind can help establish a more complex relationship with the donor," especially with one who already feels an allegiance to the institution. This individual attention is always important in securing donations, but the entire process is better facilitated when the donor already has a connection with the institution, as in the case of alumni/ae donors.

Perhaps more than other collectors, alumni/ae collectors who become donors usually want their collections to be preserved intact and to be used by students and scholars (see, for example, Lindseth 2016, 34). Such was clearly the case for Rev. McEllhenney. On 23 May 1991, in a letter to an editor at Seren Books, one of R. S. Thomas's publishers, McEllhenney wrote,

> [I plan] to give the RST collection to the library of a theological seminary with the requirement that it be maintained as a unit. There it will be available for others who have been drawn to RST as I have been drawn.

McEllhenney's desire to keep his collection together as a unit reflects a concern of many donor/collectors (Berger 2014, 178). Although this desire can sometimes present the receiving library with challenges (Berger 2014, 178–9), the Thomas Collection was attractive enough and manageable enough in size to overcome those challenges. And in McEllhenney's desire to make his collection available to others, one could hardly wish for a clearer statement—to paraphrase Bernard Mandeville—of a private vice (if book collecting should be considered a vice) turned into a public benefit.

Uniqueness of the Thomas Collection

Drew's R. S. Thomas Collection is certainly not the only one of its kind, nor is it the largest collection of materials related to the famed

Welsh poet. For example, substantial collections are found at the National Library of Wales (n.d.) and the R. S. Thomas Study Centre at the University of Bangor (n.d.). Still, it is unique, particularly in the United States, and that uniqueness underscores the value of special collections. Although portions may be accessible in other American libraries, the material within the Thomas Collection is of particular value because of its diverse nature and the completeness of the collection. As noted above, Rev. McEllehenney collected everything he could find related to Thomas and his work. The determination of a dogged collector—the "completist"—is evident throughout the collection (even down to collecting a coffee mug!).

Moreover, the nearly sixty letters between McEllhenney and Thomas constitute an especially interesting component to this collection. Private correspondence, one might argue, is necessarily unique, and the McEllhenney–Thomas correspondence gives Drew's Thomas Collection an even more distinctive quality. In addition to the correspondence, McEllhenney has also donated a series of archival materials related to his own research into Thomas and his work. As mentioned above, these materials helped McEllhenney craft his monograph on R. S. Thomas. For researchers, such material offers a unique perspective on Thomas (from McEllhenney's point of view) and an insider's tour of the scholarly approach to understanding Thomas and his work. These archival documents provide insights that go beyond the printed word and present an example of how scholarly texts are researched, developed, written, edited, and published. In many ways, seeing the drafts and corrections of McEllhenney's work can better demonstrate the scholarly process of creation than reading the final product. McEllhenney's archival material includes numerous drafts of his book on Thomas, as well as research materials, interviews with Thomas and others, and even page proofs from his publisher. These are materials that could not be found elsewhere.

An additional aspect of the collection's uniqueness is its ability to transcend a specific topic. Extending from literature to theology and nature writing to Welsh nationalism, the collection is unique in its scope. While many collections have a strong, single focus, the Thomas Collection is more expansive and so can prove useful to more diverse interests.

Interdisciplinary Appeal

The increasing importance of interdisciplinarity across academia has been well established (Klein 2010; Gibson and Mack 2012). Not surprisingly, the term figures prominently on the Drew University Theological School website (see, e.g. Drew Theological School, n.d.). Rev. McEllhenney's own interest in R. S. Thomas might be seen as interdisciplinary, as he was, from early on, convinced that "Thomas's poetry would be of particular interest to pastors" (McEllhenney – Thomas Correspondence, February 9, 1993). Indeed, part of Drew's interest in McEllhenney's Thomas Collection lies in the fact that Thomas's poetry exhibits wide-ranging religious concerns and so is of interest to theology students.

As McEllhenney himself attests, part of what drew him to reading (and collecting) Thomas's work was the poet's clear and fearless attempts to openly discuss his own doubts about God and his own occasional lack of faith in religion. Thomas's poetry supported McEllhenney's conviction "that doubt is the crack in conventional religion that allows the light of true belief to get in" (McEllhenney email to authors, September 17, 2020). This discussion of belief and doubt formed the foundation of McEllhenney's book on Thomas and is at the heart of the material within the Thomas Collection. Poetic struggle with theology, philosophy, faith, and God—it's all right there on the shelves and in the boxes of Drew's special collections. It could not be more appropriate for an audience of seminarians, theologians, and researchers. However, the interdisciplinary possibilities of the collection extend far beyond that theological audience. Indeed, McEllhenney saw this as well when offering the collection to Drew. As he recently put it: "the search for the Still Center, the Ground of Being, may be found in poetry and art that is doubt-laden, not overtly religious, perhaps even patently anti-religious" (email to authors, September 17, 2020).

Poetry, literature, and art are also disciplines that are able to take advantage of the value of the Thomas Collection. Such areas bring rich resources to explore a poet's oeuvre, biography, and personal perspectives. From the MFA program in poetry to undergraduate classes in English, poetics, and nationalistic literature, to memoir writing and personal reflection, the Thomas Collection is a valuable, hands-on teaching tool for classes that visit the archives. Students in literature-related majors and graduate programs have been able to engage the Thomas Collection from completely different perspectives than that of their seminary colleagues.

One particularly interactive way in which the collection has supported academic programs at Drew is as a model for student authors. Students in the MFA and other graduate programs have used the Thomas material for inspiration in their own work. Classes have visited the archive to read and review Thomas's work (among others) as creative stimulus, particularly in areas related to writing about the natural world. Undergraduates in writing classes have been inspired by Thomas's poetic memoirs and personal struggles. Seeing first-hand these moments of inspiration in the reading room demonstrates just how much of an impact the Thomas Collection can have at all levels of literary study in the university.

The final, and perhaps most unexpected, discipline that has tapped into the Thomas Collection in recent years is that of environmental studies. In recent years, classes focusing on environmentalism and writing have come to the archives and taken advantage of the materials in the Thomas Collection. Thomas's poetry has elements of what Christopher Morgan (2009, 51) calls a "romantic-realism" in its discussions of nature:

> [R]omantic in the sense that R. S. Thomas's experiences and explorations of nature continue, ultimately, to be experiences and explorations of the self and of God... and yet realist by his consistent acknowledgement of nature as not merely sublime in its aspect or nurturing in its action, but equally as fierce in its tumult, ruthless in its purpose, deadly in its possibilities, frightening in the harshness of its very discompassion towards itself and its human interpreters.

This duality of the sublime and the reality of nature, evident throughout much of Thomas's work, is perfect for an environmental studies curriculum that includes classes on nature writing, eco-criticism, and literary analysis. What better way to learn about writing about the natural world than to explore a collection devoted to a man whose poetic work was often dedicated to that very topic?

These environmental studies classes also provided an opportunity for Rev. McEllhenney to see his collection at work first-hand. During a class visit to the archives in October 2019, Rev. McEllhenney himself was a guest lecturer. He discussed with students his collecting habits and history. The class (ENGH206 Nature Writing) was taught by Dr. Summer Harrison and was focused on the "tradition of writing about the natural world," including exploring "the role of writing in the human relationship with the environment" (Drew University Course Catalog, Fall 2019). Students in the class looked at a variety of collections, including both the Robert Frost Collection and the R. S. Thomas Collection. Rev. McEllhenney was on hand not only to talk about the collections but to answer questions, and, at the end, he read aloud some of Thomas's poems. This interaction between an alumnus and current students—between a donor-collector and potential future donor-collectors—left a deep impression on all involved and exemplified how special collections can use material "to deepen and enlarge the understanding of students in a wide variety of disciplines" (McEllhenney, email to authors, October 16, 2019).

The Gift That Keeps Giving

As the preceding discussion demonstrates, Rev. McEllhenney's donation has introduced new students to the joys of book collecting and to the wonders of special collections. Although initially aimed largely at attracting Drew Theological School students and faculty, this donation has proven to have wider interdisciplinary appeal and to have enticed undergraduates to engage with library collections in new ways. This has led to a greater awareness and use of the Thomas Collection and to an even stronger relationship between Rev. McEllhenney and Drew's special collections.

A wonderful example of how this relationship has expanded over time is the addition of a new collection to Drew's special collections. This collection, consisting of more than 100 volumes of books by and about C. S. Lewis, came to Drew as a result of its relationship with Rev. McEllhenney. In October, 2019 (shortly after the Nature Writing class session), Rev. McEllhenney reached out to the archives with an offer to connect us with Ellen McGill, a friend of his who was looking for a place to donate her late husband's large collection of C. S. Lewis material. We were only too eager to accept the donation. Although Lewis is well-represented in Drew's library, there were few (if any) first editions or rarer publications. This became a perfect marriage of a collection rich in scholarly materials, which needed a home, and an academic library that needed it—an engagement facilitated by a donor matchmaker! In many ways, the Frost and Thomas Collections brought the C. S. Lewis collection to Drew and so illustrate how a deep relationship with a generous alumnus is the gift that keeps on giving.

In their study of academic libraries and engaged alumni, Griffith and Kealthy (2018, 203) present a "base interaction model for the alumni – academic library relationship." This model highlights the pivotal role played by academic libraries in creating engaged students and, in turn, engaged alumni who support libraries. The McEllhenney donation illustrates quite strikingly how an engaged student can become an engaged alumnus whose donation to the library—in this case, specifically to special collections—has helped to engage new students. Ideally, this cyclical model should perpetuate itself. As Michael L. Taylor (2018, 129) has noted, "it is important to include current students in the category of potential donors. As alumni, they may one day be in a position to give."

As is evident from this case study, what alumni can potentially give to an institution's special collections cannot be measured solely in the number of books donated or in the rarity of manuscripts and archival material given. Rather, it is also measured in research done, connections made, exhibitions curated, publications produced, classes taught, students inspired, and more. Rev. McEllhenney's Thomas Collection thus confirms the claim that "libraries can benefit from alumni who have a deeper relationship with the library that extends well beyond graduation" (Griffith and Kealthy 2018, 204). In this particular case, sixty years beyond graduation seems to be just the beginning of Drew's relationship with John McEllhenney. Other donor/ alumni relationships are out there for other institutions large and small. One never knows exactly where these relationships will lead, but the possibilities are endless and the outcomes often unexpectedly rewarding.

References

Allen, Susan M. 2012. "Seeking Gifts of Rare Materials: Things to Consider." *Journal of Library Administration* 52: 233–43. *https:// doi.org/10.1080/01930826.2012.684503*.

Berger, Sidney E. 2014. *Rare Books and Special Collections*. Chicago: Neal-Schuman.

Brittingham, Barbara E. and Thomas R. Pezzullo. 1990. *The Campus Green: Fund Raising in Higher Education*. ASHE-ERIC Higher Education Report 1. Washington, DC: School of Education and Human Development, George Washington University.

Brown, Tony. 2006. *R. S. Thomas*. Cardiff: University of Wales Press.

Casey, Anne Marie and Michael Lorenzen. 2010. "Untapped Potential: Seeking Library Donors Among Alumni of Distance Learning Programs." *Journal of Library Administration* 50, nos. 5–6: 515–29. *https://doi.org/10.1080/01930826.2010.488597.*

Clark, Charlene K. 1986. "Private Support for Public Purposes: Library Fund Raising." *Wilson Library Bulletin* 60 (February): 18–21.

Clotfelter, Charles T. 2001. "Who Are the Alumni Donors? Giving by Two Generations of Alumni from Selective Colleges." *Nonprofit Management and Leadership* 12, no. 2 (Winter): 119–38.

Cox, Steven. 2004. "Libraries and Donors: Maintaining the Status Quo." *The Southeastern Librarian* 52, no. 3: 34–41. *https://digital-commons.kennesaw.edu/seln/vol52/iss3/7.*

Dartmouth College Rauner Library. n.d. Accessed November 20, 2020. *https://www.dartmouth.edu/library/rauner/rarebooks/rare_book_collections.html.*

Dow, R. F., S. Meringolo, and G. St. Clair. 1995. "Academic Collections in a Changing Environment." In *Academic Libraries: Their Rationale and Role in Higher Education*, edited by G. B. McCabe and R. J. Person, 103–23. Contributions in Librarianship and Information Science. Westport, CT: Greenwood Press.

Drew University. n.d. "Comic Book Collections." Accessed November 25, 2020. *https://www.drew.edu/library/2020/11/11/comic-book-collections.*

———. "Harry A. Chesler Collection." Accessed November 25, 2020. *https://www.drew.edu/library/2019/08/18/harry-a-chesler-collection-of-cartoon-art-and-graphic-satire.*

———. "R.S. Thomas Collection." Accessed July 22, 2020. *https://www.drew.edu/library/2019/08/19/r-s-thomas-collection.*

———. "Richard L. Walker Papers." Accessed September 10, 2020. *https://www.drew.edu/library/2019/08/19/richard-l-walker-papers.*

———. "Robert Frost Collection." Accessed September 10, 2020. *https://www.drew.edu/library/2019/08/19/robert-frost-collection.*

Drew University Theological School. n.d. Graduate Division of Religion. Accessed December 1, 2020. *https://www.drew.edu/theological-school/academics/doctor-of-philosophy/graduate-division-of-religion.*

Gibson, Craig, and Daniel C. Mack. 2012. *Interdisciplinarity and Academic Libraries.* ACRL Publications in Librarianship 66. Chicago: Association of College and Research Libraries.

Griffith, Andrew S. and Ceire Kealty. 2018. "Are Academic Libraries Utilized to Produce Engaged Alumni?" *Library Management* 39, no. 3/4: 200–6. *https://doi.org/10.1108/LM-09-2017-0096.*

Hawley, E. Haven. 2016. "Reflections on the Meanings of Objects." In *Forging the Future of Special Collections,* edited by Arnold Hirshon, Robert H. Jackson, and Melissa A. Hubbard, 3–10. Chicago: Neal-Schuman.

Hernández Montes, Benigno. 1984. *Biblioteca de Juan de Segovia: Edición y comentario de su escritura de donación.* Bibliotheca theologica hispana, serie 2a, textos 3. Madrid: Consejo Superior de Investigaciones Científicas, Instituto "Francisco Suárez."

Keith, W. J. "R. S. Thomas." 1978 – . *Dictionary of Literary Biography.* Detroit, MI: Gale Research Co.

Klein, Julie Thompson. 2010. *Creating Interdisciplinary Campus Cultures: A Model for Strength and Sustainability.* The Jossey-Bass Higher and Adult Education Series. San Francisco, CA: Jossey-Bass.

Konzak, Elizabeth and Dwain P. Teague. 2009. "Reconnect with your Alumni and Connect to Donors." *Technical Services Quarterly* 26, no. 3: 217–25. *https://doi.org/10.1080/07317130802520252.*

Kuhn, Jim. 2016. "Affinities and Alliances: Thoughts on Acquisitions, Collection Development, and Donor Relations." In *Forging the*

Future of Special Collections, edited by Arnold Hirshon, Robert H. Jackson, and Melissa A. Hubbard, 11–29. Chicago: Neal-Schuman.

Leonhardt, Thomas Wilburn. 2011. "Key Donor Cultivation: Building for the Future." *Journal of Library Administration* 51: 198–208. *https://doi.org/10.1080/01930826.2011.540550*.

Lindseth, Jon A. 2016. "Where Does the Collector/Donor Community See Special Collections Today?" In *Forging the Future of Special Collections*, edited by Arnold Hirshon, Robert H. Jackson, and Melissa A. Hubbard, 31–5. Chicago: Neal-Schuman.

Little, Paul L. 1987. "Gifts, Donations, and Special Collections." *Public Libraries* 26: 8–10.

McEllhenney, John G., ed. 1982. *Proclaiming Grace and Freedom: The Story of United Methodism in America*. Nashville, TN: Abingdon.

———. 1992. *United Methodism in America: A Compact History*. Nashville, TN: Abingdon.

———. 1996. *John Wesley: A Man Who Shook the Spiritual Earth*. Madison, NJ: General Commission on Archives and History.

———. 2002. "'My World Stock Fluctuates a Good Deal!': An Appreciation of R. S. Thomas from the Western Side of the Atlantic." *New Welsh Review* 56 (Summer): 21–8.

———. 2013. *A Masterwork of Doubting-Belief: R. S. Thomas and His Poetry*. Eugene, OR: Wipf and Stock.

——— and Charles Yrigoyen, Jr. 1984. *200 Years of United Methodism: An Illustrated History*. Madison, NJ: Drew University.

———, Charles Yrigoyen, Jr., and Kenneth Rowe. 2008. *United Methodism at Forty: Looking Back, Looking Forward*. Nashville, TN: Abingdon.

McEllhenney – Thomas Correspondence. R. S. Thomas Collection. Drew University Library.

Morgan, Christopher. 2009. *R. S. Thomas: Identity, Environment, and Deity*. Manchester: Manchester University Press.

National Library of Wales. n.d. "Thomas, R. S. (Ronald Stuart), 1913–2000." Accessed November 20, 2020. *https://archives.library. wales/index.php/thomas-r-s-ronald-stuart-1913-2000.*

Nelson, Veneese C. 1988. "Buried Alive in Gifts." *Library Journal,* April 15, 1988.

Perry, S. J. 2019. "The Innocence of R. S. Thomas." *Essays in Criticism* 69, no. 3 (July): 325–48. *https://doi.org/10.1093/escrit/cgz017.*

Poetry Foundation. n.d. "R. S. Thomas." Accessed December 4, 2020. *https://www.poetryfoundation.org/poets/r-s-thomas.*

Princeton University. 2015. "Scheide Donates Rare Books Library to Princeton; Collection is Largest Gift in University's History." February 16, 2015. *https://www.princeton.edu/news/2015/02/16/ scheide-donates-rare-books-library-princeton-collection-larg-est-gift-universitys?section=featured.*

Purcell, Aaron D. 2015. *Donors and Archives: A Guidebook for Successful Programs.* Lanham, MD: Rowman and Littlefield.

Taylor, Michael L. 2018. "Special Collections Exhibitions: How They Pay Dividends for Your Library." *RBM: A Journal of Rare Books, Manuscripts, and Cultural Heritage* 19, no. 2 (Fall): 121–32. *https:// doi.org/10.5860/rbm.19.2.121.*

University of Bangor. n.d. "R. S. Thomas Study Centre." Accessed November 20, 2020. *https://rsthomas.bangor.ac.uk/index.php.en.*

Washington University Libraries. n.d. Accessed November 20, 2020. *https://library.wustl.edu/about/alumnifriends/notable-gifts-givers.*

Wedgeworth, Robert. 2000. "Donor Relations as Public Relations: Toward a Philosophy of Fund-Raising." *Library Trends* 48, no. 3 (Winter): 530–9.

CHAPTER 10

The Millennium Project

Nature, Environment, and Time in the Future of Special Collections: Considering the Case of Bridwell Library

ANTHONY J. ELIA

*I*n preparation for writing this essay, I spent a long while thinking about the questions that concern theological and special collections libraries. Then COVID-19 hit and other considerations took priority in our lives and work. This pandemic brought up various thoughts that we had not really contemplated before, but one question in particular stood out, and that was: *How do we continue to work within a profession where our human presence has been central to our mission and livelihood, and yet, by its own virtue during a pandemic, we are forced to abandon that physical, human presence and adapt to an increasingly virtual environment?* Never in the history of special collections, I would imagine, has our profession had to ask such a question.

Several months into the pandemic, two other things prompted me to reconsider my understandings of collections, libraries, museums, and the whole enterprise of theological education in relation to acquisition practices. First, a road trip in early July around the American west brought me face to face with both our country and its variegated landscape—whether we call it *nature* or *environment*, the recognition that we exist in spaces that are tied to rock, soil, water, and air is fundamentally crucial to how we live and function in the world. And in that greater landscape, this country is made up of many different peoples, all of whom contribute in one way or another to the social fabric. In recognizing this more viscerally on the road, the relationship between people and places and what that means has become centrally important to my work and what I want to cultivate with colleagues.

Second, in good part due to this trip, I embarked on a research project to read more extensively in areas related to understanding that experience with the outdoors—fields like environmental history, nature writing, wilderness studies, environmentalism, and imperial ecologies. It occurred to me, while reading some of these works, that research about the history of the environment often had connections to the formation of empires and nation-states, which in turn manifested in the establishment, collection, cultivation, and maintenance of museums, exhibitions, and curatorial spaces—even gardens and landscaping around such institutions, which reflected the imperial designs of an empire.

Thus, I expanded my readings to include curation theories and philosophies, the histories of modern museums, and the social psychology of collections. As a result, many of these scholarly works prompted me to ask far more probing questions about my work and the role of the library. What does nature and the environment have to do with how we classify knowledge and categorize information? What do considerations about landscape and the imagination mean for how we devise our collections, or even perpetuate the histories invested in the institutions we have inherited over time? How do these considerations play into both the history of collection development policies in special collections *and* work with best practices moving forward? And what are the moral, ethical, and social implications of all of these considerations?

Simply answered, I firmly believe that a responsible library of the future (especially one that is *theological*, contains *special collections*, and has the support and backing of its parent institution) can and should strive to excel in its position of museum quality and, in so doing, must be ready to ask the tough questions—both about its own history and legacy *and* about its role as a part of the environment. Though I have yet to understand fully and articulate satisfactory answers to my own questions here, they nonetheless guide me in attempting to understand better the meaning of the task at hand—specifically, preparing for the future with an eye on moving into the next half millennium, which, while sounding outlandish to some, is precisely what we need to do. Most of us are trained in historical sciences and do not think it odd to look back half a millennium but, because we have no evidence for the future, nor will we know what it holds, it is absent from our thinking. But this is where we must begin, and the so-named *Millennium Project* is a methodology to take us there.

The basic structure of this essay includes four parts. *Part I: First Considerations* will explore how we understand theological libraries and museums within the context of time and nature. By exploring the fundamental categories and language we use to talk about these spaces, my hope is that we can articulate a distinct vision for the future of both Bridwell and other institutions, especially around special collections. *Part II: Recognitions* looks back on the history of Bridwell, while reassessing the legacy of Decherd Turner, Bridwell's first director, whose vision and method of collecting must be recognized through an holistic lens, whereby the institutional role of the library really emerged into what it is today and can grow into tomorrow—an organic and encompassing entity that weds the theological library with the museum space. *Part III: The Future of Bridwell and Special Collections* speaks to both Bridwell's strategic plan for the coming generations and how special collections in other theological libraries may seek to plan and accommodate their own futures, while facing restrictive budgets and administrative constraints. *Part IV: Conclusion—Bridwell Library in 2520 CE* is a reflection on what can and cannot be predicted in such long-term planning but also seeks to articulate the ways that particularities of Bridwell's preparedness in the short-term may afford it a boundless future of growth and importance as an institutional library and museum.

Part I: First Considerations

A Story of Time

In the fall of 2019, I went with a colleague to meet the president of a local religious organization, who was well-regarded and well-known in the Dallas-Fort Worth area. Our conversation was focused on the collection and preservation of archival materials related to the founding and history of the group and its association, which included a variety of materials from letters and journals to recordings on cassette tapes and VHS. As the conversation progressed, the president, who was extremely personable and interested in our assistance, paused and began to provide the context of his faith's view of the world—both this world and the next. He began to outline the plans for the community, its understanding of the philosophical, theological, and teleological enterprise that constituted a cosmic projection for his group in the city of Dallas. At one point he noted: "Most organizations have a three-, five-, or ten-year plan. For us, that is not enough. We look at the world and the universe in far more expansive terms—we have a five-hundred, one-thousand, and five-thousand-year plan." Both my colleague and I were more than surprised but had to reserve ourselves under the circumstances. Over the subsequent months, I thought more and more about this and recognized that, while this is not necessarily a *practical* consideration or imposition, it was something that had deep and ethical foundations in the way a community thinks about its descendants, children, and heirs. In many ways, this echoes the "seventh generation principle" of stewardship, which is commonly attributed to the Iroquois and is related to environmental sustainability. For seven generations into the future, we must consider what positive or negative impacts we will have on those who will come after us. In these circumstances, then, this conversation with a religious leader about the preservation of archives and the legacy of its collections was directly tied to a sustainability ethics of the world we had in front of us. Moreover, such a seemingly unusual game plan, which effectively looked centuries and even millennia into the future, echoed other traditions, such as those of Native Americans, which looked "only" 150 years—or seven generations—into the future.

Libraries and Theological Libraries: An Ontology

The theological library is something that has long been part of what we often describe as the "Western tradition," in great part because it reflects the heritage of the Abrahamic faiths. Most notably in the United States and Europe, the libraries that have represented Christian theological schools and seminaries, as well as Jewish and Islamic schools, have become part of this same tradition and evolved into what we know them as today. In the twentieth century, institutions of higher learning and their libraries have constituted singular structures of meaning, comprised of parts with elemental components: books, journals, shelves, tables, chairs, patrons, staff, faculty, and students. Times change and we add further elements to this form: computers, LED lighting, compact shelving, internet, wireless, digital reference, databases, maker spaces, info commons, and more. We adapt, we learn, we interact, we move ahead. What a library is becomes ever more elusive but also ever more understood, as it is the paradox of knowing it when you see it, while recognizing that there are many dynamic and new understandings of institutions and professions. Our ideas of tradition and traditional positions do not always remain but sometimes melt away into merged job responsibilities, downsizing, and changing needs in the workplace. New language and terms are used to describe a reorientation toward patron behaviors and the sciences of predictability: user experience librarians, embedded librarians, maker librarians, STE(A)M liaisons, GIS and data curation specialists, community engagement professionals, social media assistants, and market research librarians. Though these designations are not all likely to be found in the present theological library lexicon, some of them have been and may likely be adapted to in the coming years.

The ontologies (or, essential aspects of identification), then, of the theological library are about adaptability and change. They require us as library and theology professionals to make plans for sustainability as well as innovation in order to achieve the greatest flexibility and engagement with future students, faculty, staff, and donors. The ontological question, then, is not simply in the statement, "A library is…" but in the blended complexity of human diversity in the plural: "Libraries are… theologies are… and theological libraries are…" We cannot isolate ourselves into camps that do not allow for growth and creativity, since this would be the death knell for our libraries, our institutions, and potentially our religious traditions. Theological libraries, then, exist and thrive on the principles of diversity—diversity of people, ideas, perceptions, representations, and meanings. How we articulate these considerations is part of the exercise we are called to undertake in this process of living and working in the world, and it is our responsibility to enact the ontological principles of the theological library in this process.

Museums, Library-Museums, and Collection Spaces: Some Considerations

Since 2007, the International Council of Museums (ICOM) provided the following as the definition for a bona fide museum:

> A museum is a non-profit, permanent institution in the service of society and its development, open to the public, which acquires, conserves, researches, communicates and exhibits the tangible and intangible heritage of humanity and its environment for the purposes of education, study and enjoyment.

During the last couple years, though, with an increased move toward situating museums within frameworks that democratized, decolonized, and recognized marginal voices, a social and political redrafting of the definition took place, which caused further debate and less agreement. As John Fraser (2019) writes in his essay titled, "A Discomforting Definition of Museum," the move among members of the ICOM was to assert that museums play a more "activist role" in both their identity and their function. The updated recommendations for defining a museum in 2019 follow:

> Museums are democratising, inclusive and polyphonic spaces for critical dialogue about the pasts and the futures. Acknowledging and addressing the conflicts and challenges of the present, they hold artefacts and specimens in trust for society, safeguard diverse memories for future generations and guarantee equal rights and equal access to heritage for all people. Museums are not for profit. They are participatory and transparent, and work in active partnership with and for diverse communities to collect, preserve, research, interpret, exhibit, and enhance understandings of the world, aiming to contribute to

human dignity and social justice, global equality and planetary well-being.

Bridwell Library does not have the word "museum" in its name, nor does it promote itself in those terms. But by either of these standards—the older ICOM definition from 2007 or the newer proposal from 2019—Bridwell Library could conceivably stylize itself as a museum. Due to its long history, generous backing, and thoughtful vision of strategic endowments, the library has not only managed to survive but to thrive through difficult times and to evolve into a space that is demonstrably more exhibitionary in the manner of a museum. Over thirty years ago, a major gift secured this fate and established a professional-grade exhibition hall with equally valuable exhibit cases.

With this expansion and remodeling, the library took on a more specific tone that could now be considered akin to the pedagogical and even sociological work of a museum. Yet, because the library was just that—a library that supported and fostered the needs of students and faculty—the museum qualities have been more in the background than the foreground. But this does not always have to be the case. The shared qualities of the library's functional quotidian efforts that support our patrons may be balanced by the unique holdings put on display, interpreted, and written about. Thus, to be more intentional about how we consider such a space, I prefer to describe the entity we call Bridwell a library-museum. There are two important components to this designation, namely the existence of major endowments and the extent and value of the holdings, together totalling more than most individual theological institutional endowments in the United States.

Another reason for considering the "museum" designation for a place like Bridwell is that the considerations and interests on a global scale of the ICOM similarly reflect the concerns and issues that theological libraries are dealing with today. Bridwell may not be overtly oriented toward solving the major issues of the world or demanding social justice in public ways, but that does not mean that we cannot continue to be good stewards of our planet and strive to make the world a better place. The spaces in which both the collections reside and the multitude of unique items are put on display are, by their very nature, political spaces because they reflect human thought and action. No matter how hard we try, even the most uneventful or innocuous of activities, objects, or projects requires some level of political negotiation.

In sum, then, the understanding of a place like Bridwell can and should be considered through this more panoptic lens. It does not require some official action, per se, but is a reflection of reorientation of vision both by Bridwell itself and for its broad constituency. It is important, too, that we recognize that such a case is more of an exception than a rule but, that being said, there are ways in which such models can be established, grow, and thrive in other contexts, which I will detail in Part III.

On Nature:
or, Library-Museum and the Artifices of False Boundaries

In William Cronon's masterwork of environmental history, *Nature's Metropolis: Chicago and the Great West* (1991), the author introduces us to the imaginative enterprise of his youth, which dictated false projections that "cities are bad" and "nature is good." As he matured, he questioned many of his preconceived notions about Chicago and cities in general, especially as he reflected on the reasons for these ideas being tinged with the particularities of moral judgments from his youth—mostly drawn from the memories of gray clouds, smokestacks, and cold, wet urban landscapes set under the pall of dark skies. These were scenes that he had conjured and remembered in contrast to the bucolic scenes of Wisconsin farmlands, rural Illinois cornfields, and the majestic shores of Lake Michigan. The common denominator in this thinking was the concentration of people—how many or how few there were in a given area. But this was also about how, in that concentration, humans have constructed spaces, making them supposedly less natural. One of Cronon's key points has to do with our imagined concept of nature as an idea—something that demarcates how we think about spaces, create artificial boundaries, and articulate distinctions between those inhabited places. Chicago, after all, grew not in an isolated bubble but through the expansion of the Western plains, the tapping into resources like forests for timber and iron deposits for the railroads, and the use of agriculture and livestock to feed the burgeoning city. Similarly, the idea that either a city or a building, such as a theological library, is somehow distinct or separated from nature is an equal fiction—one that must be recognized and corrected, but also one that must be considered for how it requires nature to establish, cultivate, and sustain human institutions.

Similar to Cronon's critique of nature was an earlier distinction made by the German biologist Jakob Johann Uexküll (1864–1944), who is attributed with first using the expression *Umwelt* (environment) as that which describes our perceived spatial-temporal surroundings (Uexküll 1926). Cronon and Uexküll provide us with distinct considerations for not just how we might think about environmentalisms or environmental histories broadly speaking, but about the very fundamental understanding of and approach to how we categorize the foundational elements of our world. As we look to the roles that libraries play, we naturally question what they have done historically as well as what they can provide for the future. Drawing on the proposals and considerations of thinkers like Cronon and Uexküll, these theories of nature, space, and environment may guide our reexamination of the library itself and then of the needs of special collections for future generations.

A further aspect of this consideration of nature and environment comes in the form of boundaries within the library and its collections—especially important as we change administrative structures, go through staff reductions and turnovers, or consider evolving operational standards and best practices. This, too, involves adaptability, but when we discuss the needs of special collections and archives, for example, the question arises now as to whether one of these categories is inherently part of the other or if they are inherently separate? This question may be obvious and easy to answer for some institutions, while for others it is more complex. For Bridwell, this matter has a long history. While it is fairly well-defined on the one hand, it requires more fine-tuning on the other.

To consider how we understand both nature and environment in the context of libraries, and particularly Bridwell, we must recognize specific uses of these terms and how they play out in both our preservation of the past and our more expansive look toward the future. What many library administrators understand very well is the necessity to build robust relationships with facilities and maintenance specialists and managers, because the physical relationship between a building's contents—especially the rare materials, the special collections, and archives—and its surroundings is crucial. The concepts of environment and nature are central to how we must understand our facilities. Immediately upon assuming my current position, the most pressing concerns were facilities issues. At every library I have served, the facilities were absolute priorities on the lists of responsibilities. At Bridwell, the concern for making sure that all environments meet the standards for temperature, climate, and humidity, for example, are measures of what is necessary to maintain a space properly. When water seeped through drainage pipes, between gutters, and under windows, it was a major concern. In one case, water had come through a gap in the roof, and we were forced to perform an expedient mitigation and repair. But this plays into what Cronon discerns about nature: Was nature, which constituted the outside world of earth, flora, and the elements, somehow what required us from keeping it out, as we might all assume? Or, should it be embraced as part of the organic nature of the building itself?—not to let water "invade" the spaces of our stately building and precious contents, of course, but to recognize the animate nature of the library's physical, organic, and holistic relationship to the elements of nature. The building—like all buildings—is indeed very much an organic, moving, shifting, and perhaps even a pulsing entity. And while many readers of this essay may think it is a rabbit hole of a concern, what remains is a necessary truth about how we are able to best equip ourselves and our cultural institutions with the knowledge, tools, and approach to most effectively understand our buildings, our collections, and how they fit within the categories of nature and environment. In doing this, we recognize environments of space, culture, pedagogy, accessibility, and research, especially as they are connected to special collections. We must also consider and evaluate not only how the past and the trappings of an historical structure affect the present conditions of our collections but, even more importantly, how our actions today around building maintenance, upgrades, and renovations will affect the future of these collections in a building that should last a long time and protect its contents. Indeed, it is no secret that many buildings constructed today have projected "lives" of only twenty-five to fifty years, after which they will either need to be renovated or replaced. That approach to architectural design and sustainability has its own problems. For us, it is imperative that we act as the best stewards of our controllable circumstances, contending with operational costs in light of longer-term strategies of both the library and the greater institution. This, then, will support the visions we have for hundreds of years to come, not simply decades.

Part II: Recognitions[1]

Becoming the director of Bridwell Library was an honor but also a tremendous responsibility, which has taken some time to grow into. Equally, it is a position that requires a fair amount of patience for the consideration of the ontologies mentioned earlier. In this process of self-definition—of the institution, of the library, of the collections, of its identity—we collaborate to come to some consensus around our common goals. With these responsibilities, too, it is only right for us to recognize those shoulders on which we stand. Thus, the characters of those who established, gathered, cultivated, and enhanced the collections and the entire experience we call Bridwell (or, in some cases, "the Bridwell") should be held in highest regard for what they have provided and what has now lasted for more than seventy years. Eight directors and dozens of staff have been crucial to the success of this institution, and the earliest cultivators of the collections, especially Decherd Turner, have been recognized for setting Bridwell in a direction that allowed it to flourish and grow into what it is today.[2]

In the period before Bridwell's establishment, Kate Warnick's contributions as the first theology librarian (1924–49) fostered and led the library through times of development that made the theological library a respectable and cherished place. As the first director of Bridwell from 1950 to 1980, Decherd Turner established an encompassing and creative space for collecting—one which possessed qualities embodied in both a theological library and a museum space. Without Turner's enterprising ideals, creative impulses, collaborative undertakings, and enduring curiosity, we would not be having the conversations we have today, nor would I be speaking of ontologies or considering Bridwell as a library-museum space. Some may question even the museum designation, because nowhere in our charter or official description is there the description of museum. But as we entrust our materials of great quality and value into the hands of specialists, feature ever more extensive professional exhibits, and support a full-time staff of curators, digital designers, conservators, and exhibition programmers, the role of exhibition spaces and defined exhibits are intermingled with what characterizes the singing of the muses—the museum space and idea.[3]

For thirty years, Decherd Turner expressed the collecting principles of an eclectic personality through a vision that projected the Bridwell brand as one that was both-and: both a Methodist theological library and a special collections repository of great prestige. Yet, in many ways, Turner went far beyond the collecting principles of the originating documents or the notions of Mr. Joseph Sterling Bridwell, the Perkins family, and other major founding donors. Turner was a man of particular interests, who clearly saw the role of special collections and the library itself as expansive, holistic, and even organic. The specificity of Methodistica and Wesleyana certainly had their place, but so too did the manuscripts, incunabula, and so-called monuments of early printing, which are among Bridwell's cherished prizes. Yet these, too, merely scratch the surface of what Turner procured. The archival collections themselves are exponents of fields of knowledge and inquiry that burst beyond the predictable limits of a premiere theological collection, and the multitude of fine art, antique furniture, historic sculptures, occult archives, and a plethora of cultural artifacts are both breathtaking and stunningly disparate.

Nearly three quarters of a century on, a re-assessment is in order. In many ways, the often unarticulated and under-the-radar collecting habits of the first Bridwell director make sense when we consider the conditions and circumstances of the mid-twentieth century world and a time when the legacies of old-world museums were still very much on the minds of directors, curators, and conservators. The particularity of Turner's visions, along with some of the collections he inherited from SMU's original antiquarian collections (e.g., the A. V. Lane Egyptological Collection) were in so many ways the manifestation of what is commonly referred to as the *Wunderkammer* legacy—the "cabinet of wonders" that stands as the origin of the modern museum. The relationships between the "cabinet's owner" and the establishment of museums echoes the matrix of relationships among donors, curators, directors, and administrators. For Turner, his strengths were in these very matrices of power and persuasion, whereby he was able to turn chance encounters or introductions into major acquisitions of collections or works of art—some of which today are of significant value.

Many tales of Turner's methods still circulate among us. Two years ago, I wrote an article for one of our newsletters about a modernist painting a colleague had found in storage at Bridwell. I liked it so much that I had it installed in my office. Some months after, I received a lovely letter from the artist, who was unknown to me but had somehow come across the article online. The remarkable part of this story is that the painter was ninety-five-year-old Marlinde von Ruhs—an internationally acclaimed artist who was still active painting and who had, for many years, been living in Guadalajara, Mexico. When I called her in Mexico a few weeks after receiving her letter, she told me that Turner was quite persuasive in his wishes to acquire the painting for Bridwell—even though she was not in the market to sell. His impression of the work was that it fit well within the collections of the theological library, broadly defined as they were.

Stories like this demonstrate a number of points to consider, but not least is the consideration of modern and contemporary art as contributing to theological reflection, inquiry, and research. What we should consider, though, is that Turner's own seemingly haphazard collecting was not all that erratic. Instead, it foretold the need to preserve in areas that might easily be discarded and forgotten—like the parapsychology, occult, and astrology materials. It also encapsulated a vision of theological and religious studies where there were very few boundaries or limits: cultural artifacts of Qing era statuary, Meiji period Shinto shrines, and Tibetan Buddhist manuscripts, along with paintings from European modernists, convey the broader richness of an institutional repository and museum-space, while also recognizing that these materials both instruct and inspire those who enter this place. Theology, thus, cannot be simply a rigid and inflexible enterprise of letters between itinerant preachers or Protestant hymnologists; it must be an expansive, holistic, organic, and living presence of the spoken, written, sung, and artistic human experience. This is the legacy of Turner and Bridwell broadly speaking, and one which inspires us to move forward with fortitude, grace, and a commitment to an awe-inspiring future.

Part III: The Future of Bridwell and Special Collections

Contexts, Communities, and Commodities:
or, How to Plan the Future Through Differing Means

As I noted in Part I, the successes of Bridwell are derived from a long historical complex of donations, investments, creativity, vision, and the constant commitment of an expansive community of stakeholders who, since the beginning, have wanted to see the library thrive. I cannot emphasize this more strongly because, in many ways, I now believe that the greatest inhibitors to the successful growth of both an institution and its library are the unwillingness to take risk on innovations and the undervaluing of the library itself as something decreasing in value rather than increasing in value. Institutions may have the greatest collections, the greatest spaces, the greatest staff, but, if their self-image does not match their potential, this will immediately stanch the potential for growth and transformation into something greater.

A major problem for many theological libraries is not simply a balanced budget or even underfunding. Rather, it is the overall environment of fiscal competition within the institution itself. If the library is seen as merely "a department" that requires subsidizing, that not only perpetuates the general self-image of a dependent subsidiary that plods along, it also does not encourage faith that a fundamental administrative unit within a theological institution can re-establish itself as something more extraordinary, visionary, and central to the overall success of that school.

Among the ingredients required, then, are a) the willingness of library admin and staff to innovate around the unique qualities of the library; b) the actual cultural, social, and bibliographic artifacts with which to engage (e.g., special collections and archives); c) the administrative trust, openness, and vision of the institution to afford open conversations among departments, especially development and fundraising, finance, recruitment, alumni relations, and the library; and d) a frank discussion about how to raise monies, fund new endowments, and attract a more diverse base of the public in the theological institutional space.

Theological schools, seminaries, and their libraries often focus narrowly on their labors—the "that's all we can do" model. Instead, the approach should be more than engaging with the routine patron, but with consumers of information, spaces, aesthetics, and comfort. This does not mean that all theological libraries will become the Met or the Louvre. What it does mean, though, is that all theological libraries have the potential to establish and grow into spaces of intellectual, theological, and even commercial exchange that will foster and enhance the greater institution itself. This can begin by eliciting monies to establish funds supporting theological artwork, youth-oriented projects, or even highly stylized internships. Developing from the ground up the cross-campus relationships, the clear channels of communication, and the overall willingness to enact new ideas into something concrete will yield new opportunities.

This evocation is not a recipe for how to start or build a museum or, as I have now stated, a library-museum. Instead, my suggestion considers the components and roadblocks to what could potentially be outstanding curatorial components of almost any theological library. Beyond the proclamations of the ICOM and how they have defined "museum" in the last two decades, we also face the general connotations of the word in public and among theologically minded colleagues. The term "museum" itself has, for many, a fairly unattractive reputation—that of being boring, old-fashioned, and a waste of time. Yet in recent years we know—both from the most recent ICOM statement and from contemporary and recently updated museums themselves—that these institutions have worked vigorously to remake their identity as anything but boring.

The takeaway then, for most theological libraries, might best be found in the following prescription: Institutions should collaborate internally to understand their archival past, while engaging with the immediate present and preparing for the impending future. In so doing, they must not limit their engagement to a discrete group of incoming students, for example, but engage the expansiveness of the public, which is interested in a wider palette of offerings—in the arts, in music, in social justice, in community affairs, in collaborative discussions, in lecture series, and much more. Expanding beyond a traditional understanding of a library will yield greater returns in not just monetary gains or donations but the cultural and social capital that actual money cannot buy.

I do not propose that all theological schools or theological libraries aim to build or establish their own "museums" here. Instead, the purpose of my considerations are to offer new ways to think about our libraries and institutions broadly speaking. Perhaps most important to the way that I think about our institutions is to remember that the more organic and holistic of an approach one takes, the greater the rate of success there will be in that institution. Indeed, even for our own libraries and theological schools, the words of Abraham Lincoln continue to ring true: "A house divided against itself cannot stand."

From Gloom to Social Work?

Among the vast literature on museums and cultural institutions, two very different yet fascinating approaches may be touched on when considering the potential scenarios for the library-museum of the future, which overlaps well with Bridwell and its own vision. First, in a century-old essay by John Cotton Dana, titled "The Gloom of the Museum" (1917), the author explores the historical backgrounds to the rise of museums in relation to the formation of nations and empires in Europe.[4] The glorious beauty of objects that were acquired would eventually have complicated relationships with those very empires, especially as cultural artifacts and artworks often came from places where they should have remained. As materials in museums came to reflect expansions of the state, the role of custodian of artifacts would become increasingly important. In recent times, the critical self-assessment and appraisal of not just artifacts or cultural objects but the very historiographies and provenances of cultural heritage are in constant need of reevaluation. The "gloom," though, of Dana's title is in part the recognition that the contents of a museum (or, for us, a library-museum) have multiple layers of history, meaning, and interpretation—many of which had not been discussed in the public square. But this then allows us to transition to an approach that has to do with not simply our holdings but how we show and interpret them, as well as how this can serve the public good. This second consideration comes from a fascinating book by Lois H. Silverman, titled *The Social Work of Museums* (2010). Silverman's assertion is that the museum serves a particular set of purposes that have evolved over time and are required to be more purposeful, interactive, and central to the work of society and its transformation toward the good. As Silverman writes:

> Fundamentally, museums offer interactive social experiences of communication in which relationships are activated and people make meaning of objects. This communication yields beneficial consequences: people may meet fundamental human needs like the need for self-esteem and self-actualization; achieve change in essential areas such as knowledge, skills, values, and behavior; build and strengthen social connections and relationships, including social capital; address social problems; and promote social justice and equality. (21)

Taken perhaps a step further, Chet Orloff explores in his article, "Should Museums Change our Mission and Become Agencies of Social Justice?" (2017), whether museums should take on the role of arbiters of social justice and change as prescribed by the International Council of Museums (ICOM). Orloff's concerns elevate the conversation toward the particular issues of social change, and specifically justice around immigration, and how that plays out in smaller, local, money-strapped institutions. But we may apply the central tenet of his critiques here to how museums or library-museums should consider not simply practices of collecting but of curating, exhibiting, and engaging in critical scholarship around relevant and pressing topics facing our global society. There are ways that both the financially secure and the smaller, budget-strapped institutions can contribute to giving voice and support to social struggles, justice, and work. Institutions are often inventive places or, more precisely, they have creative staff who are able to find ways to improve the environment and cultivate a socially evolving and supporting space. This is, in fact, how we as a library, a theological library, and a museum space can transition from Dana's gloom to Silverman's and Orloff's social work. The library-museum of the future will demand those changes, because the people who use the library will require it long before that.

Accessibility

With these positions in mind, we can consider how changes to the vision of a library like Bridwell may coincide with adapting to cultural changes. Among the most central considerations, then, would have to be accessibility. Accessibility may be understood in a host of ways, but essentially it concerns the idea of a broad public gaining entry and access to materials with fewer restrictions and roadblocks. Part of the democratization of information and knowledge requires us to offer not simply more opportunities for access but more information about materials we already hold. Most special collections have backlogs and unprocessed items. These areas would be included in an accessibility plan, where increased or reconfigured staffing might evaluate such backlogs and develop specific plans to make materials known and available. The other part of the accessibility framework will be to engage more thoroughly with the digital humanities and web access for patrons. With this in mind, Bridwell itself continues to work diligently in this area and will further opportunities in the future.

Printing, Presses, and the Legacy of Typography

Bridwell Library has a rich legacy in the area of printing, typography, and traditional presses. The centerpiece of this triad is the Ashendene Press and collection, founded by Charles St. John Hornby. For decades, the themes of printing and typography played significant roles in the historical contexts of Bridwell's pedagogy, research, conservation, and curation. In the last couple years, there has been renewed interest in exploring these areas more deeply and constructively, and recent acquisitions in typography, lettering, and font design have contributed to this area of Bridwell's history. Though these themes may seem more antique and less contemporary, there are burgeoning fields of digital font and letter design, especially as we evolve in virtual and online spaces. Bridwell is in a unique position to bring its historical works and holdings into contact with digital innovators of typography, such that we may provide internships, events, lectures, and research fellowships around these topics, and perhaps even establish a program or institute for the future of print design. The world of typographic experimentation continues to be an expanding and illuminative field that is driven by digital programming, market branding, and innovative visual associations. By tapping into this future of psychology and design, Bridwell will be poised to engage in a highly productive and strategically important endeavor. Additionally, there are various avenues to take in both traditional paper publishing and digitally born publishing, where new publications will carry the Bridwell Library imprint.

Calligraphy, Art Production, and New Book Arts

In the year prior to COVID-19, I had the opportunity to meet members of several calligraphic guilds in the North Texas region. Many of these talented individuals had a long history and expansive reach within the national and international networks of professional calligraphers. Bridwell is ready to engage in creative projects and possible commissions with calligraphers, who may design and create a series of hand-drawn works that are specific to Bridwell's areas of theological and biblical studies. A move toward a more concerted approach around arts production will benefit not simply the artists involved, but the broader community of global researchers. And the hope is that we will afford opportunities to artists from traditionally underrepresented communities to explore themes relevant to contemporary society and theological reflection. Furthermore, when an institution of any size promotes and supports commissions of calligraphy, art, and artist books, from modest compensations to major remuneration, the library effectively acquires a unique item that will never be found in any other institution. As a result, this specificity will build the library's credentials and attract donors, researchers, and patrons for years to come. And pedagogically, these works will serve as additional entry points into theological discourse. Among other ideas that we have considered are increased engagements with younger demographics, high school groups, and children, especially from communities without easy access to or knowledge of the work of a theological library and special collections. Such circumstances may afford opportunities for students to experience a place like Bridwell in a way that may help them form new and positive ideas about libraries, archives, collections, and museums—perhaps even giving them inspiration for future careers. These same groups eventually may be encouraged through volunteer opportunities or even competitions to create their own hand-made books and other works of calligraphic art. One day, such undertakings and community-focused engagement may be seen as useful by future researchers seeking to understand the imaginations and visions of our children in a complex, evolving, and transitional era of American life.

The Library-Museum as Performative Space with Special Collections

Since coming to Bridwell in 2018, I have had the pleasure of working with a number of insightful and intellectually thoughtful individuals. Some have provided useful and, at times, provocative ideas about how the space of a library may serve not simply to host musical performances, but how the articulation of such performance may be incorporated into a conversation among the extant holdings, future acquisitions, and planned commissions.[5] It should also be recognized that Bridwell is physically situated exactly between Perkins School of Theology and the Meadows School of Music. This reality—along with the interests of faculty with shared appointments in both schools— affords Bridwell a unique position to articulate a future with more than simply unused space in mind. Spaces, like walls, are themselves meant to provide both utility and imagination for the work we set out to do. Therefore, the future vision of such spaces shall be more than thoroughfares for patrons to access the collected works of Wesley or the most recent biblical commentaries from Europe. The aim will be to create a space that enhances the patron's experience there, drawing them in and helping them see how the building itself is a dynamic structure containing art, artifacts, sculptures, rare books, archives, and an occasional musical event or theatrical rendition. Performance, after all, is not simply in the moment when an instrument or voice is sounded, but in the total experience of those involved in the process. Bridwell, then, should consider itself in a constant and perpetual state of performance, a waltz or tango of the library-museum with its extensive community of patrons.

Part IV: Conclusion—Bridwell in 2520 CE?

What will there be in this place in five hundred years? Perhaps we must look back in order to look forward. When we consider our collections in one way but our spaces and library buildings in another, we are not getting the entire picture of what we should be imagining. It is easy to rely upon our projections of books, manuscripts, and other cultural items in our mindscape because the work that we do demands that. We are, after all, in a theological space—a school of theology—where we discuss and debate and consider the refinements of what it means to be in relationships with the divine, with each other, with the world. And these are generally mediated through the cultural objects and images found via books and artifacts. Yet, we must also consider the spaces where we learn—now more than ever, since we have been subjected to a disembodying pandemic that makes us certainly more aware of ourselves and our physicality in a way that we were not so keen to observe or recognize before. The whole concept of presence today is something that has far more meaning and value than it may have had a year ago.

So, what does this mean, then—that we must recognize and consider the physical space, the environment, and the fluid articulation of nature in the broader scheme of theological education, libraries, our collections, and the museum territory that enumerates and defines a place like Bridwell? The campus and space of SMU, along with Perkins School of Theology and Bridwell itself, have been dissimilar throughout time. The years between 1920 and 1970 are the same duration of time as those between 1970 and 2020, yet they are vastly different in how they were experienced and even how the buildings, land, and space related to one another. The Bridwell building did not even exist in 1920, and the campus had not been "fully" transformed into the lush landscape of subtle rotating gardens, aged live oaks, and perfectly cut sod squares. The earth appeared dry, the land had not been completely cultivated or torn open and covered over with macadam. There were likely no cars on campus a century ago, and certainly no parking lots (though Ford had already opened a plant in the area in 1915).

The cultivation of the campus over a hundred years also reflects the harnessing of nature and the environment of water and earth. The budget of the university's groundskeeping in 2020, and especially its monumental grass plantings, is likely to have exceeded the budget for the entire university of 1920. In 1870, the land was an aggregation of dry ranches, and in 1820 or 1770 it was a scrub-covered dry earth that had been possessed under various treaties by the French and, prior to that, the Viceroyalty of the Kingdom of Spain. In 1670 or 1570 or even 1470, we can easily establish the histories and prosopography of books and manuscripts in the Bridwell's collection, but all that we can say of the land was that it was inhabited and utilized by the Caddo tribes and that there was likely a small dry-bed river or stream that ran under the space that is now Bridwell Library. Is it then even worth predicting what might come in fifty, a hundred, or five hundred years, especially when the differences of the last five hundred could never have been imagined at the time?

Theological schools of 1820 were institutions that are virtually unknown today. The demographics, curricula, and expectations of two centuries ago were quite different than what they are today. So too were their libraries and research needs. Education, information, resources, libraries, museums, nature, and the environment are all things that change; they are also things that are very much connected. As Bridwell and other institutions and libraries take their steps into the future, we must recognize this greater holistic enterprise.

At the start of this chapter, I asked the question: How do we continue to work within a profession where our human presence has been central to our mission and livelihood, yet by its own virtue during a pandemic, we are forced to abandon that physical human presence and adapt to an increasingly virtual environment? The short answer is adaptability. The longer answer involves our participation in a more studied, self-reflective position that requires greater openness, more expansive thinking, increased inclusion of diverse stakeholders, and a willingness to take risks. As the libraries and library-museums of the future will be more hybrid, they will find the best elements of the physical and the virtual and emerge as the most effective institutions possible. While I have also written these considerations with Bridwell specifically in mind and the privilege that comes with having specific means and endowments to support many such programs, I also recognize, having worked in several smaller institutions with extremely tight budgets, that there can be opportunities to do many of the same things, such as commissions, community art projects, and eliciting donated works of art. But this will certainly involve more legwork, coordination, creativity, crowd-sourcing, and fundraising to accomplish those goals. It is not impossible. And I still firmly believe that our greatest resources are our staffs and their collective creativity—the seeds of innovation.

I have written this essay in the hopes that we can have the thoughtfulness, consideration, and courage to look deeply into the future, not necessarily to predict what might happen, but to provide a guiding spirit of our present. For we know—or at least hope to know—those things which are around us. We recognize what is in our world, and we can facilitate small actions into incremental change. We will never know what will come so far into that crystal ball of the next half-millennium, but it is not about our knowing—it is about our preparing. And, like the president of that Dallas religious organization, whom I mentioned at the outset, our responsibilities are in how willing and able we are to commit to our responsibilities as stewards and custodians of the present cultures around us and to do the best in making the world better for those who come after.

References

Dana, John Cotton. 1917. "The Gloom of the Museum; With Suggestions for Removing It." In *The Gloom of the Museum*, 10–30. Woodstock, VT: Elm Tree Press.

Fraser, John. 2019. "A Discomforting Definition of Museum." *Curator: The Museum Journal* 62, no. 4: 501–4.

International Council of Museums. 2007. *ICOM Statutes, adopted by the 22nd General Assembly*. Vienna, August 24, 2007.

Orloff, Chet. 2017. "Should Museums Change Our Mission and Become Agencies of Social Justice?" *Curator: The Museum Journal* 60, no. 1 (January): 33–6.

Silverman, Lois H. 2010. *The Social Work of Museums*. New York: Routledge.

Small, Zachary. 2019. "A New Definition of 'Museum' Sparks International Debate." *Hyperallergic*, August 19, 2019. *https://hyperallergic.com/513858/icom-museum-definition*.

Uexküll, Jakob von. 1926. *Theoretical Biology*. London: Trübner & Company.

Notes

1   There are many people to recognize and thank for all the work done in our libraries and communities. It is often a risk to list names, because invariably you miss someone. I will say that the current staff of Bridwell continues to impress me with their creativity, focus, and hard work, and I want to mention that their approaches to their many labors are much appreciated. Everything they do facilitates our greater goals of re-imagining the library and what can be accomplished with its resources and collections. Special thanks are in order to Jane Lenz Elder, Ellen Frost, Jon Speck, Kimberly Hunter, R. Arvid Nelsen, Leslie Fuller, Rebecca Howdeshell, Timothy Binkley, Frances Long, Robert Tifft, Michelle Ried, Lara Corazalla, Jesse Hunt, Seth Miskimins, Mehret Negash, Robert Edwards, and to the countless others in SMU Libraries and Perkins School of Theology. Additional thanks to Deans Craig Hill and Holly Jeffcoat for their tireless support and leadership.

2   There are too many to thank for their great and enduring contributions, though, most recently, my two predecessors— Dr. Valerie Hotchkiss and Roberta Schaafsma—had tenures of more than a decade each and provided multiple contributions to our special collections. Notably, Dr. Hotchkiss significantly expanded our incunabula collection and developed a variety of engagement programs with the public and international researchers, including fellowships and annual lecture series.

3   One consideration of the "museum" designation may be to evaluate the ratio of cultural materials, artifacts, and rare books, for example, in relation to staffing costs. For example, if an institution holds at least x-number of items (determined by the institution), which in value exceed the annual salary of any given staff member, then that is the benchmark that determines museum status. Certainly, there will be critics, but some modest framework should be in place to articulate these determinations.

4   First published in 1917, the essay has been reprinted and discussed in museum circles for more than a century.

5   Drs. Christopher Anderson and Marcell Steuernagel have been tremendously helpful as interlocutors of tonal philosophies, acoustics, and general performance theory, which continues to be much appreciated and helpful in the strategic thinking around musical spaces.

Contributors

Christopher J. Anderson is special collections librarian and curator of the Day Missions Collection for the Yale Divinity Library in New Haven, Connecticut. He has been a member of Atla since 2007 and has served the association on a variety of committees and working groups. He is currently a member of the editorial board for *Theological Librarianship*.

Matthew Baker is head of the Burke Library at Union Theological Seminary (Columbia University Libraries). He has also been the collection services librarian at the Burke. He previously taught at the American University in Cairo, Egypt, and once upon a time studied English literature. In addition to academic roles, he has been a grocery stocker, an HVAC tech, a house painter, a caregiver, an elementary school teacher, an ESL instructor, a waiter, and a haughty record store clerk.

Nell K. Carlson is curator of historical collections at Andover-Harvard Theological Library, Harvard Divinity School. She holds an MTS from Harvard Divinity School and an MSLIS from Simmons University.

Stephen D. Crocco has been the director of the Yale Divinity Library since 2015. Prior to Yale, he was the James Lenox librarian at Princeton Theological Seminary and, before that, the library director at Pittsburgh Theological Seminary. He has a PhD in religious ethics from Princeton University and an MLS from the University of Pittsburgh.

Caroline Duroselle-Melish is Andrew W. Mellon Curator of Early Modern Books and Prints, and associate librarian for collection care and development at the Folger Shakespeare Library, Washington, DC. As the curator of early modern book collections, she oversees the Reformation pamphlets collection. Her publications reflect her research interests in the history of libraries, the Renaissance book trade, and the production and reception of early modern illustrated books.

Bruce Eldevik was reference and special collections librarian at Luther Seminary. He retired in 2016, but continues to volunteer at the library, working on projects in the spellbinding Rare Book Room.

Anthony J. Elia has been J. S. Bridwell Foundation Endowed Librarian and director at the Bridwell Library, Perkins School of Theology, Southern Methodist University since 2018. He has written essays on various topics about theological librarianship, including how cybersecurity, ethics, and history play distinct roles in the future of the profession. His current research is on the role of physical environments and ecology in the history of institutional development.

M. Patrick Graham is the Margaret A. Pitts Professor Emeritus of Theological Bibliography at the Candler School of Theology, Emory University. He directed the Pitts Theology Library at Emory for 23 years, served on the Atla Board of Directors, has published in biblical studies and theological librarianship, and was the recipient of a *Festschrift* upon his retirement in 2017.

Jonathan Lawler is the archivist and digital collections manager at Southeastern Baptist Theological Seminary. He received an MA in archives and public history from New York University and a Master in Ministry from Northwest University. His experience includes managing archival repositories, teaching as a part-time lecturer in the Information School at the University of Washington, and writing on a variety of topics related to archives and special collections. *Soli Deo gloria!*

Jesse D. Mann is the theological librarian at Drew University (Madison, NJ, USA), where he also teaches in the history of Christianity. Trained as a medieval historian, his research focuses on medieval ecclesiology and political thought, Muslim-Christian relations in the Middle Ages, and book history. Currently, he is collaborating with Professor Ulli Roth (Universität Koblenz) on a critical edition of the *opera minora* of Juan de Segovia (d. 1458). Mann also has more than 20 years of experience in the rare book business.

Russell Pollard, MLS, MDiv, now a retired member of Atla, was head of Technical Services, then collections management librarian, and twice interim librarian at the Andover-Harvard Theological Library, Harvard Divinity School. As collections management librarian, he was responsible for collection development and special collections. He chaired the Atla Bibliographic Systems Committee and Nominating Committee, and served on the board of directors, from 1990–93. He is an active member of Christ Lutheran Church, Natick, Massachusetts, and, until recently, served on the Candidacy Committee of the New England Synod. He lives in Ashland, Massachusetts.

Brian Shetler is the head of Special Collections and Archives at Princeton Theological Seminary. Prior to this, he served as head of Special Collections and Methodist librarian at Drew University, where he worked closely with donors to build collections. Brian received his MSLIS from Simmons University with a focus on archives and rare book librarianship and his PhD in book history & print culture from Drew University, supplementing both degrees with training in book conservation at NEDCC and paleography studies at University College London. His research has focused on the history of printing in early modern England, particularly related to the work of John Wilkes, Geoffrey Chaucer, and John Wesley. Recent publications have focused on the history of libraries in medieval Europe, the role of special collections in information literacy, and Methodism and the macabre.

Armin Siedlecki studied religious studies at the University of Saskatchewan (Saskatoon, SK) and at Wilfrid Laurier University (Waterloo, ON) before obtaining a doctorate in biblical studies from Emory University (Atlanta, GA). Since 2001, he has been working in the cataloging department at the Pitts Theology Library, where he serves as head of cataloging and rare book cataloger. He first encountered the Richard C. Kessler Reformation Collection in 1997 when he worked as a graduate student assistant on the collection's annotated bibliography. He has been a member of Atla since 2002.

Mary Ann Teske is the catalog and collection management librarian at Luther Seminary. Prior to joining the Luther Seminary library staff in 1988, she worked as an elementary school library/media specialist in both Sartell and Minneapolis, Minnesota, and was a missionary librarian with the American Lutheran Church at the Lutheran Theological College, Umpumulo in Mapumulo, South Africa.

Shea Van Schuyver is an application programmer at Southeastern Baptist Theological Seminary (SEBTS) in North Carolina. Prior to working in the IT department, she worked as a digitization assistant in the Archives and Special Collections department of the Library at Southeastern. She graduated with a bachelor's degree in information technology and systems from the University of Texas at Dallas in 2016 and is currently pursuing a master's degree in marriage and family counseling from SEBTS.

Index of Persons

A

Adams, Richard Manly (Bo) 22

Albrecht of Brandenburg 10

Alcott, Amos Bronson 69–70

Amsdorff, Nikolaus 12

Anderson, Christopher 236

Anderson, Clifford B. 187, 189, 196

Anderson, Elmer L. 97–8

Arndt, Johann 97

Asper, Hans 42

Astrup, Nils 100

Aurifaber, Johannes 9

Azam, Sara 146

B

Bach, Johann Sebastian 21

Baier, Herta 186

Balkenende, Jan Peter 196

Barfield, Owen 195

Barth, Hans Jacob 184

Barth, Karl 177–96

Barth, Markus 182–3, 185, 187, 196

Barth, Nelly 186

Barth, Verena 184

Bauer, Ferdinand Christian 68, 81

Beach, Harlan Page 141

Donne, John 32

Dooyeweerd, Herman 180

Døving, Carl 100–1, 113

Drewes, Hans-Anton 185, 195–6

Duffy, Joan 146

Dugdale, William 104

Dürer, Albrecht 100

E

Eck, Johann 39

Eckermann, Johann Peter 68

Edelman, Leah 126

Edwards, Jonathan 192, 194–5, 198

Edwards, Robert 236

Elder, Jane Lenz 236

Ellul, Jacques 186

Emerson, Ralph Waldo 69, 71

Emser, Hieronymus 55

Erasmus, Desiderius 16, 18, 32, 145

Estelle-Holmer, Suzanne 145

F

Fabricius, Johannes Montanus 46

Fenwick, Alan 32

Flacius, Matthias 9

Folger, Emily 30

Folger, Henry 30

Francis, Convers 65–88

Fraser, John 224–5

Froben, Johann 99

Frost, Ellen 236

Frost, Robert 201, 204, 207, 212

Fuhrmann, Wilhelm David 82

Fuller, Leslie 236

Fürstenhauserin, Helena 46, 48–9

G

Gaskell, Roger 62

Gatch, Milton McC. 34, 63

Geoffroy, Françoise 50

Geoffroy, Jehan Barbas 50

Gerbert, Martin II 51

Gerhard, Johann 97

Gesenius, Heinrich Friedrich Wilhelm 82

Gillespie, Thomas 183

Gillett, Ezra Hall 120

Goetz, Ronald 182

Gullixson, Thaddeus F. 92

Gutenberg, Johannes 110, 112

H

Hadidian, Dikran Y. 183

Harinck, George 189

Harmsworth, Robert Leicester 31

Harris, Mark 87

Harrison, Summer 211–12

Hartfelder, Karl 5

Hätzer, Ludwig 45

Hedge, Frederic Henry 69–70

Hegel, Georg W. F. 81

M

MacDonald, George 195

Maimonides (Moses ben Maimon) 80

Mandeville, Bernard 208

Marchesinus, John 98

Marot, Clément 46

May, Johannes Gottlob 62

McAlpin, David Hunter 120

McCormack, Bruce L. 183–4, 187

McEllhenney, John Galen 200–13

McIntire, Carl 197

Meiners, Christoph 84

Melanchthon, Philipp 11, 32, 98, 120

Miller, Frank R. 101

Miskimins, Seth 236

Montgomery, John Warwick 158

More, Henry 70

Morgan, Christopher 211

Muller, Crafft 94

Munby, A. N. L. 33

Murner, Thomas 44, 55

N

Negash, Mehret 236

Nelsen, R. Arvid 236

Neven, Gerritt 187

Newell, William 87

Nichols, John 107

Ninck, Renate 184, 186

Norlie, Olaf Morgan 100

Noyes, Charles 76, 78

O

Oecolampadius, Johann 31, 40–1

Oettinger, Eduard Maria 82

Orloff, Chet 234–5

P

Parker, Theodore 69–70, 87

Parr, Samuel 83–4

Pearson, David 72

Perkins family 230

Peter, Niklaus 184

Peters, Elizabeth 149

Petreius, Johann 94

Petri, Adam 6, 98

Petzenstein, Johannes 12

Peypus, Friedrich 98

Phillipps, Thomas 31–56

Plantinga, Alvin 196

Pratensis, Felix 21

Preus, Dikka 93

Preus, J. C. K. 93

Puchinger, George 189–90

Q

Quenstedt, Johannes Andreas 97

R

Radde, William 82

Reinhardsberg, Gufer von 51

www.ingramcontent.com/pod-product-compliance
Lightning Source LLC
Chambersburg PA
CBHW031416270326
41929CB00010BA/1479

U

Uexküll, Jakob Johann 227
Ulhart the Elder, Philip 94

V

Van de Velde, Jan Frans 34, 37
Van Deusen Hunsinger, Deborah 195
Van Ess, Leander 34–5, 45, 120
Van Huyssteen, J. Wentzel 196
Van Kirschbaum, Charlotte 182
Van Liesveldt, Jacob 94
Van Loon, Hans 187
Van Til, Cornelius 188
Vanden Block, Henricus 35
Vos, Geerhardus 188

W

Walker, Richard L. 204
Warnick, Kate 229
Wayno, Jeffrey 125
Weiss, John 88
Wente, Norman G. 93–4
Wildi, Hans Markus 185, 187, 195
Williams, Charles 195
Winchester family 142
Winchester, Elhanan 67
Winger, Howard W. 94
Winsor, Justin 136
Wohleber, Chandra 62
Wolprecht, Wolfgang 12

Woodall, Guy 66
Wren, Christopher 104, 111

Y

Young, Andrew 196

Z

Zeller, Eduard 81
Zellweger, Max 181
Ziegenbalg, Bartholomew 94
Zwingli, Huldrych 31, 111, 120

www.ingramcontent.com/pod-product-compliance
Lightning Source LLC
Chambersburg PA
CBHW031416270326
41929CB00010BA/1479